Saltwater
Fly Fishing

ALSO BY JACK SAMSON

Line Down! The Special World of Big Game Fishing   1973

The Best of Corey Ford (edited)   1974

The Sportsman's World   1976

The Worlds of Ernest Thompson Seton   1976

Falconry Today   1976

A Fine and Pleasant Misery (edited)   1978

Successful Outdoor Writing   1979

The Bear Book (edited)   1979

The Pond   1979

The Grizzly Book (edited)   1981

The Great Fish   1983

Modern Falconry   1984

Hunting the Southwest   1985

Chennault—A Biography   1988

Saltwater Fly Fishing

Jack Samson

STACKPOLE
BOOKS

Published by
STACKPOLE BOOKS
Cameron and Kelker Streets
P.O. Box 1831
Harrisburg, PA 17105

Printed in the United States of America

10 9 8 7 6 5 4 3 2 1

First edition

Knot illustrations by Mark Olszewski

Library of Congress Cataloging-in-Publication Data

Samson, Jack.
    Saltwater fly fishing / Jack Samson. — 1st ed.
      p.   cm.
    ISBN 0-8117-1653-8
    1. Saltwater fly fishing.   I. Title.
  SH456.2.S26   1991
  799.1'6—dc20   90-23235
                                                         CIP

To Victoria

Contents

Foreword

Jack Samson goes back a long way in saltwater fly fishing. He was with me when I fished in the very first International Invitational Sailfish Fly Tournament at Islamorada in the early 1970s, and I was fishing against him when he won the International Billfish Fly Tournament in Flamingo Beach, Costa Rica, in 1989. Between those two tourneys, Jack sailed over and waded a lot of salt water—fly rod in hand.

I don't know of anyone—with the possible exception of myself—who is as devoted to fly fishing as Jack. Like me, he will stand in a salmon or steelhead river until sundown, waiting for that elusive strike. He is equally at home on a permit or bonefish flat and usually the last one to quit. He shares with me the love of tarpon fishing with a fly and was with me on a memorable day off Homosassa, Florida, when I battled a two-hundred-pound-plus fly-hooked tarpon that finally got away in the shallows after a battle that lasted more than four hours.

But it is his ability to write about fishing the vastness of the sea and the endless flats that makes Jack different from all the other saltwater fly fishermen around today. Not since Van Campen Heilner has an angler put on paper the *feel* of fishing the depths of blue water or of fly fishing in the silence and enormity of a bonefish or tarpon flat.

Billy Pate with his world-record Atlantic
blue marlin taken on a fly off Cuba in 1978.
It weighed ninety-six pounds.

I am happy that I was able to help Jack, in the late 1960s, with his first attempts at fishing for the big ones – tarpon and billfish with a fly. He learned fast, and we had some great times in both tarpon and billfish tournaments at Islamorada in those days.

I like to think that I have never been too busy to stop and help someone learning this great sport by giving them instruction in technique or tackle.

In Jack's case, he has more than repaid me.

> Billy Pate
> Islamorada, Florida

Preface

Writing about fishing is a lot more difficult than doing it—and not nearly as much fun. That is probably why my two greatest angling heroes have always been Zane Grey and Van Campen Heilner. They not only spent a lifetime pursuing great fish, but wrote extensively—and well—about their exploits.

My own saltwater angling career covers a lot of territory and a good many years, beginning with my childhood during the early 1930s in Rhode Island, where I grew up on the shores of Narragansett Bay with a hand line as a constant companion.

By the 1970s, I thought I had caught all the big fish I ever wanted when I finally caught, tagged, and released a one-thousand-pound Pacific black marlin off the Great Barrier Reef of Australia. That catch topped a career that included a lot of tournament fishing over much of the world—almost forty years of it.

But a strange thing happened. I found—in the later years of big-game fishing at such exotic spots as the Bahamas, Australia, Hawaii, the Caribbean, and Central America—that I was spending more time on the flats with a fly rod and less time on the blue water with heavy big-game fishing tackle. The challenge of taking the big fish on eighty-pound tackle, as I had done with the Pacific black marlin, was gone.

In its place was the genuine thrill of stalking and catching bonefish, permit, and tarpon on the flats with a fly rod. It is sight fishing, where one sees the quarry and casts to it, and it is a sporty business. A big permit on a fragile 12-pound-test leader can be the thrill of a lifetime!

I have been fly fishing in fresh water all my life and am devoted to it. But when I began fly fishing in salt water in the 1960s, it became a whole new ball game. A saltwater fish is so much more powerful than a freshwater fish of comparable size that it is no contest. My first Atlantic salmon and steelhead caught on a fly taught me that fish fresh from the sea are indeed powerful opponents. My first jack crevalle and roosterfish on a fly rod taught me that both the salmon and steelhead are in a totally different league from these deep-water sluggers! That is why this is not to be a textbook on saltwater fly fishing. Rather, it is meant to convey something of the history and *flavor* of this great sport.

I cannot thank enough those friends and guides—Billy Pate, Dick Williams, Billy Knowles, George Hommell, Hal Chittum, Stu Apte, Gil Drake, Jr., Joe Hudson, and a consortium of dedicated Florida Keys flats fishermen—who took the time to teach me the flats, the fish that inhabit them, and the techniques used to catch them. And I am indebted to the others—Lefty Kreh, Mark Sosin, Lee Wulff, Jimmie Albright, Lou Tabory, Cam Sigler, Vic Dunaway, Nick Curcione, Bill Barnes, Harry Kime, Jim Chapralis, Frank Woolner, Mike Leech, Didier Van der Veecken, Terry Baird, Mike Sakamoto, and Chuck Rizuto—for helping me gather material for this book.

Jack Samson

1
Saltwater Fly-fishing Tackle

I can remember—many years ago—reading some of the learned books on fly fishing for trout. If I had not already learned fly fishing as a small boy, I would *never* have had the courage to try the sport.

Back in the 1970s my friend Ernest Schwiebert sent me an autographed copy of his two-volume classic *Trout*. It is a well-researched and thorough piece of work on the ancient art of fly fishing for trout as only Ernie could have written it. I gave a set to my oldest son, John, who was just beginning to fly fish.

"Thanks for the books on trout, Dad," he wrote me, "but it is more than I wanted to know about the subject."

In this brief discussion of saltwater fly tackle, I will discuss only a few of the things I have found to be important. They may help the beginning saltwater fly angler without frightening him, or her, away from the sport.

I hope this chapter will not be more than anyone wants to know about saltwater fly tackle—but, after all, one has to start somewhere.

FLY RODS
If I were forced to exist with a minimum of rods for saltwater fly fishing, I would pick 9-weight and 12-weight graphite fly rods—both

A number of rod companies today make excellent graphite and boron rods for saltwater fly fishing.

9 feet long. And since airlines are both brutal and callous about the care of fine fly rods, I would purchase 4-piece "breakdown," or travel, rods. That way they can be carried in a short rod case that can be stored in the compartment above one's head in a modern jet airliner.

As a matter of fact, I have devised a system of carrying *all* my vital fly-fishing equipment with me on planes these days. What with badly handled baggage being normal on today's domestic and overseas airlines, it pays to carry important tackle with you. Steve Abel, that excellent California-based reel designer and fly fisherman, solved the problem well. He designed a carry-on tackle bag that holds his reels, extra lines, leaders, fly boxes, reel tools, camera equipment, shaving kit, passports, and personal papers—plus lightweight rain gear, insect repellent, hat, polarized glasses, boat or wading shoes, lip balm, and sun block. In addition, he devised a square plastic rod case—covered with a canvas, zip-up jacket—capable of carrying five breakdown fly rods for various line weights. If his baggage fails to turn up in any area of the world, he can still fish until it arrives.

The make and model of rod to purchase is strictly up to the individual. Excellent saltwater fly rods are made by any number of tackle companies today. Just remember that a saltwater fly rod must take a lot of punishment and it should have a lot more backbone than a comparable freshwater rod. The butt section of the rod you choose should remain comparatively flexible while the center section and tip bend. If the butt section bends too much when you lift it against a heavy fish, the rod is too soft for saltwater fish—especially the big ones.

Your best bet is to consult a knowledgeable rod maker by mail or phone and order the one he suggests. Sage, Fisher, Orvis, Fenwick, Deerfield, and USA Graphite are but a few of the rod companies making excellent saltwater fly rods.

I said if I were forced to fish with only two rods, I would choose a 9-weight and a 12-weight. That is true, but fortunately I don't have to restrict myself to only two rods. I usually carry at least three rods on any given trip and occasionally as many as five. A 6-weight can be very nice on a bonefish flat where the surface is calm and there is no wind. On the other end of the scale, a 10-weight can punch that fly into a stiff wind better than a 9-weight.

While a 12-weight rod is usually enough for dolphin, wahoo, roosterfish, and sailfish, there are times when a 13-weight is better for marlin. I have a heavy 15-weight rod that was developed by Tim Grennan, formerly of Fenwick, and I wouldn't trade it for anything when fishing for big marlin and tuna. A big albacore or yellowfin tuna requires a stout rod with which to pump it up, and Tim's "monster" rod does the trick where no other rod would work.

Californian Steve Abel has come up with a system of carrying all his fly-fishing gear in a bag and rod case when traveling by air.

If you decide to buy a two-piece fly rod, I suggest you invest in an extra-heavy rod case to carry it in. After having airline baggage handlers break three expensive graphite two-piece fly rods, I constructed my own rod case from heavy-walled PVC pipe. I plugged one end and devised a screw-in plug for the other, fastened by a heavy padlock. The case weighs a ton, is heavy to carry, and baggage handlers probably hate it, but they can't hurt it—short of a plane crash. B. B. Dunn of Boise, Idaho, makes excellent cases for big rods.

Make sure the reel seat of your rod is large enough to accommodate the foot of the reel you intend to use on it. Most good reel-seat hardware today is made from chrome-plated brass, but anodized aluminum seats will also do well in salt water. The grip on your saltwater fly rod will not be as important on the lighter, flats-fishing rod as it will be on your larger, deep-water rod. Most veteran saltwater fly rodders prefer the half-wells or full-wells cork grips and—for larger fish—an extension fighting butt is generally called for. The more rounded butts are better than the sharp-edged ones for fighting big fish.

When fishing in the tropics, one very important thing to remember is that the hot sun beats down on black-colored graphite fly rods, causing them to heat up and expand. Sometimes it is very difficult to take them apart. The best way to prevent this problem is to regularly rub the ferrules with a candle before joining the rod sections. Beeswax does the same job but is more difficult to find.

REELS

Unlike fresh water, where—except in the case of fishing for Atlantic salmon, steelhead, or king salmon—the size of the reel or the strength and smoothness of its drag is not of the utmost importance, the reel is the most important piece of tackle of a saltwater fly rodder. More good fish have been lost to cheap reels, bad drags, and reels with too small a line capacity than any other factor in saltwater fly fishing.

Your saltwater fly reel should be *anodized*—treated to resist corrosion by salt water. An expensive freshwater trout or salmon reel may work well for you in salt water the first day, but if it is not thoroughly washed and cleaned that night, it will seize up overnight and be worthless the next day. I should know, having ruined a couple of good trout reels that way while learning to fish for bonefish.

The screws, reel foot, and all the inside components of your reel should be of stainless steel. The reel pillars should be either of stain-

Reels run all the way from those for 5- to 6-weight rods to big ones for 12- to 13-weight fly rods.

less steel or anodized aluminum. Most of the good expensive reels have an anodized finish.

As a general rule, the reel you pick for flats fishing and just-offshore fishing—for bonefish, permit, mutton snapper, barracuda, redfish, sea trout, stripers, and bluefish—should be capable of holding at least two hundred yards of twenty-pound Micron or Dacron backing, plus a ninety-foot fly line.

The reel you get for bigger stuff—tarpon, dolphin, roosterfish, wahoo, sharks, and sailfish—should be capable of holding at least 350 to 400 yards of thirty-pound backing, plus a fly line or shooting head. If one plans on doing any regular fly fishing for big tuna and marlin, I would suggest getting a big reel capable of holding from six hundred to nine hundred yards of thirty-pound Micron or Dacron, plus a fly line or shooting head. A greyhounding marlin on a fly rod can make *any* fly tackle seem pretty inadequate!

None of these good saltwater reels are cheap. The least expensive are generally around $250 to $300, and the large-capacity, high-tech reels can go as high as $1,200! For that reason it is wise to be concerned about their maintenance after use in salt water. Even the best can be damaged by letting them sit for long periods of time after exposure to salt water or sand. They should be carefully rinsed in warm, soapy water, not just squirted with fresh water from a hose.

There are a lot of good saltwater reels on the market today, as opposed to a decade ago. Ten years ago there were only a few good ones around: the venerable Fin-Nor, the Seamaster, and one of Billy Pate's reels. Today one can find a number of excellent anodized reels that have both the line capacities and the drags for big saltwater fish.

Some of the better ones are the Fin-Nor, in both the direct drive and the anti-reverse models; the reliable Seamaster in a half dozen models; and Billy Pate's Salmon, Bonefish, Tarpon, and Marlin reels. Catino has two good saltwater reels; Scientific Anglers (3M) has excellent saltwater reels in the System II and System III models. Fenwick's Class 4 through 8 reels; Orvis's SSS series from 7-7 through its 11-12 tarpon reel; the Monarch M-40; the Hardy Ocean Prince; the Gehrke GR850 through GR1000; a couple of Ross reels; the STH reels; and Steve Abel's excellent #4 and #5 reels. Martin's new M12D saltwater reel holds 400 yards of 20-pound backing and is an excellent reel.

For the beginning saltwater fly rodder who doesn't want to spend much on a reel, the old reliable Pfleuger Medalist 1498 will do. It has been around for years as a freshwater reel but will hold up well in salt water if properly maintained.

SALTWATER FLY LINES

Scientific Anglers and Cortland have the field to themselves as far as saltwater fly lines are concerned. For years both companies have had the vision to see the potential popularity of saltwater fly fishing and have devoted years of research to the development of good lines that will stand up to pitting and nicks. In addition, they have developed specialized lines that are used for all sorts of saltwater situations.

I don't want to get too complicated here and frighten away any prospective saltwater fly rodders with a lot of technical information. Let me just say that there are lines for all sorts of situations in salt water: floating lines, floating lines with sinking tips, sinking lines that go all the way from intermediate, very slow sinking lines through extremely fast sinking lines that weigh from 550 grains to 850 grains. There are tapers for both bonefish and tarpon, monocore lines, and lines as long as 120 feet for salmon, 105 feet for steelhead, and regular 90-foot lines for general fly fishing. In addition, there are shooting heads that come in 30-foot lengths and shorter.

I could spend a dozen pages describing what the various tapers mean, but I suspect that you will only need a very few specialized

Leaders, both soft and hard, have come a long way in the past decade toward solving the problems of saltwater fly rodders.

lines for saltwater fly fishing. Let me tell you what I use and you can follow that or develop your own system. I doubt you will very often encounter a situation in flats fishing where you will need anything more than a standard ninety-foot, weight-forward floating fly line. For most bonefish situations you can get along very well with floating, weight-forward 6- to 9-weight lines, depending upon the weight of the rod. For those fly fishermen who like to throw shooting heads, lines come in both floating and sinking with a floating shooting head of thirty feet. Floating, shooting-taper, 6- to 9-weight lines should do fine.

For bigger stuff on the flats — tarpon and some sharks — ninety-foot floating lines and thirty-foot shooting-line in the 10- to 12-weight classes should be adequate.

Years ago, those of us who began fly fishing for sailfish and marlin used the standard ninety-foot floating fly line. But the resistance the long, fat lines put up to the water when a billfish was jumping caused leaders to part. Most of us have switched to short thirty-foot or less, fast-sinking shooting heads in the 12- to 13-weight category. They have far less resistance to the water and — with their heavier weight for the shorter lengths — are easier to cast long distances.

There are instances when one might require slow-sinking lines on the flats and there are special lines for that. There are also cases when one might need floating lines with fast-sinking tips (for steelhead) and they can be purchased. There are times when one wants a fast-sinking, ninety-foot fly line that will get down deep over wrecks or into a chum line. They make those too.

But if I were to be restricted to only two fly lines for saltwater fly fishing (as I was to rods), I would choose a floating, ninety-foot, weight-forward, 9-weight line and a fast-sinking, thirty-foot, 12-weight shooting head. That way I could catch fish on the flats and all the big fish I was after in deep water.

LEADERS

Leader material has come a long way in the last decade and now resists salt water far better than it used to. What one uses in saltwater fly fishing all boils down to whether one likes soft, medium, or hard leader material. It is easier to tie knots in soft mono, but soft mono tends to break faster from cuts and nicks. I have finally settled on my own system, but that does not mean that everybody agrees with me. I use a braided mono for my three-foot-butt leaders—in 30- to 40-pound-test strengths—and hard leader for my class tippets, which IGFA stipulates must be either 2-, 4-, 8-, 12-, or 16-pound-test leader sections. For my 80- to 100-pound-test shock leaders I prefer hard mono, but if I don't get it, I don't worry about it in such strengths.

KNOTS

There are only a very few knots saltwater fly fishermen must know, but unfortunately, they must know them *well*.

If I were restricted to the very basic knots in this sport, I would say I had to learn the double surgeon's loop, the nail knot, the spider hitch, the Albright knot, the improved clinch knot, and the 3½-turn clinch knot. Knots do not fascinate me. I tie them because I have to, but I consider them hard work and difficult to remember. It is for that reason that I prefer to use the spider hitch, or five-times-around knot, over the Bimini twist. I realize the Bimini is a strong knot, but it is difficult to learn and hard to remember. I have used the spider hitch for years in its place and *never* have I lost a fish that I could blame on a break at the spider hitch—and that includes sailfish, marlin, and tuna. Most breaks in line while fly fishing salt water occur in the tippet

DOUBLE SURGEON'S LOOPS

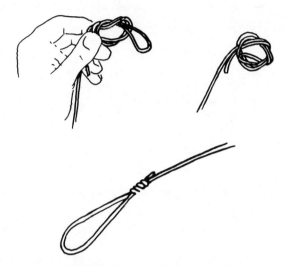

Double end of line to form a loop and tie overhand knot at base of double line. Leave loop open in knot and bring doubled line through once more. Hold standing line and tag end and pull loop to tighten knot. Size of loop can be determined by pulling loose knot to desired point and holding it while knot is tightened. Clip end ⅛ inch from knot.

SURGEON'S KNOT

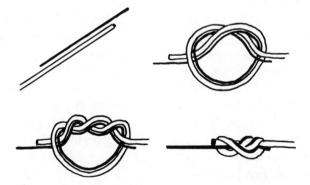

Lay line and leader parallel, overlapping six to eight inches of the two strands. Treating the two as a single line, tie an overhand knot, pulling the entire leader through the loop.

NAIL KNOT

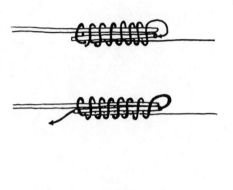

Hold coils securely. Alternately pull on long lengths and short ends to snug up tight. Trim ends. A hollow tube, as shown here, works best, but a nail will also provide a space to push the line through.

section — the weakest part of terminal tackle.

Some of the pros — Bernard "Lefty" Kreh and Bill Barnes to name a few — swear the Bimini twist is a stronger knot and that anyone intending to become a saltwater fly rodder should first learn the Bimini. Well, a difference of opinion is what makes a horse race, I always say, and I disagree. I have tested these two knots exhaustively on various Chatillon scales and the breaking variation — dry and wet — of these two knots under a steady pull is only about two to three pounds on 16-pound-test tippet. Now, granted, it depends upon who ties the knots. I tie mine very carefully, but I know people who tie terrible knots under any conditions.

I can tie a good, tight spider hitch knot to form a class tippet in about six seconds. It takes me a good two minutes to tie a Bimini twist properly. To make sure it was not just me who thought the spider hitch was as good a knot as the Bimini twist, I contacted a number of line companies and people who have a vested interest in lines and knots.

Mike Leech, director of the IGFA (International Game Fish Association), who is in charge of testing line for IGFA records, says he is of the opinion that the spider hitch, under most conditions and if tied properly, is the equal of a Bimini twist in strengths used for fly fishing.

"The spider hitch," says a spokesperson for the Dupont Line Company, "is a fast, easy knot for creating double-line leader. Under steady pressure it is equally strong, but does not have the resilience of the Bimini twist under sharp impact. It is not practical, however, with lines [leaders] above 30-pound-test." Well, since fly fishermen never go over 16-pound-test tippets for record fish, that seems no problem.

I think the liking for the Bimini twist and the distrust of the spider

---

SPIDER HITCH (FIVE-TIMES-AROUND KNOT)

Form a loop of leader length desired. Near point where it meets standing line, twist a section into a small reverse loop.

Hold small loop between thumb and forefinger with thumb well above finger and loop standing out beyond end of thumb.

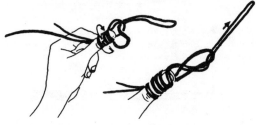

Wind double line around thumb and loop, making five turns. Pass remainder of large loop through smaller one; pull to make five turns unwind off thumb.

hitch originated with big-game fishermen. When tying knots in double line from 30- to 130-pound line, I agree the Bimini is the preferred knot, but that has nothing to do with saltwater fly-fishing knots.

Bill Monroe, of the Ande Line Company, says he thinks the spider hitch is best for fly fishermen.

"It depends on who ties it, of course," Bill said. "I've seen lots of people tie the spider hitch under all sorts of conditions and it holds. For heavy stuff the Bimini is probably the best, but for fly fishermen the spider hitch is the way to go."

I am surprised at how few people know the spider hitch, or five-times-around knot. It was learned from a Cuban fisherman years ago by "Spider" Andresen. Spider showed it to the Dupont Line Company for testing, and they named the knot in honor of Andresen. Dupont's qualification about the knot "under sharp impact" may certainly apply to shock or impact while using large, stiff big-game rods, but there is none of that with the long, flexible fly rod. I would advise any beginning saltwater fly rodder to stick with the spider hitch. Learn the Bimini twist if you must, but it may never be necessary to use it. You can always win a bet in a bar when somebody dares you to try and tie one.

Some anglers prefer the Homer Rhode loop knot when connecting a shock leader to a fly because it lets the fly swing free. There are times when I like that, but there are times when I want the fly to ride

IMPROVED CLINCH KNOT

Pass line through eye of hook, swivel, or lure. Double back and make five turns around the standing line. Hold coils in place; thread end of line through first loop above eye, then through big loop.

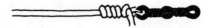

Hold tag end and standing line while pulling up coils. Make sure coils are in spiral, not overlapping. Slide tight against eye and clip tag end.

3½-TURN CLINCH KNOT

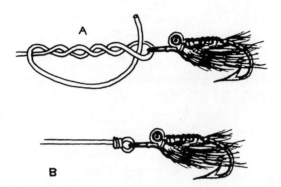

For fastening a fly to heavy 80- to 100-pound shock leader, use only three and a half turns of the clinch knot instead of the usual five turns.

straight. In that case, the 3½-turn clinch knot works best. When fishing for big fish—billfish and tuna—I would recommend the Homer Rhode loop knot be avoided. It is not a truly strong knot, and the 3½-turn clinch knot or a double surgeon's loop (even in 100-pound-test shock mono) is preferable.

For years I used the nail knot to connect backing to fly line and fly line to running line, but I think the Albright knot is stronger. I tie double surgeon's loops in the loop sections of class-tippet sections and loop them to leader butt.

The Albright special—though difficult to tie—is the only really good knot I have found to connect class tippet to heavy shock leader.

FLIES

I could spend the next one hundred pages discussing saltwater flies. Lefty Kreh recently came out with a book entitled *Salt Water Fly Patterns* and it has sixty-nine pages of color plates. I am sure he left a lot of other flies out.

Let me put it this way. There are a whole lot of saltwater flies that work and a great many others that don't. A lot of them are tied by people who want to see their names in a fly-fishing book and who never caught a saltwater fish on those flies in their lives.

ALBRIGHT SPECIAL

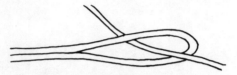

Bend a loop in tag end of heavier mono and hold between thumb and forefinger of left hand. Insert tag end of lighter mono through loop from the top.

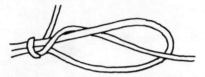

Slip tag end of lighter mono under left thumb and pinch tightly against heavier strands of loop. Wrap first turn of lighter mono over itself and continue wrapping toward round end of loop. Make at least twelve turns with lighter mono around all three strands.

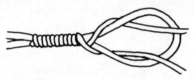

Insert tag end of lighter mono through end of loop from the bottom.

With thumb and forefinger of left hand, slide coils of lighter mono toward end of loop; stop one-eighth inch from end of loop. Using pliers, pull tag end of lighter mono tight to keep coils from slipping off loop.

With left hand still holding heavier mono, pull on standing part of lighter mono. Pull tag end of lighter mono and standing part a second time. Pull standing part of heavy mono and standing part of light mono.

Trim both tag ends.

Big saltwater poppers on #5/0 stainless hooks made up by the author for big ocean fish.

If I were told to pick one handful of flies with which to fish the rest of my life, I would fall back on the old reliable ones. I would take Lefty's Crazy Charlie and Chico Fernandez's Honey Shrimp and Dave Whitlock's Shrimp Fly for bonefish. I'd use Harry Spear's MOE epoxy fly and George Anderson's McCrab Fly for permit. Stu Apte's Tarpon Fly and John Emery's Cockroach Fly would serve me well for tarpon.

For offshore fly fishing in general, I'd take Harry Kime's Streamer Fly and Lefty's Deceiver, and for barracuda I would use a braided Fishair needlefish fly. For stripers I favor a Gibbs Striper Fly and my own poppers.

Give me a white Billy Pate Ocean Fly, tied on double #4/0 hooks, Joe Butorac's blue and white sailfish fly, and my own white poppers, tied on double #5/0 stainless-steel ocean hooks. That is all I would ever need for sailfish, roosterfish, dolphin, wahoo, marlin, or tuna.

With those flies, I'd get by anywhere.

2

The History
of the Sport

Admittedly, the records of early saltwater fly fishing are a bit obscure. In my exhaustive research of the subject, I came up with some definitive writing from early days in the United States, but foreign sources provided very little.

The very earliest writing on saltwater fly fishing I was able to find was written by the Greek, Oppian, in A.D. 176. This reference mentions fly fishing in salt water for a fish called the Scarus. Unfortunately, I have no idea what a Scarus was—or is.

Very early writing confirms, however, what we all know about fly fishing. The British author John Bickerdyke, writing in *The Encyclopedia of Sport* (Vol. 1, edited by the Earl of Suffolk and Berkshire, J. B. Lippincott Company, Philadelphia, London, 1911), said of the sport:

"Although in matters of sport, comparisons should never be invidious, by common consent there may be legitimate distinctions. Hence fly fishing is universally regarded as the highest form of angling, and it is a claim which is not advanced without sufficient reason. For example, it appeals most of all to the artistic and imaginative fancy; it demands special knowledge; it requires delicate skill; its exercise is at once costly, and beset with difficulties of an exceptional nature."

He got that right—especially the part about it being costly!

As for saltwater fly fishing in areas other than the coasts of North America, I was surprised to discover that the Australians have been doing it for several hundred years—at least in one spot near Yorkshire, particularly around Scarborough. F. G. Aflalo, in the same *Encyclopedia of Sport*, writes:

"It is, however, at Filey Brigg, a curious natural pier or breakwater, that this rock-fishing assumes its most artistic form, for cod, mackerel, and billets are caught here by casting with salmon flies, and the fish may be seen dashing at the baits in the clear water close to the rocks."

The British also brought their considerable fly-fishing skills to South Africa and used them in salt water as well as in fresh. Around the turn of the century they were taking saltwater species from the bays of the Indian Ocean. I hate to tell the experts—who claim the first bonefish caught on a fly rod came from the Florida Keys—that it ain't so. This quotation from the *Encyclopedia of Sport* (p. 121, vol. 4) is to the point:

"The best boat fishing, however [in South Africa] is in the estuaries and lagoons, where lighter tackle, with even fly rods for the smaller kinds of fish, can be used with advantage. Among the fish caught in lagoons are the Kabeljaauw up to one hundred pounds, *bony-fish* [my emphasis] up to fifteen pounds, and rock cod and grey mullet up to ten pounds."

I am assuming "bony-fish" were the same as our bonefish. They are quite common on the flats of the Indian Ocean. But while there were scattered accounts of the fly rod being used in salt water in many places in the world for centuries, it is really on the East Coast of the United States—particularly in New England and the Florida Keys—that the sport began.

One of the first written accounts of fly fishing for saltwater species appears in a book, *Camping and Cruising in Florida*, written in 1878 by Dr. James A. Henschall. He describes catching tarpon, redfish, sea trout (weakfish), snook, jack crevalle, bluefish, and "bone or ladyfish" on freshwater fly rods. Bonefish and ladyfish are two separate species of fish.

An April 1919 issue of *American Angler*, in an article written by Fred Ellsworth, went on to say that "tarpon have been taken on a fly in Florida for a long time, and they are being caught in the Panama Canal by that method."

Most outdoor writers were inclined to give Florida credit for being

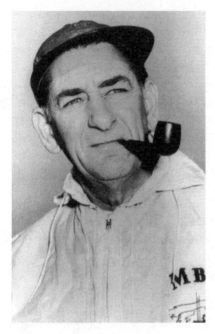

A veteran of the New England saltwater fly-fishing scene — Salt Water Sportsman *senior editor Frank Woolner.*

the place in America where saltwater fly fishing began, but the facts point toward New England. A book entitled *Fly Fishing in Salt and Fresh Water,* published in England in 1851, describes the catching of whiting, pollock, mackerel, bass, and silver mullet on flies. Since the majority of early New England settlers were from England, it makes sense to assume some of them brought fly-fishing gear to the new world.

Salt Water Sportsman reported that Genio Scott, author of *Fishing in American Waters,* wrote of fly fishing for striped bass in 1875. Tarlton H. Bean wrote in *The Basses, Fresh Water and Marine,* published in 1905, that anglers from the famous striped-bass clubs of New England sometimes used flies and black-bass fly tackle to cast for striped bass in the strong currents near the rocky shore "using a considerable length of line and manipulating it on the surface of the water."

As early as 1875, Baltimore newspapers reported that at least one fly fisherman was taking shad on trout flies below tidewater on the Susquehanna River. But it was not until just after World War II that fly fishing in salt water really took off—both in New England and the Florida Keys.

Two of the early experimenters with the long rod—for both striped bass and bluefish—were Hal Lyman and Frank Woolner. Hal began experimenting with streamers. Frank and his brother, Jack, developed a type of striper fly they called the Snake series, which was later widely copied on both the East and West Coast and called a number of things, among them the Candlefish and Tomahawk. It was a sparse streamer fly of bucktail or hackle with a long body of Mylar tubing. The object was to develop a fly that had little resistance to the air, allowing one to cast it a long distance. They even experimented with packing the Mylar tube with fish meal to attract the stripers by scent, but the meal corroded the tube and the stripers apparently didn't care for the scent of fish meal. In those days nobody worried about whether a baited fly was a fly or not. People sold the stripers they caught on the open market so anything was fair game.

Lee Wulff—perhaps more famous for his expertise at catching Atlantic salmon on a fly—nevertheless was involved in trying for saltwater species in those days too. Lee was and is a proponent of the single-action reel with no appreciable drag mechanism. He even used such reels on billfish with considerable success.

Two of the most famous early fly fishermen in the New England area were the Gibbs brothers—Harold and Frank. Both were excellent fly fishermen in the Massachusetts and Rhode Island region and the Gibbs Striper Bucktail became a must in the tackle boxes of all serious saltwater fly rodders of the area. Harold fished a lot on the Warren

Nelson Bryant, outdoor editor of the New York Times, *is an expert Martha's Vineyard striper fly fisherman.*

River in Rhode Island, and in addition to his famous bucktail tied a number of fine streamer patterns, including the Magog Smelt.

But it was the Gibbs Striper Fly that started a number of fly fishermen on the road to striped bass. J. Edson Leonard, one of the early saltwater fly fishermen, knew Harold Gibbs well and fished with him for years. Ed Leonard became one of the greatest fly tiers in America and wrote *The Essential Fly Tier* in 1976. Ed said he still had one of Harold Gibbs's striper flies that Gibbs had given him in 1949. He said it had a bright blue feather strip along the side of the white bucktail wing, a gill-like barred cheek, a silver-tinsel body, and a sparse red throat.

That fly caught stripers for decades and still does so. But Gibbs once told Leonard that a plain white bucktail would do just as well when the stripers were working in the shallows.

Ed Leonard's own streamer fly for stripers, the Galli-Nipper, is one of the best ever designed, although he says he claims only part ownership for the fly. He says its principles are as old as the wet fly itself — modesty at its best.

A charter skipper named Phil Schwind was getting considerable attention on Cape Cod in the 1940s. Fishing out of Eastham, he was market fishing for stripers and using fly rods — deadly tools when casting big, bushy streamers in combinations of white and green and white and yellow. And over on Martha's Vineyard, Nelson Bryant was just beginning to try for stripers with a fly rod in the late 1940s and early 1950s. Nels, never one to worry about the discomforts of Mother Nature, used to fly cast from an aluminum canoe just outside the surf line. As far as I can find out, he was the first to successfully catch stripers on a fly on the Vineyard, using a sand eel imitation much of the time.

There were a lot of people experimenting with fly tackle in the late 1940s and early 1950s — Paul Kukonen of Worcester, Massachusetts, among them. Paul designed a number of excellent saltwater fly patterns and was among the first to advocate using short four- to six-inch Monel or stainless-steel wire leaders ahead of the fly for bluefish.

But down in the Florida Keys fly fishermen had long been catching saltwater game fish on the long rods. Frank S. Pinckney wrote *Tarpon or Silver King,* a book published in 1888, in which he tells of a Dr. George Trowbridge catching a baby tarpon of one pound three ounces on a fly — putting him well up there among the first to do so.

A father-and-son team, A. W. Dimock and his son, Julian, regularly caught tarpon on flies about the same time and wrote a marvelous work, *Book of the Tarpon*, published in 1900. They took black-and-white photos of leaping tarpon that are a wonder today, considering the limitations on photographic equipment in those days.

A tremendous shot in the arm for saltwater fly rodders was the construction of the Florida East Coast Railway from Miami south to Key West in 1912. That island-hopping railway with its massive arched bridges opened up miles of the best bonefish, permit, and tarpon flats in the world to light-tackle anglers. By 1917 the famed Long Key Fishing Club was organized, and dedicated light-tackle anglers of the caliber of Zane Grey, Vic Barothy, Edward Vom Hofe, inventor of the famous big-game fishing reel that bore his name, President Herbert Hoover, Andrew Mellon, and a host of others joined the club.

The club awarded pins to members who caught tarpon, bonefish, permit, sailfish, wahoo, kingfish, amberjack, and barracuda. It is assumed that a lot of the wealthy members used fly rods, as the rules stated that members fishing in the competition were to use "a rod of wood . . . the tip not less than five feet in length . . . or weighing more than six ounces."

International guide and sportsman Vic Barothy said members at the club who fly fished used stiff 9½-foot and 10-foot bamboo salmon rods with a lower butt extension, and that they used a revolving Vom Hofe reel on the rods instead of fly reels. The two favored lures for the fly rods were the Feathered Minnow and the William Mills Tarpon Streamer. Unfortunately, the great club was destroyed in the violent hurricane that swept the Florida Keys in 1935—its fishing records with it.

During the same era the Pirate's Cove on Key Largo and the famous Rod and Reel Club of Miami Beach, Florida, were organized in 1928. Two club members, Red Greb and Homer Rhode, both of Miami, were fly fishing for tarpon and bonefish and designing flies for both.

George Sand, in his excellent book *Saltwater Fly Fishing*, wrote that Holmes Allen of Miami was the first man to take a bonefish with regulation fly tackle. He wrote that the incident took place in the waters of Card Sound in the Florida Keys in 1924 and that Allen was fishing with a white "crippled minnow" streamer fly.

It is generally believed that certainly one of the first fly fishermen

The legendary Joe Brooks, fly fisherman and writer, did more than anyone else to popularize the sport of saltwater fly fishing.

to catch bonefish on a fly was one Colonel L. S. Thompson of Red Bank, New Jersey, who used to fish at the Long Key Fishing Club with the veteran guide J. T. Harrod. It is said he used to fish for baby tarpon with a fly rod, using a #6 Royal Coachman trout dry fly, and regularly caught bonefish on that fly. But he considered it just an accident and was not fishing for bonefish anyway.

About this same time, 1938, the Tamiami Trail—the highway that runs west from Miami to Florida's west coast—was completed and a lot of fly fishermen began to catch snook, tarpon, and ladyfish on flies. Holmes Allen and some of his avid fly-fishing chums—Bob Aiken, Hayes Armstrong, Stewart Miller, and Red Greb—made regular trips inland along the narrow strip of canal.

Another saltwater fly-fishing pioneer of that day was Dave Newell, who began fishing with the long rod on Florida's west coast "when Luke Gates got me started over at Casey's Pass, on the Gulf Coast, on snook, sea trout, jacks, and redfish." I spent many a happy day with him fly fishing for Atlantic salmon on Canada's beautiful Miramichi River in the last years of his life. We had grand days fishing with his favorite guide, Harley Stuart, and also with another longtime fly fisherman, Hugh Grey.

Other pioneers of saltwater fly fishing in those early days were Howard Bonbright, Frank Baxter, Bo Randall, and Lee Cuddy. Bonbright's Tarpon Fly was sold in Abercrombie & Fitch stores from the

Captain Lee Cuddy is a veteran Florida guide and the man credited with catching the first sailfish on a fly—a forty-seven-pound sail caught June 4, 1964.

1920s on. It is still listed in a lot of fly catalogs.

Of course there were any number of Florida Keys guides who were constantly experimenting with flies and fly rods for all kinds of fish. Yet because they were not famous or well known, their exploits seldom came to light. One such fine fly caster was Bonnie Smith, wife of veteran Keys guide, Bill Smith. Bonnie moved from Georgia in the mid-1930s with her two sisters, Beulah and Frankee.

Bonnie got into fly casting when the excellent fly-rod guide Preston Pinder taught her about fly rods and reels and how to cast a fly. Bonnie took to the fly rod like a duck to water and proceeded to teach her two sisters the art. All three women eventually became accomplished fly fishers and all also married guides. When these guides went off to World War II, the women took over their husbands' guiding businesses, and by the time the men came home the wives had earned names for themselves.

Bill and Bonnie Smith helped Joe Brooks buy a house in Islamorada, and Joe set off on a quest to catch with a fly rod nearly everything that swims. It was here, after the war, that Joe—fishing with Keys guide Captain Leo Johnson, Bill and Bonnie Smith, Joe's wife, Mary, and Miami tackle-shop operator Ralph Miller—set out on his quest to catch a permit on a fly.

It took him a couple of years, but finally at Content Key he caught a five-pound-ten-ounce permit using a Johnson Golden Minnow fly-rod spoon. He considered it the first permit caught on a fly rod, but he wanted to catch one on a fly — not a fly-rod spoon. The following year, guided by Bonnie Smith, he succeeded in catching a twelve-pound-eight-ounce permit at Content Key, using a white bucktail fly on a #1/0 hook. That was in May 1951. The following year, Eddie Miller of Miami caught a fourteen-pound permit on a fly at Key Largo, and Bonnie Smith caught a permit on a fly while wading a flat at Islamorada soon afterwards — the first women to do so.

Ten years later, Joe went on to catch a twenty-three-pound permit on a fly at Bimini in the Bahamas while fishing with a veteran Bimini guide, "Bonefish Sam" Ellis, and Don McCarthy. That great fish held the fly-rod record for a decade before it fell to Chuck Walton's thirty-pound permit on a fly at Sugarloaf Key in 1970.

I was stationed for a brief time in 1943 at the old Thirty-sixth Street Airport in Miami (now Miami International Airport) while attending navigation school in the Army Air Force during World War II. Being the same fishing nut I am now, I fished every chance I got. My buddies and I used to go down to Biscayne Bay and charter boats for sailfish and smaller stuff. I didn't use fly rods in salt water then, only for the excellent bass fishing on the Tamiami Canal. In salt water I used short rods and level-winding reels. To show you how times have changed, a fishing guide in those days — bringing his own boat, outboard motor, and guiding skills — would charge between $20 and $35 a day!

In a new era — the 1950s and 1960s — saltwater fly fishing began to take off like a rocket. *Everybody* who had been dedicated to flailing the great freshwater rivers and lakes seemingly discovered bonefish, permit, and tarpon all of a sudden. Anglers of the caliber of Stu Apte, Billy Pate, Joe Brooks, Joe Lopez, Chico Fernandez, A. J. McClane, Mark Sosin, and Lefty Kreh seemed to suddenly appear in the Florida Keys and Bahamas. Even the tackle companies produced some excellent saltwater fly fishermen such as Scientific Anglers' Leon Martuch and Orvis's Leigh Perkins.

Stu Apte, an airline jet pilot by profession, burst upon the saltwater fly-fishing scene with his uncanny ability to catch big tarpon on a fly. He both fished and guided out of Islamorada in the 1950s and 1960s, taking one world record after another. His Stu Apte Tarpon Fly and his Stu Apte blood knot are just two of his contributions to the sport.

Stu Apte has held innumerable tarpon records on a fly; he caught the first Pacific sailfish on a fly (136 pounds) in 1965. It is still a record on 12-pound-test tippet.

Both Lefty Kreh and Mark Sosin were easterners—Lefty from Maryland and Sosin from New Jersey—who became enamored with fly fishing for stripers and bluefish. They were instrumental in organizing the Salt Water Flyrodders of America and in setting up the record-class rules for saltwater fly fishing that exist today. By the 1970s the administering of the organization had become difficult, and it was turned over to the capable hands of the IGFA in Fort Lauderdale, Florida.

I did much the same thing while editor-in-chief of *Field & Stream* in the late 1970s. The magazine had kept records of both freshwater and saltwater fishing for nearly eighty years, but by the mid-1970s the keeping of the records had fallen to one magazine employee, Mary Ball. Mary was known as "Mike" Ball on the masthead probably because early editors assumed a woman did not carry enough authority to handle such an impressive task. At any rate, I turned over the entire record keeping of the *Field & Stream* Fishing Contest to the IGFA, which is doing a magnificent job with it today.

Both Lefty and Mark later spent a great deal of time fishing in the Florida Keys, Bahamas, and elsewhere in the tropics. Lefty went on to write the definitive book on saltwater fly fishing, *Fly Fishing in Salt Water,* and Sosin went on to do great things in the area of television fishing shows with "Mark Sosin's Salt Water Journal."

Mark Sosin was one of the early founders of the Salt Water Flyrodders of America. He later went into television and did much to educate and entertain the public about saltwater fishing with Mark Sosin's Saltwater Journal.

Billy Pate, a South Carolinian, began catching big fish on a fly in the late 1950s and early 1960s, setting successive records for tarpon on a fly. He then went on to become the first man to catch both species of sailfish and four species of marlin on a fly. He set the world record for tarpon on a fly with a 188-pound monster, caught at Homosassa Springs, Florida, on May 13, 1982.

A. J. McClane, a fishing editor of thirty years for *Field & Stream* when I was editor-in-chief in the 1970s, had pioneered fly fishing for bonefish in the Bahamas and wrote profusely about the sport in the magazine—particularly about Deep Water Cay, the excellent bonefish and permit island owned by his longtime friend, Gil Drake, Sr. Gil Drake, Jr. and his wife, Linda, later became premier bonefish, tarpon, and permit guides at Key West.

The fly fishermen who flocked to the Florida Keys in those days were legion: Bill Barnes, Jim Lopez, Bob Stearnes, Bill Levy, Chico Fernandez, Winston Moore, Jim Chapralis, Bermuda's Pete Perinchief, "Pop" Hill and his son Gordie, Del Brown, Pat Ford, Dave Chermanski, and baseball great Ted Williams. All were in search of flats fish like bonefish, tarpon, permit, mutton snapper—anything that would take a fly and fight.

In the area of big fish, Dr. Webster Robinson and his wife, Helen, were off Key West trying to catch sailfish on a fly. "Doc" Robinson began experimenting by casting flat-bottomed cork popping bugs with big fly rods—culminating in his catch of a sailfish of 74½ pounds in 1962. Robinson was to go on in the next few years to take a 145-pound striped marlin on a fly from the waters of Baja California.

Lee Wulff was busy taking bonefish, tarpon, permit, and billfish on a fly and writing excellent books about it. His superb *Fishing with Lee Wulff*, published in 1972—the same year I fished with Lee and his wife, Joan, in Iceland—is a classic. In it he writes about flats fishing as well as taking sailfish and marlin on a fly.

Out on the West Coast, Harry Kime had been experimenting with fly fishing for saltwater species for years. After spending a lifetime fly fishing for freshwater species, Harry suddenly discovered Baja and Mexico. Up until then he had fished for trout and salmon in California, Iceland, and British Columbia, but when he found out what Pacific yellowtail and dolphin did on a fly rod, he gave up fresh water and became a saltwater fly rodder. And this was at almost age sixty!

Harry's experiments led to the first practical flies for dolphin, yellowtail, and sailfish. His later fishing at Casa Mar, Costa Rica, led to the development of some excellent tarpon flies.

Harry fished from Loreto in Baja and caught yellowtail, dolphin, roosterfish, sailfish, and marlin—all from a wooden skiff—back in the

The late Dr. Webster Robinson and his wife, Helen, developed the method of teasing up and catching billfish on a fly rod. "Doc" later went on to catch striped marlin on a fly off Cabo San Lucas, landing a 145-pound striped marlin in the early 1960s. Although he caught dozens of sailfish and three or four striped marlin, Webster never entered any of his fish for IGFA fly-rod records.

late 1950s and early 1960s. Like his friend Ray Cannon—who really discovered Baja and loved to fish with a fly rod—Harry began fishing off Loreto when *nobody* went there.

There was no Baja highway then, and Harry flew to Loreto with Ed Tabor, one of the great Baja bush pilots of the early 1960s.

"I hit the Sea of Cortez more than thirty years ago," Harry told me in 1989. "The fishing was fantastic. I fished for Pacific yellowtail in the cooler months and dorado in the summer months. I kept all the yellowtail to feed the natives, but released all the dorado—I had no ice in the skiffs I used at Loreto. I was very happy with the Loreto fly fishing for a decade, but I finally started fishing for sailfish. I used only a nine-inch molded rubber squid as a teaser. I stopped the skiff when the sailfish hit and cast a seven- to nine-inch fly when the sailfish was at close range. This fishing was south of Cabo San Lucas—on the Mexican mainland—between Mazatlan and Manzanillo."

Harry, at eighty years old, was still fly fishing happily at Casa Mar in 1989, catching tarpon off the mouth of the Rio Colorado. I talked to him in October 1989 while fly fishing for big snook. We had been discussing sailfish and marlin. Harry had lost count of the number of sailfish he had taken on a fly, but he was not optimistic about taking marlin on a fly.

"I have hooked several marlin, but only boated four in the past twenty years," he said. "Marlin up to two hundred pounds sound

The late Harry Kime with a batch of fly-caught yellowtail taken off Mulege, Baja, in the late 1950s. Kime pioneered the sport of saltwater fly fishing on the California coast and in the Sea of Cortez, taking yellowtail, dorado, roosterfish, sailfish, and striped marlin long before anyone else thought of trying it.

possible, but larger than that on a fly—most unlikely."

I spent a lot of time in south Florida in the 1960s and fished with Billy Pate, Stu Apte, and such veteran guides as Jack Brothers, Dick Williams, Lee Baker, Hank Brown, Billy Knowles, George Hommell and Jimmie Albright. Even after I joined *Field & Stream* in 1970, I continued going to the Keys—fishing in the annual Gold Cup Tarpon Tournaments and the bonefish tourneys.

The first billfish fly tournament was sponsored by Billy Pate off Islamorada in the early 1970s. I fished with Pate on that one in terrible weather. Only one sailfish was caught on a fly. It was won by Rip McIntosh of Palm Beach, Florida. The sport was slow to catch on.

The first official fly tournament for sails and marlin—the First International Invitational Billfish Fly Tournament—was held May 2–6, 1989, at Flamingo Beach, Costa Rica. It was sponsored by Billy Pate and George Hommell of Wide World Sportsman of Islamorada, Florida, and saw a field of sixteen boats and thirty-two anglers enter from all over the world. It was a far cry from the tiny Islamorada tournament more than a decade and a half earlier. It was so international, a Japanese team took second place.

The 1980s have been the decade of saltwater fly fishing. Young people have discovered the marvelous solitude of the bonefish, tar-

Veteran Florida flats guide Hal Chittum, who is responsible for a number of tarpon fly-rod world records.

Chico Fernandez, one of the real pioneers in saltwater fly fishing and an outstanding tyer of saltwater flies, with his world-record channel bass, caught May 12, 1981, at Oregon Inlet, North Carolina. The fish was caught on 12-pound-test tippet and weighed forty-two pounds five ounces. It is still the largest channel bass ever caught on a fly. IGFA lists the fish under red drum.

pon, and permit flats in an era when the freshwater streams, lakes, and rivers are becoming overcrowded and polluted.

Tackle stores on the East Coast, around the Gulf of Mexico, and on the West Coast of the United States have begun to carry saltwater fly tackle they did not know existed a decade ago. Rod, reel, and line companies have seen the mushrooming growth of the sport and are now catering to the army of fly fishermen heading for the flats and deep water with the fly rod in hand. Boat companies making 18- to 30-foot, center-console, deep-water boats for fly fishermen are experiencing a boom in business. Those making flats boats doubled their business in the last few years.

In the Florida Keys smart, young, and enthusiastic guides of the caliber of Sandy Moret, Rick Ruoff, Steve Huff, and Flip Pallot—aided by such venerable experts as Stu Apte and Chico Fernandez—have opened a saltwater fly-fishing school to help fly fishermen explore the possibilities of the flats and blue water.

Silvio Calabi, publisher of *Fly Rod & Reel*, reported that by 1989 saltwater fly-fishing tackle accounted for 25 percent of the *entire* fly-fishing tackle market.

Saltwater fly fishing is an idea whose time has come.

3

Wind Knots and Turtle Grass—Bonefish

A solitary great blue heron stood guard over a vast flat, shimmering in the June heat of the Bahamas, and arctic terns wheeled and dove at a school of minnows close by the wooden skiff.

"Tide's about right," said Ray Pritchard, bonefish guide from the nearby settlement of Alicetown, a collection of weather-beaten shacks perched on the southeastern tip of North Bimini. "She's been comin' in for about two hours. The bones should be workin' up onto the flat pretty soon."

I squinted into the morning glare and glanced at the big, tall, white house topped by a huge circular balcony that straddled Paradise Point to the north.

"Strange-looking place," I said. "What's the big balcony for?"

"Roller skating, folks say."

"Roller skating?"

"Rich man who built the big house—years ago—liked to roller skate. He made all his money by inventing the hubcap in the States. So he built that big balcony and poured a cement floor on it so he and his guests could roller skate."

"Jesus."

"Yeah. Lots of rich guys and their women come here to stay in that house over the years—writers like Hemingway, Van Campen Heilner—lots of them. Some of them, like Heilner, damned good fishermen too. My father used to take them bonefishing before the Big War."

The Big War. Here it was 1968, Korea had been over for more than a decade, and the Vietnam War was raging in Southeast Asia—and tearing our land apart at the same time—and yet, for men of my generation, ours was still the Big War.

"I remember his book on saltwater fishing," I said. "He used to write about Bimini and bonefish. He really loved this place."

"He caught a lot of bones here," Ray said. "My father said he used to take him and a friend out even on full-moon nights. They caught some big bones down off south Bimini."

"What do you use to catch them?" I asked. I had never seen a bonefish, much less caught one. I had heard Bimini was the best place to go to catch big ones and had flown in the night before on one of the rickety Grumman flying boats of Chalk Airlines. The clerk at the desk of the Big Game Club had recommended "Bonefish Ray" as the best guide around.

"Conch, mostly," Ray said, tossing me a piece of the battered bait. "We dig it out of the conch shell and hammer it for a while till it gets easy to work with. It stays on the hook better than crab—though sometimes bones like crab better."

I looked at the spinning rod and reel resting across the seats of the wooden skiff. The monofilament looked to be about 12-pound-test. The open-face reel could have held several hundred yards of it. A chunk of conch was impaled on a #3/0 stainless-steel hook. There was no sinker on the line. I guessed that the weight of the conch was enough to carry it out.

"Bones," Ray said suddenly and stood up, a hand shading his eyes. "Nice school. Some big ones in it." He took the long wooden pole and jammed an end of it into the sand beneath the boat.

"Get ready," he said softly, handing me the rod. "When I point, try to throw the bait where I say. Then close the bail and wait. I'll tell you when to strike."

I was wearing polarized glasses and looked where Ray was looking. I could see nothing but the glassy surface of the flat. A soft breeze rippled the surface as I looked, but I could see no signs of fish.

"Where are they?" I whispered, standing up.

"There," Ray pointed, holding his arm steady, "About fifty feet off. They're moving slowly toward us—feeding on the bottom. About a foot of water. See the little puffs of sand?"

There was a bright sun shining and the bottom was white sand. I could see nothing but that.

"Okay," Ray said suddenly, "They're turning left a iittle. Try to get the bait about there." He pointed.

I had used a spinning rod off and on since the 1950s, mostly for largemouth bass. I was fairly good with it, although I was primarily a fly fisherman. I opened the bail with my left hand and cast the chunk of conch. It landed with a *splat* where Ray had pointed. I closed the bail and raised the rod tip.

"Good." Ray whispered. "They're movin' toward it . . . good, good. One's goin' for it. He's takin' it. Okay, just raise the rod tip."

I did so, slowly, and suddenly the rod was almost jerked from my grasp. An area in front of us erupted in a sea of splashes, and the reel screeched as a fish headed directly away from us in the shallow water. My line tore a searing slash in the surface of the flat. I was too surprised to do anything but hang on to the throbbing rod.

"Whooee, mon!" Ray shouted, jamming his pole into the sand and shoving the skiff forward. "Big bonefish. Keep that tip up!"

That was truly a battle. That bonefish must have run at least two hundred yards on the first run, churning up bottom sand and bits of turtle grass. It finally slowed, and we fought it for twenty minutes— me pumping and Ray poling. By the time I got that strong fish near the boat, I was soaked with perspiration and my right arm was almost dead.

Ray dropped the pole across the boat and grabbed a large aluminum dip net as the bonefish lay on its side, its gills pumping. With one swoop he scooped up the fish and held it wriggling in the mesh, gleaming in the morning sunlight. We looked at each other and Ray reached out a hand.

"Good fish, mon," he said, laughing. "Go about nine pounds. Good fish for your first one. Hey mon, how you like bonefish?"

I looked from him to the squirming fish.

"My God," I said. "What a fish! I wonder if I could catch one on a fly rod?"

"Fly rod?" Ray asked. "Hell, mon, why didn't you say somethin'?

Maybe we could have borrowed one from the club. Two or three fishermen come over here from Miami and fish with a fly rod once in awhile."

That was the beginning. We didn't borrow a fly rod that day, but we caught two more small bonefish on the spinning rod, and I was hooked—literally.

Van Campen Heilner, in his book *Salt Water Fishing*, published in 1937, ended his chapter on fishing for bonefish at Bimini with this quotation:

"Whom the gods would destroy

They first make a bonefisherman."

Amen.

The following year I was asked by Al Rockwell to help make Cat Cay, a few miles south of Bimini, a great big-game fishing club again. The club had once been known as a premier marlin and bluefin tuna angling center during the heyday of "Uncle Lou" Wasey, a New York advertising man who had leased the island from the Bahamian government in the 1930s.

But the posh island had been leveled by the ferocity of Hurricane Betsy, which had smashed into it in 1965, demolishing the docks,

A nice bonefish taken on Andros Island, Bahamas.

crushing dozens of palatial homes, and leaving the island strewn with palm fronds and wrecked sports cars. The wealthy club members, for the most part, had never returned to the lovely island. Rockwell and a consortium of investors had purchased the island in 1969 with the idea of restoring it as a plush private club.

I had been doing a lot of big-game fishing over the years—having been on the professional tournament circuit from the Bahamas and Florida to Baja and Kona—and had gained a name as a marlin and bluefin angler. I had even written a successful book on the sport, *Line Down!*, and Rockwell, with whom I hunted and fished a lot, decided I was just the man to put the Cat Cay Club back on the map as a prime fishing resort.

The public relations work I was doing for the island was just that—work—but the real find was a small bonefish flat on the east side of the tiny island. It must have been very popular with the members before the advent of the hurricane, but by the winter of 1969 nobody had fished it for four years. I was the only fisherman among a few hundred construction workers rebuilding the island.

I had been a fly-rod trout fisherman all my life, but I had never wet a fly line in salt water. In addition to trout, I had fished for Atlantic salmon in Quebec and the Maritime Provinces of Canada, but it had never occurred to me that the fly rod could be used in the ocean. The small bonefish flat at Cat Cay gave me my first chance to experiment.

The trip to Bimini the year before had given me my first exposure to bonefish, but I had no idea how to go about pursuing them with fly tackle. I had several good split-bamboo fly rods that I used for trout and salmon, a good Hardy reel, and a Zwarg salmon reel, but common sense told me they were unsuited for the task.

Fortunately for me, one of the longtime employees of Abercrombie & Fitch in New York, Emil Schmidt, was an expert on saltwater fly fishing. My office was only a few blocks from the venerable old store, and Emil made up a list of what I would need to attack the bonefish problem. He recommended a 9-foot, 9-weight fiberglass fly rod, a floating, weight-forward, 8-weight fly line, and twelve-foot leaders tapering down to both 8- and 4-pound-test tippets. He suggested I purchase a Fin-Nor saltwater fly reel with a capacity of two hundred yards of twenty-pound Micron or Dacron backing, plus a ninety-foot fly line. His list of flies included Bill Curtiss's Blue Tail Fly, Lefty Kreh's Black Beauty, Chico Fernandez's Bonefish Special,

Bonnie's Tailing Bonefish Fly, Bob Nauheim's Crazy Charlie, Jimmie Albright's Frankee-Belle Bonefish Fly, Carl Navarre's Greenie Weenie, and George Hommell's blue Evil Eye—a thoroughly professional selection.

I almost went into shock at the price. I had no idea saltwater fly gear—the reels in particular—could cost that much! Had I known what the same outfit would cost today, I would gladly have paid the price and kept quiet. But, with only a few shortcuts, I outfitted myself and headed for Cat Cay.

Looking back on that time today, I realize how ill-prepared I was for bonefishing. I knew nothing about the habits of the fish, the ecology of a bonefish flat, the techniques needed to catch one on a fly, or what to do with one after I hooked it.

I began by wading the small flat barefoot—a serious mistake. I almost immediately cut myself on sharp shells, rough coral rocks, and wore off a lot of tender skin on coarse sand. A pair of tennis shoes helped, but did nothing to dull the sharp spines of the black, bottom-hugging sea urchins.

It took me a week to realize that the almost invisible, silver ghost-like shapes I was seeing flitting by me on the flat were bonefish. I had been casting flies at boxfish, needlefish, all sorts of snappers, barracuda, and small sharks. I lost a number of flies to the sharp teeth of the snappers before I learned what they were.

I began trying for bonefish in March, and it was late April before I learned enough to find the fish on the incoming and outgoing tides and figured out the pattern of their feeding. Even then I threw flies into the middle of bonefish schools, short of the schools, and behind the schools, spooking innumerable fish with the leader. I frightened fish by wading right up to them, by waving my arm when they were close, and by false-casting right over the school. I wore bright shirts until it dawned on me that the fish were fleeing from the flat when I approached. I lost so many pretied tapered leaders that I had to learn to tie my own good knots in desperation. I read everything I could find on fly fishing for bonefish—including Stanley Babson's marvelous work.

By late April, I was an expert on surface glare, wind-ruffled surfaces, twenty-five-knot winds that whipped a fly line unmercifully, and overcast days when I could see nothing. I was also becoming an expert on badly burned skin and chapped lips, but I had hooked and lost two small bonefish on a fly.

The last day of April was a day of triumph. I was crouched down—on a still, clear morning—close to the small channel that separates North from South Cat Cay. The tide was pouring in from the Gulf Stream to the west, and as I stared into the clear water ahead of me, I saw a school of bonefish making its way up the channel. They were not feeding, but heading for the flat behind me. I had on a Phillips Pink Shrimp—a favorite of the legendary Joe Brooks—tied on a #4 hook. As the fish approached, I dropped the fly a good twelve feet ahead of the school and allowed it to sink. I had not yet learned to strip the fly with my left hand so the rod tip gave a jerking motion to the fly.

To my utter amazement the lead fish swung to its left and took the pink fly as it sank toward the bottom. I was so in shock that I failed to set the hook. It was probably a good thing, as it is better not to strike. The swimming fish hooked itself and—feeling the bite of the hook—streaked for the flat behind me. I had enough sense to raise the rod tip and the battle was on.

The rest of the small school stayed with the hooked fish for part of the fight, but finally left for deeper water. I was running and stumbling across the flat, in knee-deep water, trying to keep up with that churning bonefish. It headed south along the curve of the flat and easily took 150 yards of line before I had enough sense to follow it.

The fish finally wore itself out fighting that rod and dragging line, and I managed to work it into very shallow water along the east side of south Cat Cay. I had no net, so I gradually eased it up on the dry sand and fell upon it like a ravenous osprey. What a triumph! A frigate bird, circling lazily high above in the clear blue sky, cocked its head at my whoop of joy.

I carried that bonefish back to the boat docks and showed it to every bored construction worker in the area. I had my photograph taken with it and would have had it mounted had there been a taxidermist anywhere near Cat Cay. As it was, one of the Bahamian cooks asked me if he could have it to eat. I had no way of preserving it anyway, so I gave it to him—reluctantly. It weighed exactly eight pounds four ounces on the kitchen scales—a figure I shall never forget.

From that day on my fly fishing for bonefish was all downhill, as the saying goes. I got better and better, and by late May 1969, I was convinced I was an expert on the subject—like most beginners. Twenty years later I realize there is a whole lot I still have to learn

The Crazy Charlie Fly is probably the best all-around fly for bonefish.

about the subject, but at least I am smart enough to know that now.

I was fortunate enough to have my own 17-foot Boston Whaler at Cat Cay (that I ran across the Gulf Stream from Fort Lauderdale with the help of my oldest son, John) and it gave me considerable mobility to fish bonefish flats—although the bigger whalers drew too much water to be ideal bonefish boats.

I was able to run the whaler (equipped with an 80-horsepower outboard) up to Bimini regularly. It was only about a nine-mile run, up past Gun Cay to the entrance of Bimini harbor, and I was able to fish with Ray Pritchard and Mike Hinzey for bonefish at least once a week all that summer. The late Mike Hinzey was an all-around fisherman and skippered the *Striper II,* an old wooden Hatteras that was a great marlin boat. But Mike also liked to fish for bonefish, and we had many a great day on the flats.

In late summer I was able to spend several days on Chub Cay at the Ocean Reef Club, where the veteran bonefish fly fisherman Lou Dougherty taught me a lot about spotting bonefish schools and how to fish for various tailing fish. It was there that I saw my first permit taken on light spinning tackle. Lou was a marvelous caster and spent most of his free time on the bonefish flats.

A. J. (Al) McClane came down to Cat Cay that summer to fish with me and brought his wife, Patti, and Bing McClellan. We caught some nice bonefish on flies from my Whaler and it was there that A. J.

taught me a lesson about bonefish I will never forget. He tossed a big Zaragosa plug, with three sets of gang hooks on it, out on the flats where it was almost immediately struck by a fish. When I asked him what he thought had hit it, he shrugged and continued to play it.

"Could be anything," he said casually. "Barracuda, jack, snapper, bonefish."

"Bonefish!" said the world's biggest bonefish expert, with at least two months of fly-fishing experience to back it up. "Hell, a bonefish won't take a plug!"

When McClane had the fish to the boat, he handed the rod to Patti.

"Here, Patti," he said. "A nice bonefish. Should go about eight pounds. Bonefish will sometimes take a plug," he told the shamefaced expert. "They feed mostly on crustaceans, shellfish, worms, lots of things, but now and then they will take small baitfish—and plugs," he laughed.

Later I was to fish with A. J. at both Deep Water Cay and Chub Cay, and I have seldom seen anyone who knew more about bonefish or was a better fly caster for them.

By fall, when my public relations tasks were over and Cat Cay was well launched as a big-game fishing island and successful club, I was able to fish a few more Bahama islands for bonefish—Andros, Grand Bahama, and Treasure Cay—before returning to my New York City headquarters. But by that time I was an incurable saltwater fly rodder, fishing for striped bass with the likes of Nelson and Danny Bryant up at Edgartown on Martha's Vineyard, the Sherman brothers in New York, and Al Ristori off Montauk.

But it was bonefish that had me hooked, and I traveled to the Florida Keys every chance I had to fish with Billy Pate and such veteran Islamorada guides as Billy Knowles. It was Knowles who added at least twenty feet to my casting distance. With a right arm the thickness of my thigh, he had been throwing big tarpon flies on #3/0 hooks into the wind for years.

Like most freshwater fly casters of the "old school," I had learned to fly cast over small bodies of water. It had never been necessary for me to cast flies long distances. Most trout streams required a cast of not more than twenty to thirty feet. Accuracy had always been more important than distance to me. Even on the relatively open surfaces of bass ponds, a fly caster seldom had to cast more than forty feet to a weed bed. I had learned to cast a fly accurately—for distances up to perhaps sixty to seventy feet—on the big trout rivers of the west, but the bonefish flats were a different ballgame. With a thirty- to forty-knot wind blowing in one's face, throwing a fly eighty feet to a school of cruising bonefish took a lot of know-how. I never mastered it during my Cat Cay days, but I did learn how to cast on the flats from Billy Pate and guides like Billy Knowles.

Since I am a right-handed caster, the stiff winds blowing from my right baffled me for a time. The heavy line and fly needed for tarpon would come whistling back on the forward cast low and dangerous to both me and the guide. Knowles showed me how to shift the big 12-weight fly rod in my right hand as I started the forward cast so that the tip moved from my right up through the vertical as the rod came forward. That way the line and fly would come forward over my left shoulder rather than my right.

Pate showed me the double haul—that little trick that is so valuable to anyone attempting to cast a distance with a fly rod. It seemed difficult to learn at first—akin to rubbing one's stomach and patting one's head at the same time—but it turned out to be a simple technique to master. Over the years it has become second nature to me, and I use the double haul at all times while fly casting in both fresh and salt water.

The double haul consists of giving a sharp, short jerk—of approximately six to eight inches—on the fly line with the left hand just at the instant the fly is being picked up from the surface with the right hand. Since it is done at the same time the rod is being loaded (picking up the line, leader, and fly for the powerful backcast), it dramatically increases the speed of the line.

That short, fast jerk of the left hand consists of the first part of the double haul. The second part is another fast but slightly longer tug on the line by the left hand as the line begins to move on the forward cast. These two almost imperceptible movements of the left hand speed up the moving fly line and can add considerable distance to a cast. The double haul takes some practice, but once learned it becomes a natural part of fly casting.

Williams, Brothers, and Albright were a few of the original guides who had fished the Keys during and after World War II, and they had marvelous stories about the early days. It was Williams and Albright who discovered the now-famous Buchannan Bank to the west of Islamorada, where tarpon pass by in single file each spring and early summer. Now, anglers and guides speed out in a matter of minutes to Buchannan Bank in modern fiberglass flats boats powered by enormous outboard engines.

Back in 1945 and 1946 it took the veteran guides hours to putt-putt out to the bank in heavy wooden skiffs powered by small outboard motors.

"We had to get up pretty early in those days," Dick Williams told me once, when we were entered as angler and guide in one of the annual Invitational Bonefish Tournaments at Islamorada back in the early 1970s.

"Hell, if a customer wanted to fish an eight-hour day and wanted to fish for tarpon at Buchannan," he said, poling the boat along the west side of Nine-Mile Bank, "we had to leave before daylight. With two hours out and two back, we only had four hours on the bank before it was time to go in."

Jimmie Albright, considered the dean of Keys guides today, began his fishing career before World War II as mate on a deep-sea fishing boat out of Fort Lauderdale, Florida. During the war he fished for bonefish with Bonnie Smith. Bonnie was holding down the family business while her guide-husband, Bill Smith, was in the service.

When both Bill and Jimmie returned from the service, Bill taught Albright the tricks of Keys guiding and they both made names for themselves in the business. Joe Brooks, fishing editor of *Outdoor Life*, and the man who probably did the most to popularize saltwater fly fishing in the period after World War II, fished often with Albright. Joe was convinced he was the first saltwater fly rodder to take bonefish on a fly purposely, although there is some evidence he was far from the first.

Joe, a marvelous fly fisherman and a great writer, put it his own way in his book *Salt Water Game Fishing*.

"The first two tailing fish to be deliberately fished for with flies and caught," he wrote, "were taken by the writer, while guided by Captain Jimmie Albright, at Islamorada."

That was in June 1947. Joe, Jimmie, and Allen Corson towed a skiff out to Peterson Key in Albright's larger boat, the *Rebel*. Brooks cast a Red Greb streamer fly—a grizzly-winged fly with a white chenille body, tied on a #1/0 hook—and hooked and landed two bonefish approximately eight pounds each from a tailing school of fish, no

Expert guide Jimmie Albright (right) with Joe Brooks and three fly-caught bonefish taken in 1947 in the Florida Keys.

mean feat in those early days. Joe stipulated *tailing* bonefish, and was convinced he was the first to do that.

For my money, a lot of the Keys guides probably contributed the most to early fly fishing for bonefish. Bonnie Smith was given one of the fine bamboo fly rods built by the legendary George LaBranche of dry-fly trout-fishing fame, and became an accomplished saltwater fly rodder and guide. Bonnie is generally credited with being the first woman to take a permit on a fly, and her husband Bill caught a bonefish using his own flies in 1938. There were reports of other anglers, such as Milton Bugbee of Islamorada, catching bonefish on flies by accident during the same general period.

Unlike the Bahamas, where schools of small bonefish in the two- to three-pound category are common, large fish are the rule in the Florida Keys. I would estimate that the average bonefish caught in the Keys would weigh in the vicinity of five to six pounds. This is why fly fishermen flock in such numbers to places like Islamorada, Marathon, Key Largo, and Biscayne Bay. Bimini and Andros are about the only two Bahamian islands where big bonefish can be consistently caught on a fly. But they are caught all over the Keys—Islamorada being about the best spot. The current IGFA book on saltwater fly-rod bonefish records would also indicate this.

Tippet Class	Weight	Place	Date	Angler
2 lb.	11 lb. 12 oz.	Andros Island	3/15/83	Rod Neubert
4 lb.	15 lb.	Bimini	3/17/83	Jim Orthwein
8 lb.	13 lb. 4 oz.	Islamorada	11/6/73	Jim Lopez
12 lb.	14 lb. 6 oz.	Islamorada	9/22/85	Vic Gaspeny
16 lb.	13 lb.	Bimini	3/4/86	Jim Orthwein

These, like all records, will be broken by other fly rodders. After all, the all-tackle record for bonefish is a whopping nineteen pounds, caught in South Africa in 1962 by Brian Batchelor. Lefty Kreh, the great saltwater fly rodder and an angler who probably has caught as many bonefish on a fly rod as anyone alive, says he has seen some giant bonefish at Andros Island. There is no question that Bimini holds giant bonefish as does the small Shell Key, just to the west of Islamorada. Veteran bonefish guide Bill Curtis, fly rodder, and the inventor of the fine Blue Tail Fly for bonefish, has guided the Biscayne Bay area just south of Miami for decades. He has caught huge bonefish, some weighing more than twelve pounds.

Lefty likes a 5- to 6-weight fly rod for bonefish with a reel that holds at least 150 yards of eighteen- to twenty-pound Micron or Dacron backing. For distance on wind-free days, he would advocate going to a fly rod with a matching 7-weight, floating, weight-forward fly line. I would agree up to that point, but there are places I like to have a 8- to 9-weight rod and matching line. I have seen bonefish at such spots as the Andros Island Bonefish Club that turned my knees to water. Some of them had to be thirteen to fourteen pounds! For those fish—and the big ones at Bimini during spawning season in mid winter and early spring—I would feel a whole lot safer with a 9-foot graphite, 9-weight rod with an 8-weight, floating, weight-forward fly line and a reel with no less capacity than two hundred yards of twenty-pound backing and line. I hooked a bonefish off Islamorada in 1978 that took all two hundred yards and a ninety-foot fly line off a Pate Bonefish reel and never slowed down when the 12-pound-test tippet snapped! Neither I nor the guide had any idea how big that bonefish was.

The bonefish, *Albula vulpes,* is an incredibly strong fish. It is a distinct species of very bony, primitive fishes that date back at least 125 million years. It is distributed around the world in warm tropical waters. It is a bright, silver color with dark streaks on the sides. Although the bonefish has a hard, rubbery mouth with no teeth, it does have a set of granular plates in the upper and lower mouth that can instantly grind molusks and crustaceans to a pulp.

It is just because the fish does not have teeth that it is not necessary to strike it when it takes the fly. The bonefish picks up a fly and slides it back into the mouth. When the angler feels a slight tug, or sees the leader twitch, it is only necessary to raise the rod tip to set the hook. After that, keep the rod tip up and play the fish off the reel. Most bonefish are lost to the saltwater fly rodder in the first few seconds of a run because the line is held in the left hand when that swift run begins.

Once there were only a very few people trying bonefish flies— Lefty Kreh, Chico Fernandez, Joe Brooks, Bill Curtis, Bill Smith, Winston Moore, Jimmie Albright, George Hommell, Lee Cuddy, Nat Ragland, Al Pfleuger, and a few others. Now there are hundreds, some of them excellent tiers as well as fine bonefish fly fishermen.

The selection of bonefish flies is so large that only seasoned guides can tell the novice what really works for a specific area. A whole new category of bonefish flies has been developed since Marathon guide Harry Spears developed the hot-glue Epoxy Fly some years ago. Harry's original Mother Of Epoxy, or MOE Fly, started a whole new trend in bonefish and permit flies for the fly rodder. They work well, but are not as easy to cast as the traditional, smaller, feathered bonefish flies.

High-tech materials, sharper and better hooks, and advanced fly-tying equipment have all made a big difference in the past few decades. Flies today are tied all over the world for large companies, and individual tiers in the United States are turning out exceptional flies, including the saltwater variety. Some of the most outstanding of these today are Dick Nelson, Ben Estes, Bob Kay, Steve Baily, Mitch Howe, Jack Montague, Eric Otzinger, Bob Johns, Hagen Sands, and Tom Evans.

Jimmy Nix, John Vanderhoof, Hawaii's Terry Baird, Dan Blanton, John Barr, the legendary Harry Kime, Bill Catherwood, Ralph Kantz, and California's enthusiastic Nick Curcione are spearheading the tying of large offshore flies for big-game fish.

With the world becoming such a noisy and crowded place, a bonefish flat offers peace and serenity found almost nowhere else these days. While casting from a flats boat is a comfortable way to stalk bonefish, I prefer to wade a flat.

In the Bahamas, I take a canteen of fresh water, wear a belt pack, and sometimes spend a whole day on the vast flats—just wading. There is the odor of decaying vegetation and the taste of salt air on the lips. There are the wheeling gulls and frigate birds, the planing flight of pelicans, the hovering of ospreys, and the company of herons.

The hot sun beats down on endless stretches of white beach and the flats are alive with life. Wading a flat at low tide can be an absorbing pastime. There are innumerable small fish in the shallows and predator fish constantly prey upon them—silently circling the rim of the flat. Barracuda and small sharks will herd schools of bonefish and then slash through them like hurled lances. Rays, needlefish, boxfish, various snappers, and baitfish schools constantly move through the clear water. The bottom is studded with sea urchins, conch shells, starfish, marine worms, and all sorts of shellfish. Spiny lobsters peer from beneath rusting oil drums and beds of turtle grass sway with the current.

The constant cycle of life and death—predators feeding on prey in a fine balance—reminds one that there is a grand scheme to all of nature. And fly fishers worth their salt learn that we are but a tiny, integral part of that vast plan.

4

Blues and Stripers

One of the few bright lights of my eighteen-year stay in New York City, while editor-in-chief of *Field & Stream*, was that I was able to fish for bluefish and striped bass with a fly rod. The other was belonging to the Campfire Club of America in Chappaqua, New York, about forty miles up the Bronx River Parkway from Manhattan. There I could fish for sunfish, trout, and largemouth bass with a fly rod on one of the club's three lakes. As for Manhattan itself, I could think of very few redeeming features.

Nelson Bryant, outdoor editor of the *New York Times*, felt the same way I did about the huge, dirty, and noisy city, but Nels had the advantage of living on Martha's Vineyard. From that ideal perch he was able to send in his regular outdoor columns by mail and seldom visited Manhattan.

Nelson and his brother, Danny, were perhaps the first anglers to fish for stripers with fly rods. Nels regularly caught Vineyard stripers on a fly thirty years ago using a Gibbs Sand Eel fly.

I used to fly up to the Vineyard in the late 1960s and fish with Nels and Danny. We would run out from Edgartown in Danny's center-console boat—loaded down with fly rods and canned beer—in the late afternoon to try for big stripers close to the rocks along the shore.

Fighting a big bluefish off the shore of New Jersey.

I kept a 17-foot Menemsha Boston Whaler in Rumson, New Jersey, in the first few years I was with the magazine as managing editor, and got in some excellent fishing for both bluefish and stripers along the north Jersey shore.

During good years there would be a substantial run of early bluefish toward the end of May, or when the water heated up to 60 degrees. These were big blues in the five- to twelve-pound category and a real treat on a fly. In a chum line of ground-up menhaden and hog-fry minnows, a white fly on a fast-sinking line worked just fine.

I fooled around with a lot of flies for this purpose, but finally ended up by trying my own on #1/0 stainless-steel hooks. Not being an original-type fly tier, I copied what I thought were the best around. I settled on a variation of Keith Fulsher's Thunder Creek series of minnow flies that the late Jimmy Daren carried in his cluttered Anglers' Cove shop in Manhattan. Keith's were different in the way the bucktail was attached to the hook, which in turn led to the shaping of the head and body. The few turns of red thread at the neck looked just like a minnow's gills.

In order to get the minnow to sink properly, I tied the fly with a full body wrap of .030 lead wire, then tied only a half-body wrap so that the fly would not sink too quickly. My unweighted flies were for when there was no current. With a current, one fished these flies dead drift—with no action—just the way the chum and dead minnows floated. One just had to watch the line and when it stopped, strike!

Fishermen who have never caught a twelve- to fourteen-pound bluefish on a fly rod have a great thrill coming. It was necessary to use #2 piano wire as a short leader for bluefish, as they have a formidable set of teeth. That 24-pound-test wire went through the eye of the hook easily.

By the end of June there was usually a run of smaller blues that would come around Sandy Hook and the Atlantic Highlands, and they were suckers for these same flies, plus some I dyed a red tinge to match the color of the red meat in the menhaden chum. I was never fond of the taste of bluefish, but I sure liked catching them on a fly. I probably never reached the level of enthusiasm of Gardner Grant and a few of those dedicated fly fishermen of the Hudson River area, but I got pretty good. I fished with the Shermans, Gary, his brothers and father, and with that marvelous saltwater fly rodder, Steve Sloan, and I got so I knew the area, the water, and the fishes' habits fairly well.

My three sons were growing up in Cape May, New Jersey, by the time I became editor of the magazine, and I used to commute down to that lovely little south Jersey town on weekends. We kept the Whaler there for years, but I never could seem to score on either blues or stripers with a fly rod there the way I had been doing up near the mouth of the Hudson River.

The bluefish can be a formidable opponent on a fly rod.

I had absolutely no luck casting flies from jetties or from the beaches at marauding schools of bluefish. My sons and I caught them from the whaler by trolling umbrella rigs, and I caught them by flinging Hopkins lures and lead-headed eels in the surf on the big spinning rods, but the fly rod didn't seem to work there.

I haunted the jetties and bridge pilings near Cape May with a fly rod and popper bug until my youngest son, Jim, decided I was never going to catch a striper in Cape May County. I think I finally caught one of about five pounds when he was a sophomore in high school and just barely escaped his dire prediction!

Al Ristori introduced Nels Bryant and me to the joys of striper fishing in the late fall at Montauk Point. One bitterly cold November, Al called us both and invited us out to Montauk.

"The stripers are on Shagwan Reef," was all he said, and hung up. Al was then not a fly fisherman—at least not for big fall stripers—and I had never fished for them with a fly rod either. That particular day we all used conventional and spinning gear, throwing big surface plugs and heavy spoons as a late November wind whipped up the surface of the Shagwan Rip. Boats were all around us, and several hundred striper fishermen were clustered along the rocky shore beneath the big lighthouse, heaving lures into the surf. We caught big stripers— some up to thirty pounds or more—until our arms were tired. I was half-frozen and covered with striper scales before darkness settled and we had to quit, but I will never forget that day!

When I began pursuing stripers in the fall with a big fly rod and popper bugs, I used to go to Montauk in late October and November and charter boats out of the Montauk Marina. Later, Bill Lattimore, who kept a trailered 21-foot Mako at South Hampton, and I fished the big reef with fly rods each fall up until it got too cold to take it. Many a time I have had to quit fly casting because my hands were too cold to hold the cork handle of the rod.

Ah, but those big Shagwan stripers were a thrill when they smashed that chugging surface popper as it bobbed in the churned-up surface of the rip. A 9-foot, 9-weight fly rod was none too big for some of those bruisers, some in the thirty- to forty-pound class. I never caught anything close to the big record stripers, but I did land a few in the twenty-five-pound class on a fly rod, and that was indeed a battle. What made it such fun was the current in that savage rip. The stripers would take the popping bug on the surface and then turn and go away on that current at full speed. Turning one took a big saltwater reel loaded with at least four hundred yards of twenty-pound backing, and turning it was only half the battle. The long fight to get the fish back in sometimes took half an hour in that raging sea. Just keeping one's footing in the rolling, pitching boat was difficult enough without being tied to a battling striper.

But catching stripers was not the entire reward. I will never forget my first taste of a properly cooked striper at Montauk. Nels and I were staying at a local motel there and brought home several stripers of what Nels called "eating size." He filleted them in the kitchenette of the motel, opened up several cans of tomatoes, and slowly broiled them in the spicy sauce. Dusted with a little salt and black pepper, they were enough to make one weep!

In the spring and summer months there was some good fly fishing for stripers along the shores of Long Island Sound and at Montauk. On quiet mornings we used to go out and flip flies as close as we could to rocks along the shore—dropping flies like Lou Tabory's Sand Eel and Don Avondolio's Silversides Clone in the stillwater. Tabory, one of the finest saltwater fly rodders ever to stalk stripers, helped me learn to cast the big saltwater flies at Campfire Club of America back in the mid-1970s, and I credit him with adding yards to my casting distance—in one lesson!

For some strange reason I was ending up with wind knots in the leader, and the fly was striking the leader when I tried for distance. Lou properly diagnosed my problem and suggested I try to "roll" the line as it went forward by hunching my right shoulder a bit and at the same time turning my right thumb a bit to the right on the forward cast. It did the trick, and I straightened out my cast and was able to get the fly to the 100-foot mark on the Campfire long-distance range.

It has always amused me to read in the many outdoor magazines about anglers who claim to be able to cast a fly 100 feet. I have fished with some of the finest fly casters in the world, and I swear I can count the ones who could cast a fly over 100 feet on the fingers of one hand. Lee Wulff, Ernie Schwiebert, Billy Pate, Lou Tabory, Lefty Kreh, Al McClane, Nelson Bryant, and Stu Apte are about the only pro fly fishermen who come to mind. There are a number of professional bonefish, permit, and tarpon guides who can cast that far, or farther—like Billy Knowles, Sandy Moret, and Steve Rajeff—but they are *supposed* to be able to do it. Hell, if I spent three hundred days a year on the flats in all kinds of wind, I'd be able to cast 120 feet, too!

Veteran striped-bass fly rodder Lou Tabory giving casting lessons to members of the Campfire Club of America in the late 1970s.

But if you want to separate the men from the boys in fly casting, just set up a distance range on a quiet pond some time. At the Campfire Club of America there is such a distance range, and at two annual outings each year nearly a thousand members try at qualification in order to get a gold pin. One of the events is distance fly casting.

Out of those thousand members only a handful each year try their hand at distance. Lots of them—and they are almost all expert fly fishermen—try for accuracy and obstacle casting and do well. But for a decade or more I watched them cast for distance. The marker out at 85 feet qualifies one for a "special." The marker at 100 feet is almost *never* reached, except for a few veteran saltwater fly fishermen like Nick Heineman and visiting instructors like Tabory. One hundred feet is a *long* way to cast a fly! Before you say you can do it, remember that the standard fly line is 90 feet long. Have you ever cast the *entire* fly line through the top guide of your fly rod?

I have never fished for stripers with a fly rod on the West Coast of the United States and it looks as though I am not going to have a chance to do it. From what the experts out there tell me, the striper stocks have been terribly depleted. Pollution seems to be the main villain, but overfishing by commercial boats and netters has certainly contributed to it. I have been reading for years about the marvelous San Francisco Bay striper fishery and I understand it is nearly gone. Nobody writes better about fishing for a striper on a fly than Russ Chatham, and I haven't seen much by him in the last few years about that grand sport.

When I was editor of *Field & Stream*, Larry Green was my West Coast editor, and he kept me deluged with fine stories about striper fishing with fly rods. The purple Striper Grabber Fly, invented by Larry, is said to be one of the truly great flies for California linesides.

Michael Fong was another writer who did a lot of fishing for, and writing about, striped bass in the San Francisco area, and Mike told me the fishery had dropped to very low levels. That veteran saltwater fly fisherman, Cam Sigler, is still fishing for West Coast stripers on a fly, but that is because Cam never gives up fly fishing for *anything!* Only a year ago he almost set a world record for striper on a fly rod, missing the mark by ounces. His catch was a hefty striper of twenty-four pounds eight ounces—on *6-pound-test tippet*! Cam says about the only place that good striper fishing can be found now on the West Coast is at the mouth of the North Umpqua River in Oregon.

About 1970 it was estimated there were almost two million striped bass of sixteen inches or better in the San Francisco Bay complex. All these fish, and the rest of the northern California and Oregon fishery, were the result of a stocking of 132 striped bass from the Navesink River in New Jersey in July 1879.

That stocking, by United States Fish Commission fisheries biologist Livingston Stone, and a stocking three years later of three hundred more stripers from the Shrewsbury River in New Jersey, developed the entire West Coast striper fishery. Up until a few years ago the striped bass were plentiful in two areas along the Pacific coast—the San Francisco Bay area and the Coos Bay area of Oregon. Fishing was also sporadic on the Columbia River system between Oregon and Washington. Additional stockings—in Humboldt Bay in 1889, the Santa Ana River in California's Orange County, and San Diego in 1903—did not turn out well.

The striped bass, smarter than the fisheries biologists, went north from the original area stocked by Stone at Martinez, California, on the south shore of Carquinez Strait, and headed for large river estuaries in which they needed to feed. They established themselves in San Francisco Bay and Coos Bay, and by 1922 there were enough of them to see a commercial fishery established there.

The Pacific grew the biggest striped bass, as is often the case with Pacific waters. All the striped bass fly-rod records are from either California or Oregon. Joe Brooks set a world record back in the 1950s when he took a twenty-nine-pound-six-ounce striped bass on a fly rod, using a 12-pound-test tippet and a big, balsawood, white popping bug. The weight record lasted almost twenty years until it was broken by Russ Chatham with a thirty-six-pound-six-ounce striper landed on 15-pound-test tippet.

Today's fly-rod world record is held by Beryl E. Bliss, with a whopping sixty-four-pound-eight-ounce striper taken on a fly from the Smith River in Oregon, July 28, 1973. There are hopes that the once-great striper fishing on the West Coast will return with sensible fisheries management and considerable cooperation from commercial fishermen, sport fishermen, developers, and those responsible for industrial pollution.

For it is indeed a great fly-rod game fish.

5

The Chrome-plated Bomb – Tarpon

While there is no doubt that saltwater fly fishing began in New England for the striped bass, it is also true that Florida is the spot where the sport came of age.

Early fly fishermen raised on trout and bass probably either took their vacations there to escape the bitter winters up north, or retired in Florida and began experimenting with fly rods. The gear was rather primitive by today's standards. The rods were usually 9-foot, split-bamboo rods, the line was linen or waxed shoemaker's twine, and most anglers used salmon reels. Some were made by Bogden, Zwarg, or Vom Hofe, and would handle saltwater fish, but all gear had to be carefully washed down with fresh water after a day's use in the corrosive salt.

Fly fishing for tarpon is a sport that appeals to a certain type of flaky fisherman. It combines all the best elements of hunting, stalking, and explosive action that seem to satisfy the masochist in those of us who have become addicted to the pursuit.

But it was one day in Islamorada, when I was out with guide Dick Williams, that I became a tarpon addict. We had been chasing bonefish schools all morning, and Dick had brought along the huge, 12-weight, 9½-foot fiberglass fly rod used for tarpon. We were an-

*Florida Keys guide Jimmie Albright (left)
and fly rodder Bart Roth with Roth's
138-pound tarpon taken on a fly at
Islamorada on March 7, 1955.*

chored close to one of the highway bridges when suddenly a school of tarpon began to swim by close to us. They were in a channel, but only about six to eight feet deep. Dick slid the rod from its gunwale holder, stood on the casting platform, and dropped a small, orange fly just ahead of the cruising fish. To my utter astonishment, the lead fish turned like a trout, opened its huge mouth, and engulfed the fly.

What happened next was pure frenzy. The fish—one of about one hundred pounds—blasted into the air, hit the water, and came out again in an explosive leap that saw the silver fish do three cartwheels in midair. When it hit the surface, it came out again and made a series of frantic leaps across the channel toward the bridge. On the sixth or seventh jump the hook pulled out and the line fell slack in the water. Dick grinned and began to reel in.

"Jeezus!" was about all I was able to say.

"That," Williams said, "is called jumping tarpon."

"Aren't you pissed off that you lost him?" I asked.

"No," said the guide, "that's the fun of it—the jumps. If he stays on, the real work begins."

That got me interested, and for the rest of the day we hunted tarpon. I didn't catch any, but I jumped two, one of about 75 pounds and another of perhaps 125 pounds. Both gave me more excitement than any fish—with the possible exception of big marlin—I had ever hooked. From that moment on I was hooked.

That was in 1969, and for the next decade I fished for tarpon with a fly every chance I got. The season in the Keys runs from early April through late June, when the tarpon migrate through the Keys and up the west coast of Florida.

I fished with most of the well-known guides and was entered in the annual invitational fly-fishing tournaments for a couple of years. I never won any of them, but I sure had a lot of fun competing against tournament-quality anglers like Stu Apte. But the man who taught me more than anyone else about fishing for tarpon with a fly was Billy Pate.

Billy is the kind of angler who is never too busy to help a novice learn the sport. My biggest problem was knots, and Billy taught me how to tie the ones that hold big fish on a fly rod. Pate currently holds the world record for tarpon on a fly, a 188-pound monster caught at Homosassa, Florida, May 13, 1982.

But he lost a bigger one than that. I know because I was with him, his ex-wife Patti, and guide Hal Chittum at Homosassa a year later. It was June and it was hot and we had been out for a couple of hours that morning. Billy had cast to a few fish and one had taken the fly, a fish of about seventy pounds. It had put on a grand show, jumping and tearing up the calm surface of the flats. Billy finally subdued it and we went back to search for big fish. I was more interested in taking action photos of the jumping tarpon than I was in fishing that day. It's a good thing I was. I probably would have had a heart attack if the same fish that struck Billy's fly had hit mine!

A lot of care goes into the knots, lines, backing, leaders, and hooks used to fish for tarpon with a fly rod. Pate uses 100-pound-test shock mono between the hook and the 16-pound-test mono tippet. He prefers the shooting head to the standard ninety feet of standard fly line because he can cast it more quickly and it presents less drag in the water.

It must have been about noon when Hal Chittum saw the school of tarpon coming. He was standing up on the poling platform and pointed out the school with the long pole. Billy nodded and got ready. When the school was within about sixty feet, he began his cast.

"Billy, there's a big fish in the center of the school," Chittum said softly. "Try and drop it pretty far back."

I was poised to one side with the camera ready to photograph the first jump. When the fish took the fly, I was peering through the lens finder, but I heard the huge splash the tarpon made when it broke water. I looked up in time to see the fish half out of the water. I heard Billy grunt as he struck the fish.

"Big fish!" he said, leaning back with the rod tip high.

"It may go over two hundred!" Hal said, jamming the pole into the bottom to get the boat moving. At the same time, he flipped on the switches that started the two electric trolling motors that jutted down from the stern.

The big tarpon made two more leaps as it went away from us, then dove and began swimming. Pate leaned into the heavy rod and checked his drag on the big reel. I glanced at my wristwatch. It was 12:20 P.M.

That big tarpon went directly north along the shore opposite the mouth of the Homosassa River and across the big flats. For the next hour we were all busy lending Billy moral support, taking photos, and waving away other boats that came close to see what was going on. The big fish—not wasting time on jumping—was pulling steadily in about six feet of water.

By 2:00 P.M. the fish began to veer off toward a cluster of mangrove islands inshore where the water grew more shallow. We could see the big tarpon clearly as it swam steadily in the clear water. Both Pate and Chittum agreed it was more than two hundred pounds. The back was at least eighteen inches across and it looked to be well over six feet in length.

The fish swam steadily into the shallow water between the small mangrove islands and we all suddenly realized that we were going to have a problem with this fish. The water was full of small coral rocks jutting up here and there, and near each island there were tangles of mangrove stumps and roots sticking up close to shore. It was 3:15 P.M. and the tarpon did not seem to be tiring. Pate put all the pressure he could on the big fish without endangering the 16-pound-test tippet. He had caught hundreds of tarpon and knew just how much pressure he could exert without risking a break.

The fish abruptly swerved off to our right and headed for the shore of a small island. It swam within a few feet of the mangrove roots, and there was a question of whether it was going to unexpectedly swim into the thick tangle of roots. Chittum could do nothing but follow the swimming fish with the boat, hoping it would move offshore.

I thought if I dove overboard and tried to swim between the fish and the roots, I could spook it back out into deeper water. I took off my wristwatch and slipped out of my slacks. Wearing just a pair of trunks, I slipped into the water and began swimming. I made pretty good progress for the first fifty yards, but soon realized the fish and boat were going faster than I could swim, so I stood up in the waist-deep water.

"Can't come back for you, Jack," Hal said.

"That's all right," I replied. "The water is warm and shallow. I'll wade along the shore until you get back."

Hal nodded and went back to his poling.

The fish suddenly swerved offshore and headed for the center of a large body of shallow water. Now, I thought, Pate will wear him down. I sat on a big mangrove root and watched the fight. The boat appeared smaller as it moved into the distance.

It was twenty minutes later when I saw the boat heading my way. I began wading out into the deeper water to save them the trip into the shallows. I was hanging onto the gunwale as Hal turned off the engine. Nobody was smiling.

"Running line parted," Hal said, shaking his head.

I looked at him. "The running line! That tested out at fifty pounds!"

Billy nodded. "Must have rubbed against a piece of coral. We thought we had the fish. It was tired and was coming in when the line parted."

There was nothing else to say. That is what big-game fishing is all about.

The 200-pound tarpon is the goal of all fly-rod anglers who pursue this great game fish. The big fish will be caught someday and Billy Pate may be the man to do it, but he didn't do it that day. The commercial boats have taken tarpon over 200 pounds in nets, and on March 19, 1956, an angler named M. Salazar caught a 283-pound tarpon on conventional tackle in Lake Maracaibo, Venezuela—so they are there. It is only a matter of time until a fly rodder takes one over 200 pounds. I at least have the satisfaction of knowing exactly what one looks like!

The tarpon is a strange, primitive, bony fish that dates far back and is a member of the herring family (*Megalops atlanticus*). It has large platelike scales and a bony mouth that makes it extremely difficult to set a hook. Since it is not taken commercially in the United States, there has been comparatively little scientific study of it and relatively little is known about its migration or spawning habits.

Billy Pate (right) and his world-record tarpon on a fly. The fish was caught May 13, 1982, at Homasassa, Florida, on 16-pound-test tippet and weighed 188 pounds. It is still a record.

Those of us who have fished for it for years have attempted to learn more about it, but the research material is scarce. Tarpon are found on both sides of the Atlantic: in Africa from about Dakar down to the mouth of the Congo River, and in the West from the Carolinas down to Brazil.

Lefty Kreh, who has caught enough tarpon on a fly to rate as an expert, says a large migration arrives in the Florida Keys in late May. He says the fish then move up the west coast of Florida in late June and July, appear off Louisiana in mid-July, and then move on to the Port Aransas, Texas, region in August. He says they move down the coasts of the Yucatan Peninsula in the fall and pass through the waters of Belize, Panama, and Colombia. Then, he surmises, they travel across the Gulf of Mexico in early spring and begin the cycle all over again.

They are not eaten in the United States, and it is probably a good thing, as commercial netters would have made them an endangered species by now were they considered edible. Interestingly, the natives of Central America find them good to eat. I have had guides ask me to keep tarpon on the Rio Colorado in eastern Costa Rica and in Belize.

Tarpon fishing with a fly rod is about half fishing and half hunting. One sights the fish, singly or in a school, and then casts to it, at least in the Keys and in spots like Belize where the water is clear.

Tarpon can be on the move or lying close to the bottom in holes. It is necessary to get the fly well out in front of moving tarpon and to let it sink before stripping it in with short jerks.

A tarpon will not smash a fly the way it will a surface plug. It comes up in a slow roll and sucks in the fly gently. If one strikes when the huge mouth is open, the fly will be pulled away from the fish. It is better to wait until the tarpon turns and starts to swim downward before striking. Then it is necessary to set the sharp hook repeatedly in the bony plates of the fish's mouth to make sure the hook point penetrates. The failure to wait until the tarpon takes the fly all the way into its mouth is the reason for most losses — that and failing to get the hook point into the bony mouth.

The sight of swimming tarpon is enough to unnerve any fly rodder. It is usually then that I — and a good many other veteran saltwater fly casters — step on the coils of fly line at my feet, forget to clear the fly of weeds or grass, find that the line has wrapped around the rod handle, and either hook the guide or the push-pole on the first backcast. It is a heart-pounding moment.

Some veteran guides have their own solution for that moment. Bill Knowles used to keep me fairly calm by using psychology. We were "staked out" at Buchannan Bank one spring back in the early 1970s, when he spotted a big tarpon swimming down the bank toward us. I hadn't seen it yet and was standing on the bow of the flats boat, rod in hand.

"There's a little tarpon about twenty-five pounds, coming down the bank," he said casually. "It might be fun just to hook it. Cast that fly out there about twenty-five yards and let it sink. Strip it when I tell you," he added.

I did so and — when he told me to — moved the fly. I felt a tug, set the hook repeatedly, and a huge tarpon of about 150 pounds shot out of the water and cartwheeled several times in the air before smashing back to the surface.

"Holy mackerel!" I yelled as the big fish began a series of grey-hounding jumps across the bank — with me holding on. "That's a *little* tarpon?"

"If I had told you how big it was," Knowles said, yanking the pole from the sandy bottom," you'd never have gotten the fly out there!"

He was absolutely right. I would have panicked at the size of it.

The fish broke off after about a twenty-five-minute battle anyway, but the fight was spectacular while it lasted.

There are about seventy to eighty tarpon flies today—tied by perhaps two dozen top tiers—that will take tarpon well. One of the first great tarpon flies was tied by Stu Apte, one of the best tarpon anglers of all time and holder of several former world records on a fly rod. It is the bright orange-and-red Stu Apte Tarpon Fly, tied on #2/0 to #5/0 hooks.

It is a grand fly and I have taken a lot of tarpon with it, but there are times when tarpon won't take bright flies and it is best to switch to darker or dull ones such as John Emery's popular Cockroach or Lefty Kreh's Black Plague. There was a time when it was thought tarpon would only take certain flies, but as the years went by it was agreed the big fish would take almost any fly at times. For instance, there is a small orange palolo worm that occurs in May at several spots in the Florida Keys, and any fly that closely imitates it, such as guide Nat Ragland's Orange Quindillon, will take tarpon. Billy Pate's Homosassa Special, which looks a bit like a Cockroach Fly, will take tarpon regularly off that north Florida west-coast town.

The old-time tarpon fly tiers such as Winston Moore, Chico Fernandez, George Hommell, Bill Barnes, Stu Apte, and Billy Pate showed the way and now there are good tiers galore making excellent flies. Mike Conner, Dan Blanton, Bob Kay, John Cave, John Emery, Phil Chapman, Beth Luscombe, Ray Donnersberger, Steve Baily, Bob Stearnes, Jack Gartside, and Pat Wardlaw are among those making real strides in the tarpon-fly arena.

There are two kinds of tarpon fishing with a fly rod: sight fishing and blind casting. I prefer the first, but there are times when blind casting can be both effective and exciting. Dropping a fly on the end of sinking fly line into deep holes in the Keys can dredge up tarpon in the early spring. It is arm-wearying work, casting a heavy sinking line over and over, but now and then the rewards are worth it. I learned about blind casting back in the early 1970s.

I went down to the east side of Costa Rica to fish for tarpon at Casa Mar, having heard much about the fine tarpon fishing in the huge Rio Colorado, which runs by the Casa Mar and empties into the Caribbean a short way off. I brought a fly rod and discovered I was the only one of a dozen anglers there with the long rod. Most were using big conventional rods, or heavy spinning gear, and jigging heavy, cast-iron lures close to the bottom. They were finding and catching tarpon, but it did not strike me as a particularly exciting way to catch the big *sabalo*, as the Spanish-speaking Costa Rican guides called them.

Fortunately for me, that was the first year that veteran saltwater fly fisherman Bill Barnes was manager of Casa Mar, the best of the tarpon and snook resorts on the Rio Colorado. He noticed my fly rod and quickly joined me in the bar, where we discussed tarpon fishing and tarpon flies with considerable help from the cold beer.

Bill told me to use a sinking line in the murky current and handed me a couple of his own flies—the red-and-white Casa Mar Special Number One and the red-and-black Casa Mar Special Number Two, both tied on a #4/0 hook. In addition, he suggested I use one of the flies I had with me, a favorite of veteran Keys guide Bob Reinamen called the Black Death. This fly had a wing of red bucktail tied at the rear of the shank; on each side were three to four wide, black saddle hackles. It had a collar of red hackle, the head was painted red or orange, and it was tied on a #3/0 hook.

Thanks to Barnes, I jumped tarpon all over the Rio Colorado for those three days and even managed to land four or five in the swift current. They were not big fish—forty-five to seventy-five pounds on average—but they fought well, as do all the silver bombs on a fly rod. There were some big snook around and I caught several fair snook on a Whistler series fly, but I never hooked anything approaching the size of the one Bill Barnes took in 1980 on a fly rod—the world record snook of twenty-six pounds.

It is not that much fun blind casting to tarpon in the big main river, but the trips far up the side channels of that mighty stream were an experience to remember. With the thick jungle foliage hanging overhead and pushing in from both sides of the narrow stream, the guide would navigate the aluminum skiff upstream with a small outboard motor. And far upstream one would come upon quiet stretches of water—deep, slow moving, and black as ink. As the flocks of parrots screeched overhead and howler monkeys roared eerily far back in the jungle, we would cast streamer flies toward the overgrown banks. The muffled silence of the jungle pressed down on us as we fished. Suddenly, a huge tarpon would engulf the tiny fly and when hooked, smash the silence to a million shattered particles, leaping and ripping

The late Harry Kime and leaping tarpon.

up the green foliage and branches on both sides of the narrow channel before breaking the leader and getting away. Sitting, panting and perspiring, in the small boat as the waves and ripples slowly subsided and the silence came down again like a blanket, it was hard to believe such power lay just beneath us.

Belize is a bit like Costa Rica at times in that you must cast flies on sinking lines to tarpon as they lay deep in the channels between the mangrove islands, but they are also seen on the flats in clear water, as at that premier tarpon-fishing lodge, El Pescador. The tarpon in Belize do not grow as large as those on the flats of the Florida Keys. I have no idea why. One would think they would be fish migrating from Florida and any tarpon of about one hundred pounds should be in the sixteen- to seventeen-year age bracket. But, as I said earlier, not that much is known about their habits.

The beauty of fishing for tarpon at a resort in Belize, such as Turneffe Flats, is that one can fly fish for tarpon and then switch to fly casting for bonefish or permit the same day. All three—plus barracuda and some fine snappers—are all in the same general habitat of mangrove islands and flats. The best time of year for this type of fishing is from about April to October.

But it is on the flats of the Florida Keys, with the mangrove islands suspended in the mercury line of the horizon and the hot May sun beating down on the casting deck at my feet, that I find myself at peace with the world. The faint breeze brings the odor of rotting turtle grass and loggerhead sponges, and frigate birds hang suspended in the currents above Lignum Vitae Key.

Whether it is a "stake out" near Arsniker Key or on a white bottom to the east of the bridges, there is that deep-buried excitement in knowing that tarpon will show. Maybe not in the next hour, but they will show.

Suddenly, the guide stiffens on his poling platform, raises an arm to shade his eyes, and bending forward a bit, stares. "Here they come," he says softly.

And the great, silver tarpon swim ever closer, like huge, sleek torpedoes flickering over the dark beds of turtle grass.

6

Flickering Shadows of the Flats—Permit

The permit is a relatively easy fish to spot on the flats, but unlike the bonefish it does not readily take a fly. Very few saltwater fly rodders are lucky enough to have caught one. Among those dedicated long-rod anglers fortunate enough to have taken one of these silvery, torpedo-shaped, forked-tailed speedsters of the flats, *one* is considered an angling triumph. The fly fishermen who have caught more than one represent a select group.

The permit and the origin of its name have been lost in the mists of angling history. It inhabits the bonefish and tarpon flats from Brazil to Florida in the western Atlantic and from Venezuela to Mexico in the Caribbean.

It belongs to the family Carangidae, which numbers among its members such notable fighters as the jacks, pompanos, and amberjacks. It is known by a number of local names, among them great pompano, round pompano, and pompano jack.

While most permit seen on the flats may average five to fifteen pounds, much larger ones have been caught in deep water on heavy tackle. Anglers have sought permit on reefs and over sunken wrecks for years because these fish are marvelous fighters. The all-tackle record permit was caught April 28, 1978, by William M. Kenney off Palm Beach, Florida, on conventional fishing gear. It weighed fifty-one pounds eight ounces. The fly-rod record is far smaller: forty-one pounds eight ounces, set by Del Brown at Key West, Florida, on March 13, 1986 on an *8-pound tippet*!

But the permit is relatively new as a fly-rod quarry when compared to such species as tarpon and bonefish. Both of these fish were sought and taken by fly fishermen, using early split-bamboo rods and salmon reels, in the Florida area shortly after the turn of the century.

The problem with permit for the fly-rod angler is that they do not readily take a fly. Unlike the tarpon and the bonefish, which will take a fly with relish, the permit will follow flies but will seldom take them. The most maddening aspect of the permit is that it will sometimes follow a fly right up to the boat, or the feet of a wading angler, before refusing the offering.

While a permit will eat all sorts of bottom-living invertebrates in addition to small fish, its favorite food is the small blue or sand crab of about two to two and one-half inches in diameter. And thereby lies the rub. It has been very difficult for fly tiers to successfully imitate this small crab with a fly that both resembles it and casts easily with a fly rod.

In the early days of fly fishing for permit, both in the Bahamas and in the Keys, anglers cast white streamer flys and such odd lures as the old Johnson Golden Minnow Spoon (fly-rod size, but hardly a fly) at permit with few results. Most permit were taken on bonefish flies, like the ones tied by the very talented Chico Fernandez of Miami, but that was usually an accident. I took my first permit on one of Chico's bonefish shrimp flies while fishing a flat at Cay Cay in 1969. The permit, a little one of about three pounds, took the fly while I was casting to a school of bonefish. I couldn't understand why the guide was so excited. I caught my second permit on a fly at Turneffe Flats in Belize *nineteen years later,* and I had been casting flies at literally hundreds of permit in the intervening years!

Permit travel in schools, although individual fish will often come up from deep water to feed on the flats during outgoing and incoming tides. They feed rapidly, flitting like ghostly shadows across the sandy bottom with only their black anal and dorsal fins and sicklelike tail standing out against the white background. Permit feed head-down, their rounded noses probing the bottom and the huge forked tail waving above the surface. It is a sight to make any fly fisherman weak-kneed.

Compounding the problem of getting a permit to take a fly is the fact that a fish concentrates on the few square inches of bottom under its nose and virtually ignores everything else. One can land a fly all around that tiny feeding area and the permit will pay no attention to it. Many permit are caught because they have a highly competitive nature while feeding in schools. A fly, which might attract little or no attention if a fish were feeding alone, is sometimes grabbed because it lands near another tailing fish.

It takes good eyes (equipped with polarized sunglasses) to spot permit. Experienced guides learn to spot these wary fish in shallow water by sighting the fleeting shadow of the fast-moving fish on sandy bottoms or by correctly reading what they term *shaky water*—surface water activated by the underwater movement of swimming permit. Veteran Key West permit guides like Gil and Linda Drake can make a fly-fishing trip for these spooky fish successful when anyone else would fail to spot a permit. And there are native guides—at such proven permit spots as Deep Water Cay and Chub Cay in the Bahamas or Turneffe Flats in Belize—with eyes so accustomed to seeing permit that it verges on the supernatural.

Gil Drake, Jr., with a permit caught by the author off Key West. Gil, who grew up guiding for his father on Deep Water Key in the Bahamas, is now a successful permit, tarpon, and bonefish guide at Key West.

Don't be fooled by the occasional claims of some saltwater fly fishermen that catching permit on a fly is easy. It is a relatively simple task to anchor over a sunken wreck, dump a load of chum over the side, and catch permit on a fly rod by jigging large white-and-tinsel streamer flies in the depths. The permit mistakes the flies for bits of floating chum. The fish put up a mighty struggle on the long rod, that is certain, but it is just as certain that this is no way to fly fish for permit. In fact, flats fly fishermen worth their salt would never be caught dead jigging for permit in deep water. But, as many a veteran permit and bonefish guide will testify, a good many fly-rod "records" were set in just such a manner.

Permit flies have come a long way in the past few decades. In contrast to the early bonefish flies that took the occasional permit, today's tiers have come up with some materials that truly imitate the favorite food of these great fish. The first successful imitation of a tiny crab was tied by Keys guide Nat Ragland. It was the first of the many "puff" flies to come out of the Keys and it took a lot of permit. With small, shiny bead eyes, it pioneered the family of flies that attracted permit. Ragland's Puff Fly was developed in the early 1960s and approximately a decade later a Marathon, Florida, guide named Harry Spears developed the first epoxy fly—a triangular-bodied, beady-eyed, hot-glue fly that sank to the bottom and really attracted permit as no fly had done before. Spears added tail feathers and some of the other Keys guides added plastic weed guards and the fly became a success.

I took my second permit, a whopper of about fifteen pounds, on one of Spears epoxy flies in Belize in the spring of 1987—a banner day in the life of a saltwater fly fisherman. That fish—for a reason known only to the gods of fly fishing—took the epoxy fly like a trout taking a dry Iron Blue Dun. It fought like a tiger for forty-five minutes before coming to the net, only to be released a few moments later. I was tempted to have it mounted but reasoned the photograph of it would serve as well as a mount.

A few new flies have come along in the last couple of years to make the frequent catching of permit on a fly rod more of a possibility. John VanderHoff, a California tier, has come up with some excellent epoxy crab flies that have gotten me some good "follows," if not actual takes.

Over the years a lot of bonefish flies have taken permit, but not regularly enough to be called permit flies. Among those that have taken permit consistently are such fine flies as Lew Jewett's Blue Crab Fly, Bonnie's Tailing Bonefish Fly, a number of the variety of Crazy Charlies tied by Bob Nauheim and Lefty Kreh, Eric Otzinger's Crab Fly, Bob John's Puff Fly, Steve Bailey's Epoxy Flies, Ben Estes's Epoxy Fly and Deer-Hair Crab Fly, Jerry Martin's Epoxy Moes, and Jack Montague's excellent line of epoxy flies—crab and shrimp Moes.

But the best of the new lot was developed a few years ago by Livingston, Montana, fly-shop owner George Anderson and two of his fellow tiers and saltwater fly fishermen, Jim Brungardt of Livingston, Montana, and John Barr of Boulder, Colorado. It is made from deer hair, dyed dark brown, and does an excellent job of imitating the permit's favorite food, the small sand crab. Anderson modified a good crab fly, tied by Dave Whitlock, by adding weight to make it sink and by attaching six tiny rubber legs to it.

Anderson sent me two of them in 1988, just before I left for the small island of Guanaja in the Bay Islands off the northeast coast of Honduras. There, at a small resort named La Posada del Sol, I tried them out on what must be the best series of permit flats in the Caribbean. In five days' fishing, New Mexico's San Juan River trout-fishing guide Chuck Rizuto and I saw 116 permit—most within casting distance of our boat.

I lost three permit to sharp coral outcroppings on the flats, but on the second day, fishing with local guide Mandy Moore, I caught an eighteen-pound permit that took the fly *a second time* after I failed to hook it on the first strike! Fortunately, that big permit was hooked on

The McCrab Fly was developed by George Anderson, Jim Brungardt of Livingston, Montana, and John Barr of Boulder, Colorado. This fly is now being widely copied and works very well for permit.

the edge of a sandy bank and sped for a deep drop-off where there were no rocks or other obstructions. Even with deep water, that fish took nearly thirty minutes to subdue on a 9-foot, 9-weight graphite fly rod.

As if that were not enough, fishing the following day with another local guide, Robert Jones, as well as Rizuto, I cast Anderson's fly (which he calls McCrab) at three permit cruising by us in about five feet of water. *All three* permit tipped up and followed that fly down to the bottom, and when I twitched it, one took it and sped off. It was a small permit of about eight pounds, but as all of us permit anglers know, *any* permit on a fly is a trophy!

Two permit on a fly in three days—my cup ranneth over! But that added up to four permit on a fly in twenty years, about a normal average, most permit fly rodders would agree.

The encouraging signs are that the sport is attracting more devotees. Young fly fishermen are discovering that with freshwater streams and lakes ever more crowded, the solitude of the bonefish and permit flats is a refreshing alternative. New high-tech materials are allowing manufacturers to make lighter and stronger rods, reels that are anodized against saltwater corrosion and capable of holding far more fly line and backing, and better lines and leader materials.

Increasingly, more fly fishermen are discovering that saltwater game fish are larger, faster, and stronger than their freshwater cousins, and what's more, will readily take a fly. All except the unpredictable permit, that is. But then, challenge is what makes saltwater fly fishing such a fascinating sport.

I have been asked a number of times what my favorite game fish is. It is a difficult question to answer quickly. There are so many great game fish to be taken on a fly rod. Some, like the tarpon and the billfish, are explosive and acrobatic, and they represent a totally different kind of experience. Atlantic salmon and steelhead trout, on the other hand, are magnificent fighting fish but are taken in a different way, in entirely different surroundings.

Considering the total experience and setting, I think fly fishing for permit is my favorite. There is the solitude: the vast expanse of flats and adjoining reefs, twisted and sea-smoothed driftwood, coral outcroppings, white sand bottom dotted with sea urchins, turtle grass, loggerhead sponges, and sea cucumbers. The flats are filled with myriad tiny swimming creatures. The clear blue sky overhead, great banks of cumulus clouds on the horizon, a hard, bright burning sun, and the whisper of a steady salt-laden wind from the sea combine to give one a sense of smallness and awe at the intricacy of such a world.

And the permit—cautious, flitting ghostly shadows against a flickering, ever-changing background; darting, pausing, tipping up briefly and then quickly moving on—present such a tenuous target.

If one caught as many permit on a fly as one does bonefish, I doubt if permit fishing would hold as much mystery and excitement for me as it does. But the fact that it is a nearly impossible task beckons me on. I have returned—salt encrusted, sun scorched, leg weary, and bleary-eyed after a day on the permit flats—still content. I have caught no fish, but I have seen several up close, have cast to a few that ignored me completely, and perhaps have had one tentative follow.

But in a small channel, water emptying from the blue sea beyond the reef onto the flats, there was a huge permit, holding steady against the current while it waited for tidbits to wash off the coral rocks. The stalk took twenty minutes to execute, most of it in a half-crouch. When the crab fly was finally delivered—landing about a foot ahead of the big fish—it turned slightly, nosed down to inspect it, then slowly

Fighting permit from a boat in Belize.

turned away and resumed its place in the current. With a heart hammering in my chest, I cast again, only to have the line glisten in the sunlight and send the big fish in a flash out through the cut and into deep water. But that one almost-take had been enough to make my day.

Walking back across a flat to the staked-out skiff as the sun sets on the rim of the western horizon in a huge ball of orange light, with thoughts of a cold beer from the ice cooler and a broiled fresh dolphin fillet for dinner, completes a day.

Walking the flats at daylight, with gulls hovering overhead, glinting white and pink in the first rays of the rising sun, gives one a sense that this will be a day of fulfillment. There is not much else that a permit fisherman needs but the knowledge that the strong winds will not blow this day and that permit will be coming up on the flats with the rising tide.

On the barnacle-encrusted coral rocks of the breakwater on the island of Guanaja, big arrow crabs can be found dead in the early morning, resting on the rocks above high tide. They all face east, their sightless eyes reflecting sunlight.

"What kills them off that way?" I asked the old guide.

"Not *killed*," he answered, holding out a hand to take my fly rod into the boat. "These are old crabs. No one knows why, but they come out on the rocks to die, early in the morning, looking into the rising sun."

I climbed into the boat as the guide pushed it off from the breakwater. The sun's rays played on the wet rocks and glanced off the tapered palm fronds overhead. Dozens of small reef crabs scuttled up the face of the rocks as a wave crest rose from below. I looked at the big crabs on top of the rocks. They already looked an integral part of the awakening day.

7

The Incredible
Pez Gallo — Roosterfish

Back in the mid-1970s, veteran southern California light-tackle angler Chuck Garrison and I were fishing for sailfish, marlin, and dorado from the small East Cape resort of Punta Pescadero in Baja California.

We had taken a couple of sails and a small striped marlin on twenty-pound mono and were cruising close to the beach on the way back in to the resort. It was mid-May and the hot sun beat down on the tattered canvas top of the 31-foot cabin cruiser. Both Chuck and I were seated in battered folding chairs, with our feet propped up on the transom, a couple of bottles of Corona Beer in our hands. The vista of white beach stretched for miles north and south, uncluttered by anything except the occasional native fisherman's shack or a solitary brown pelican.

I suddenly noticed a large black patch just outside the surf line. I stood up, whistled to the captain and mate above us, and pointed to the spot. I shrugged my shoulders and gave the skipper a questioning look.

"Pez gallo!" he said excitedly, spinning the wheel to turn the boat toward the area.

"What did he say?" I asked Garrison, who was halfway to the cabin.

"*Pez gallo*—roosterfish," he said, coming out with a light spinning rod in his hand. A silver spoon dangled from the tip on a short length of wire leader.

"Get another spinning rod," he said enthusiastically, "either with a spoon or plug. This is one fish you don't want to miss!"

The captain eased back on the throttle and the boat quietly glided up to the black patch: a school of feeding fish. I could see baitfish erupting in sprays from the edge of the patch.

Chuck heaved his spoon into the center of the school and almost immediately was into a fish. The fish he hooked made a spectacular leap and headed for the surf. I threw a Rapala diving plug close to the school and began the retrieve. A strange-looking dorsal fin cut the surface behind the swimming plug and suddenly I felt a smashing strike.

The strong fish dove and ran off to my right, and I held the rod tip high, wondering if I was using eight- or twelve-pound mono. I had not had time to look.

"Aiee!" the mate yelled, landing beside us on the cockpit deck. "*Pez gallo—grande!*" He picked up the gaff and stood ready.

He needn't have hurried. Those two fish fought all over the beach area. It took us nearly twenty minutes to get them close to the boat, and another ten minutes after that to get them to gaff. When they came aboard, we found that we had taken a pair of almost identical roosterfish of about fifteen pounds each.

The school, alerted by the commotion, had moved off into deeper water, and try as we might, we could not get them back up by casting or trolling. I looked at the great silver fish lying on the deck.

"My God, Chuck, I wonder what they would fight like on a fly rod!" was all I could say.

It would be at least ten years before I would find out.

If I had looked up the roosterfish before I began to pursue it with a fly rod, in 1986, I might have been prepared for its strength.

As it was, I hooked two on a cork popping bug before I realized the fish was a member of the family Nematistiidae. Had I known that, I would have increased my tippet strength from the puny 8-pound-test thread I was using at the time. The fact that I lost both fish on the first run *should* have told me something!

The roosterfish is identified by such local names as *papa gallo*, *gallo*, and *pez gallo* from Peru up to Baja and southern California—its known range. The local names are derived from the word *pez*, meaning "fish," and *gallo*, the Spanish word for "rooster." The name *gallo* came from the unusual, long, seven spines of the dorsal fin that the fish raises above the surface when attacking prey. They resemble a rooster's comb.

When I realized what a formidable adversary I had taken on, I resolved to return to Baja California outfitted with the proper fly-fishing gear. When I had hooked the first two roosters, I was fishing with a 6-weight rod, 6-weight, floating, weight-forward fly line, and a reel capable of holding two hundred yards of twenty-pound backing. That outfit had served me well for bonefish and permit over the years, but it was a bit light for the roosters of Baja's East Cape. Some in the thirty- to forty-pound category were being taken on conventional gear just off the surf line.

That size roosterfish is not at all uncommon from Cabo San Lucas up the east side of Baja during the peak months of May through October for this great game fish. They grow a great deal bigger than that, though. An angler named Abe Sackheim caught a 114-pound roosterfish on conventional gear and thirty-pound line off La Paz, Baja, back on June 1, 1960, to set an all-tackle world record, but most caught near shore weigh far less than that. The world record for a fly rod, when I began my serious campaign to take them on a fly in 1987, was twenty-five pounds eight ounces. That fish was taken by Harold Winkle at Mulege, Baja, May 17, 1974, on a 16-pound-test tippet.

I grew a lot smarter in 1987 after losing several more fish on heavier fly tackle. By then I was using a 9-foot graphite fly rod, 9-weight, floating, weight-forward fly line, a Pate Tarpon reel capable of holding four hundred yards of thirty-pound Micron or Dacron backing, and 16-pound-test tippets. Even with this formidable tackle, I was breaking off fish. Most seemed to be in the fifteen- to twenty-pound category, from the brief glimpses we had of them in the clear water just beyond the surf line at Baja. On the first strong run each time they were breaking leaders in the class-tippet section, just above the fly.

I had caught jack crevalle on a fly several times off the Florida Keys on 12-pound-test tippet. They had fought with the same savage run and had continued to pull long after a fish of equal size would have given up. The few I had lost broke the tippet in the same way. At the time, the guide suggested I go to a wire leader or to heavier mono between the fly and the class tippet. That did the trick.

So, in 1987 at Baja, I added twelve inches of 80-pound-test mono as a shock leader to the tippet. The IGFA does not allow more than twelve inches of shock leader if one is fishing for record fish. I started holding fish immediately. By July of that year I had caught several good roosterfish on a white cork popping bug. I started out using white streamer flies, but could never interest roosterfish in them. Didier Van der Veecken, the excellent saltwater fly rodder (and IGFA representative from Baja) at Cabo San Lucas told me roosterfish much prefer a popper to a streamer. He was right.

The traditional method of taking roosterfish at Baja has been to troll a live mullet behind a boat just outside the surf. The guides prefer a mullet of at least eight to nine inches in length on the theory that large mullet take large roosterfish. These big mullet are hooked through the lips with a hook ranging in size from #3/0 to #5/0. When a roosterfish takes the mullet, the guides advise letting the fish run some distance to swallow the bait before setting the hook.

The system works well, and a big roosterfish that takes the trolled mullet does so with a savage strike. Using that to advantage, Didier and other fly rodders have learned to troll both mullet without hooks in them or big plugs without hooks as teasers. When roosterfish attack these teasers, the teasers are hauled in and a popping bug is cast to the attacking fish. Single fish strike such teasers, as do roosterfish in schools. Casting a fly at roosterfish that are churning up the surface, their dorsal fins out of water, is a very exciting sport.

There is one big disadvantage to using live mullet. When a big roosterfish hits the live mullet, it not only tears it up badly, but the fish is reluctant to give it up. Unless a fishing partner, or mate, pulls the mullet quickly away from the attacking fish, it may swallow the mullet whole and lose interest in striking any other bait.

The hookless plug, however, works just the opposite way. When a roosterfish hits the smooth plug, it is unable to hold it and will continue to strike at it as it is being pulled in. Any popping bug that lands near it is sure to attract a savage hit. The ideal situation for the saltwater fly rodder is to come upon a school of these great fighters feeding just outside the surf line.

By the spring of 1988, I had taken some fairly big roosterfish on fly tackle. Fishing from one of the popular roosterfish resorts on the East

Cape—the best two are Punta Colorado and Spa Buena Vista—I took a twenty-four-pound-two-ounce roosterfish just south of Punta Arena, a point jutting out into the Sea of Cortez. The point harbors a multitude of roosterfish at peak season. That fish put up a monumental struggle and it was a good forty-five minutes before the big fish came to the boat in water no more than six to eight feet deep.

I was lucky enough to discover another prime roosterfish area later that year. While I was fishing for sailfish on a fly from Bahia Pez Vela in Costa Rica, Mark Tupper, owner of the excellent fishing resort up the coast from San José, said he had caught some big roosterfish on conventional gear up near the Bat Islands close to the border between Costa Rica and Nicaragua. It is only about an hour's run by boat from Bahia Pez Vela.

Fortunately, I had some of my own white-bodied cork poppers with me. I carve them from one-inch diameter #10 bottle corks, hollow out the faces to make them concave, paint them with white enamel paint, insert white and brown tail feathers in them, and mount them on #5/0 Mustad stainless-steel hooks. I make them because I have never been able to find out where to buy such poppers.

I had not brought any 9-weight fly tackle along, but figured I could manhandle roosterfish on the marlin and sailfish gear: a 9-foot, 12-weight graphite rod, a thirty-foot, 12-weight sinking shooting-head line, and a Pate Marlin reel with six hundred yards of thirty-pound Micron backing. It was probably a good thing I had such a rig. I really didn't expect to take any roosterfish of size and just went to see what kind of fish were there.

Arturo, skipper of the 26-foot, single-diesel *Cubero*, came up with several foot-long rainbow runners to troll as teasers. The water at the Bat Islands, close to the face of sheer rock outcroppings, was about eighty feet deep. Thinking roosterfish only inhabited shallow water over sandy shores, I did not have much faith in our chances of teasing up roosters.

The seas were running two to three feet, we were in intermittent rain showers, and a steady ten-knot wind was rippling the surface around us. The rainbow runner was no sooner out than it disappeared in a smashing boil of water fifty feet astern. I had looped my mono running line at my feet in a plastic bucket, so I was ready to cast. The bug landed about six feet from where the teaser had disappeared, and at the first strip the surface erupted in a geyser of spray and the bug was gone.

The big fish took out three hundred yards of line on that first run and dove nearly one hundred feet deep before it began to slow down. I was thanking the gods of fishing that I had used the sailfish rig with one foot of 100-pound-test shock leader ahead of the bug. Even with heavy tackle, it took thirty-five minutes to bring in that fish. Chuck Rizuto, trout-fishing guide from the San Juan River in New Mexico, alternated between lending moral support, giving advice, and taking photos. A roosterfish will turn a flat side toward the pull of the line and is a tremendous fighter, especially on fly tackle. I fully intended to release the fish, so Arturo used a Teflon-coated glove instead of the gaff to grasp the big roosterfish by a gill plate as it was brought alongside. It was a handful to get over the side as it struggled against the hull.

I had an idea the fish might be a world record after seeing the size of the twenty-four-pound fish I had taken off Baja. Arturo kept the fish in a big fish box filled with water as we continued to fish. I took another big roosterfish several hours later that probably would have weighed twenty pounds had we kept it to be weighed. By the time we released that fish the seas were too rough to continue fishing and we headed home.

The big roosterfish weighed thirty-one pounds twelve ounces on the accurate scales at Bahia Pez Vela. The measurements were carefully taken and the fish was photographed from every angle. It was later certified by the IGFA as a new world record and appeared in the 1989 IGFA *World Record Game Fishes*—quite a thrill for a saltwater fly fisherman!

Roosterfish are plentiful from Salinas, Ecuador, and Pinas Bay, Panama, up to Costa Rica and the west coast of Mexico and Baja. There have been some sightings as far north as San Clemente Island off southern California. If I were to advise a beginner about where to go to try for them, however, I would suggest Baja's East Cape from May to October. The area is relatively easy to reach by airline, and there are a number of good spots from which to fish. Cabo San Lucas is also an excellent spot from which to fish for roosterfish with a fly rod.

Any good 9-foot graphite fly rod will do for big roosterfish, but it is advisable to use a saltwater reel capable of holding three hundred to four hundred yards of backing, plus a fly line. A smaller reel might do for the average roosterfish, but one never knows when a thirty- to forty-pound fish will strike the fly.

The author and a twenty-four-pound roosterfish caught on a white popper near Punta Arena on Baja's East Cape.

Some roosterfish fly-rod anglers prefer weight-forward floating lines, as do I. But I have a number of friends who prefer to cast floating shooting heads, as do lots of tarpon fly fishermen. I use sinking shooting heads cut down to twenty-five to twenty-eight feet in length for bigger fish like marlin and sailfish. I think they offer much less resistance to the water when big fish run and leap, but I don't find them necessary for roosterfish.

As on all big saltwater fish, the knots are all-important when fishing for big roosterfish. These powerful fighters will quickly pull out any knot not carefully tied. I prefer a hard Mason leader for the class tippet, the same as I use on billfish. I think the 80-pound-test shock tippet is sufficient. One may fasten it to the eye of the hook with a 3½-turn clinch knot. It is also possible to use a double surgeon's loop, even in 100-pound-test shock mono, to fasten a knot ahead of the fly. This knot is very strong and can be used for billfish, big tuna, and sharks.

The saltwater fly rodders pursuing roosterfish are growing in number each year. Word has spread of the fighting qualities of this great gamefish. Anglers, particularly from the West Coast and the Southwest, are flocking to the sun-blasted deserts and long, curving beaches of Baja each spring and summer in search of *pez gallo*. It is a welcome addition to the stable of game fish sought by the growing legion of long-rod anglers.

8

Coyote Flats—Redfish and Sea Trout

With a little luck, the wind dies down early enough in the evening to allow the sand to settle in the water by morning. And when it does, the redfish and speckled sea trout have enough visibility to see the small popping bug as it gurgles on the surface of the south Texas coast flat.

Given that much of a break, the saltwater fly rodder needs the almost constant wind to hold off until only an hour after dawn, before it begins to scrape its rough and broken fingernails across the vastness of the flats.

Breakfast can be a halfhearted affair at 4:30 A.M. No amount of bacon, eggs, and steaming black coffee can erase the rude shock to the system of an alarm clock's screaming vibration in the darkness.

"Still calm out there," says Dick Negley, second-generation, south-coast fly fisherman, sliding a slice of toast across the table. "We may get lucky."

It would be a near miracle for this year. The winds had blown across the beaches, keening endlessly out of the reaches of northeast Mexico and across the delta of the Rio Grande since March. And here it is, early July. But then, the winds had died down early the night before, something unusual in itself.

Flashlight beams bob and stab in the darkness as the sleek boat is gradually loaded with the fly rods, lunches, a cooler of cold drinks, wading belts, and assorted gear. Dawn is only a mercurial suggestion on the horizon as the bow and stern lines are unhooked and the big 200-horsepower, jet-powered outboard coughs to life. Sleek as a sting-ray, the flats boat—21 feet long and modeled after the bonefish and tarpon craft of the Florida Keys—was custom built for Negley. It has a Kevlar bottom to ward off the occasional lost anchor, and only draws six inches of water in a region where eight inches is considered *deep.* The flat bottom sports no keel, and to make a turn at her cruising fifty-knot speed, Negley needs a good quarter mile of space.

The channel of the narrow harbor mouth at Port Mansfield is clogged with departing boats: bulky shrimpers; aluminum johnboats; scooters; center-console, deep-water craft; sportfishermen heading for the offshore big-game grounds forty to fifty miles out; and the occasional airboat, howling in the darkness.

The warm, fetid, salt breath of the flats blows some of the cobwebs from the mind as the boat streaks across the quicksilver surface of the

Fly fishing for redfish and sea trout on the calm, early-morning flats.

flat. To the east there is just enough light to make the sandy Spoil Islands—cast up by the giant dredges digging the Intercoastal Waterway—black silhouettes on the horizon.

As the light gathers in the east and the boat speeds quietly—the engine roar blasted rearward—wakes of thousands of fleeing fish curve outward from the probing bow.

"Mullet mostly," Dick says with a nod toward the fish. "Takes a while to learn to tell the redfish and trout wakes from the mullet, but it's mostly that they push a bigger wake—with bigger shoulders on them."

Far out on the horizon to port there are two black dots, immobile against a silver void background. They could be great blue herons—stilt legged, but . . .

"Coyotes," Dick says with a grin and a head shake. "Seems hard to believe, but they make a living way out on these flats. I guess they feed on crabs, dead fish, sea-bird young, and bird's eggs . . . most anything. They live on these Spoil Islands and just scrounge . . . like coyotes do. There's even quail on these sandy islands. Can hear them on still, quiet mornings and sometimes just before dark."

The thunder and vibration of the big engine changes gradually as the boat slows. Instead of an anchor, which would hardly be needed in less than a foot of water, a five-foot steel spike mounted on the transom is driven down into the sand to secure the boat.

With the big engine shut down, silence drops like a curtain, broken only by the slurping sound of millions of mullet surface feeding. The silver surface of the flats stretches out and away until it merges with the dawn sky, leaving the impression of being inside a giant, iridescent globe. The only horizon is to the east where rays of gold and crimson radiate upward from the hidden sun like giant fingers reaching for the day.

The water is a warm 80 degrees Fahrenheit and in all directions hardly more than ankle deep. Feeding mullet are everywhere, dimpling the surface, and leaping and falling to the surface on their sides.

"Watch for the bigger wakes," Dick says as the rods are slid from the gunwale tunnels and flexed. "It's not easy. Takes time. Drop the popper ahead of the cruising fish and gurgle it a couple of times. They strike hard—both the redfish and the specs. Sometimes you'll get lucky and a redfish will tail while feeding. The mullet tails are forked, but the red's tail is blunt—and has a reddish tint in the light. The trout don't tail."

The 9-foot graphite rod is a live thing vibrating in the hand. The 8-weight floating, weight-forward line sighs softly in the heavy air and the small balsawood popper lands with a *splat*. On the end of a nine-foot leader tapered down to 8-pound-test, its concave face pushes the water with a bubbling sound.

Off to the left, Negley casts into the rising sun, bits of water falling from his backcasts like tiny jewels. Both redfish and trout will feed, he says, among and on the fringes of the mullet schools. It is best to cast constantly, hoping for a blind strike, until a feeding target is sighted.

The wading belts hold a small canteen containing fresh water, a length of cord with a metal spike point, and cork floats to mark where fish are stashed. Some are to be kept for dinner, but only those redfish between twenty and twenty-eight inches in length, as stipulated by the Texas Parks and Wildlife Commission. The under twenty-inchers are considered too small and those above twenty-eight inches must be left as spawners.

The popper disappears in a swirl of churned water and the reel screams. The arc in the rod testifies to a good fish making a straight run toward the red-and-gold pathway of the climbing sun. With two hundred yards of twenty-pound backing on the aged reel, long runs are not a problem, but the size of the fish is still unknown. At about fifty yards out, the fish swings to the left and begins a circle. It is a strong fish, the throbbing tugs indicating head shakes as it swims.

When it finally tires, it turns out to be a speckled trout — weakfish is the local name — of about six pounds. It glistens in the morning sunlight, then churns the bottom getting away when released.

A rounded tail suddenly appears amid the forked ones of the feeding mullet, shining red in the bright early sun as the fish noses down in the shallow water. The popper lands close by and gurgles at the first strip. There is an instantaneous, vicious strike and the fish is on. There is a difference to this fish — a bullish, powerful strength. The run is long, and when it finally turns nearly one hundred yards out, there is little give to the gradually decreasing circles. Even when close, the fish streaks away again at the sight of the net, making several more strong runs before finally giving in.

After thrashing in the net, the fish is held, gleaming in the intense light, a bulky, solid redfish of about eight pounds. The distinctive, black tail spot contrasts sharply with the pink-and-white body.

"Beautiful fish," Dick says, turning it slowly for the camera. "They are all heart. The trout will fight well, but give me a bull red any time.

Saltwater fly rodder Dick Negley and a catch of small sea trout for dinner.

When one about twenty to thirty pounds hits a popper, it is unlike any other kind of fishing. We don't keep them, but the fight they put up warms those cold winter nights, that's for sure."

The wind stays down for another hour, just long enough to let several more reds and another sea trout smash the poppers. After that, the surface wrinkles as the breeze picks up from the south, promising winds of fifteen to twenty knots by midmorning. While the spinning-reel and level-winding-reel anglers may stand a chance of success with plugs and spoons, the day is over for the fly fishermen.

The slim boat skims along the lee shores of the Spoil Islands on the way in. The shallows are dotted with great blue herons, white cattle egrets, green herons, black-crowned night herons, and least bitterns – all stalking or waiting for small fish. The sandy beaches are host to flocks of killdeer, ruddy turnstones, sandpipers, sanderlings, phalaropes, yellowlegs, marbled godwits, dowitchers, and oyster-catchers.

"Maybe the wind will fall early," Dick says, "giving us a shot late in the day. If not, we have the morning. Usually, by July, the mornings are calm enough to give the fly fishermen a chance. But the real time down here" he grins "is October and November. No wind, nice and cool, and lots of fish. Keep that in mind. While the rest are bird shooting or watching football on TV, you can be catching reds and specs on a fly until your arm is tired. That ain't all bad," he adds solemnly.

Negley learned to fly fish from his father, Bill Negley, who is an all-around sportsman: fly fisherman, wing shooter, and one of the greatest bow hunters of all time.

I started out using fairly large poppers for redfish, but Dick said both he and his father had experimented with different surface poppers and found the larger ones failed to hook fish as well as the smaller largemouth bass-size poppers.

The whole Texas Gulf Coast, from Sabine Pass on the east to Brazos Island on the west, is a paradise for the saltwater fly rodder looking for that king of shallow water game fish—the red drum.

Known along the Texas coast simply as redfish, or "reds," the red drum, or channel bass, as it is called on the East Coast, is found all the way from Massachusetts to the Lone Star State. It is a superb fighting fish and a delicacy to eat, a fact that has put it in grave danger over the past few decades. The "blackened redfish" craze of the mid-1980s put a real dent in redfish populations from the Carolinas and Florida all around the Gulf Coast states.

Louisiana saw its state legislature ban commercial fishing for redfish in 1988 for three years and reduce recreational redfish limits to five reds a day with a sixteen-inch minimum and no more than one red exceeding twenty-seven inches.

After a study that showed 40 percent of the annual redfish catch was going to commercial netters using their gear illegally, the Texas Parks and Wildlife Commission voted to remove all commercial netting from state water (nine nautical miles) beginning September 1, 1988. Sport fishermen saw the creel limit dropped from five to three reds per day with a twenty-inch minimum and a twenty-eight-inch maximum.

But to the long-rod fishermen, who return most of the fish they catch to the water anyway, the new limits did not mean as much. It is as much fun to catch a twenty-inch red as it is to catch many other twenty-eight-inch fish on a fly. Also, the flies in no way injure fish, and the ones released are as good as new.

I've found that a good fly for redfish is a popper bug—the same bug one uses for largemouth bass. While speckled trout, or weakfish, will take a streamer readily, redfish seem to prefer the commotion a popping bug makes on the surface. It will strike the noisy bug with a

This sea trout fell for a small red popper on the calm flats.

vengeance as it gurgles along the surface. I doubt if the color means much to them. I do best with a red-and-white popper and one that is colored a bright chartreuse green.

The many shallow bays and flats close to the Intercoastal Waterway—that monument to mammoth engineering that created a dredged commercial shipping and barge canal from Beaumont to Brownsville—are alive with redfish. Getting to them, for the fly rodder, is the problem. Most of the area is so shallow a rowboat could not go one hundred yards without getting stuck.

In order to get into the shallow bays and coves, one needs a flat-bottomed, shallow-draft boat with considerable power. The answer has been the popular "skooter"—a flat-bottomed, center-console, flat-decked craft that sports an adjustable outboard motor with a prop or is fitted with a jet outboard motor. On many of the boats the prop can be moved up and down on the lower unit of the motor or can be operated in a tunnel in the hull. The jet outboard is a very practical innovation and allows the boatman to skim over the flats with very little chance of damage to a prop.

A number of redfish anglers use airboats to reach the shallow flats. They are probably the most practical craft for this task, but the noise is a bit much on the ears and crewmen need to wear ear protectors while operating them.

Redfish travel in schools and feed on a multitude of small critters on the shallow flats: crabs, shrimp, mollusks, and small fish. It is not a big problem to approach a school after it has been spotted providing the angler does it silently. A loud noise, such as the starting of an outboard motor or the dropping of an object in a boat, will spook them. But if one walks carefully on the mud or sand bottom, one can get within casting distance.

Wind is the real enemy of the fly fisherman along the Texas coast. The best time, by far, to fish for redfish with a popper bug is early in the day before the wind comes up. The next best time is at night under lights from a dock. Not only is it difficult to cast a popper bug in any kind of wind, but a churned-up surface makes it very difficult to locate reds. Redfish, singly or in schools in shallow water, can be spotted by the V-shape wake they make while feeding. It is necessary to drop the popper bug ahead of a feeding fish to make sure it sights the lure. Stripping it in short jerks causes the bug to make a gurgling sound and makes it a very attractive target for a red.

One of the best ways to locate redfish on windy days is to watch the sea birds. Gulls and terns follow feeding schools of redfish and sometimes hover just above them when the fish are feeding in shallow water. If an angler is lucky on a windy day, he may spot a flock of birds hovering just above the exposed tails of feeding redfish. The fish are easy to approach under those conditions, and a popper bug can be landed almost in the middle of the feeding school without spooking fish.

One needs to be aware of bottom conditions when wading flats. There are areas where the bottom is extremely soft and others where the bottom is quite firm. Finding a soft, deep bottom is not much fun when wading. It is also tiring to walk a soft-bottomed flat for any length of time.

The flats of the Texas Gulf Coast are alive with mullet schools for most of the year. These schools extend for acres on the flats and can be annoying when one is trying to locate feeding redfish. On the other hand, they can signal the location of reds on occasion. It is quite common to find redfish feeding on the fringes of mullet schools.

When wading extremely shallow flats under no-wind conditions with a fly rod, keep in mind that a redfish feeds nose-down and tail-up. While there may be thousands of forked mullet tails breaking the surface on a flat, a redfish tail is round and has a red hue to it, especially in bright sunlight.

Fly-fishing gear for redfish need not be complicated. Any good

Author and a nice fly-caught redfish.

7- to 8-foot fly rod will do for these strong fish. I like to use a longer fly rod, but that is just personal preference. I use a 9-foot graphite fly rod with 9-weight, floating, weight-forward fly line. The reel is the important piece of equipment in all saltwater fly fishing and particularly with strong game fish like redfish. A twenty-eight- to thirty-inch redfish will strip out a lot of fly line and backing on that first run. It is advisable to have a reel that is anodized against saltwater corrosion, as salt water can seize up a freshwater reel in short order. Also, it is necessary to have at least two hundred yards of backing, preferably twenty-pound Micron or braided Dacron on the reel behind the fly line. I have never found it necessary to use a leader stronger than 12-pound-test, but it is up to other anglers to choose whatever they like best.

9

King of the Snappers — Mutton Snapper

Guide Mandy Moore and I were fly fishing for bonefish on the flats at Guanaja, a beautiful little island resting like a tiny jewel in an aquamarine sea just off the northeast coast of Honduras. The island houses a fine resort called La Posada del Sol, a diving club run by a retired, professional deep-sea diver named George Cundiff.

George bought the lovely, big mansion that houses the club after its former owner, a Canadian businessman, died. The main house is made of rock and concrete and will withstand anything but the worst hurricane. George wondered if there was anything on the flats that would attract fishermen to his place in the off-diving season, and invited me to come down and find out.

What I found out was that the flats near the island contain a few bonefish schools, but a whole lot of permit. Guanaja may well be one of the premier permit spots in the world.

Mandy and I had been fishing for a couple of days and had caught a few small bonefish from the resident school just across from the hotel. I had hooked and lost a small permit that morning and was looking for another, using an epoxy fly tied on a #2/0 hook. I saw what I thought was the shadow of a fast-moving permit in water four to five feet deep, and made a long cast to it. I immediately lost sight of the fish, but kept stripping the fly.

The resulting strike was so hard it jolted my arm. Thinking I had hooked another permit, I raised the tip of the 9-foot graphite fly rod and shouted to Mandy, who was about forty feet away.

The fish made a mad dash for deep water about fifty yards away, and I held the rod high to try and keep the fish away from any coral heads in the way. The fish reached deep water and instead of swimming directly away from me—the way a permit would—this fish dove for the bottom and began a head-shaking battle. It was an incredibly strong fish and had there been any coral at that spot, it would surely have broken me off. But the bottom was sandy and the fish was unable to rub off the epoxy fly.

The fight lasted about twenty minutes, and when the fish finally began to come in, I knew I had been in a real war. Mandy had gotten the aluminum net from the flats boat and scooped up the fish as it splashed close to us. It was a big mutton snapper of about eight pounds. It was the biggest one I ever caught on a fly, and I sure hope it won't be the last. I would have released it after we had taken a photograph, but Mandy strongly insisted we eat it. It proved to be one of the best meals I have ever had!

For many years light-tackle fishermen considered the mutton snapper strictly a fighting fish of the reefs and blue holes. And while it was sought as a tough scrapper and a delight to eat, it was not considered a fish of the flats. It has been only a few years since dedicated fly-rod anglers in the southern Florida Keys discovered that mutton snappers not only frequent the flats but tail while feeding much the same as bonefish and permit.

Like the other two great game fish, they make a run for deep water when hooked, making them a challenge both on a fly rod and light spinning and conventional tackle. But while the bonefish and the permit are seldom kept to eat, the mutton snapper is prized for its fine taste by some anglers who are as interested in the gourmet aspects of the fish as in its fighting qualities.

The mutton snapper (*Lutjanus analis*) is a brightly colored snapper that occurs along the east and west coasts of Florida, the Bahamas, and throughout the tropical American Atlantic and Caribbean. It averages six to twelve pounds, but can go as high as fifteen to thirty pounds in many areas. Fish have been caught in commercial nets up to twenty-five pounds.

The mutton snapper—a marvelous game fish on a fly rod.

The fly-rod record is held by Joseph A. Few, Jr.—a fourteen-pound-fourteen-ounce mutton snapper, caught at Key West on April 15, 1985, on an 8-pound-test tippet.

The 12-pound-test tippet class was finally filled by Raz Reid with a ten-pound-twelve-ounce fish caught in Islamorada in 1990. The 16-pound class was still vacant as of January 1991.

The colorful mutton snapper has an olive green back, reddish orange on its sides, and white below. All its fins are bright red, and it has a prominent black spot just above the lateral line halfway back and on both sides. It has the same formidable set of teeth as most snappers, and fly-rod anglers trying for them would be well advised to use fairly heavy mono as a shock leader. When I caught that one, I was using only the 12-pound-test tippet with no shock leader. I was lucky.

In years past I have taken them in the Bahamas and off the Florida Keys by trolling for them along reef drop-offs with spoons, feathered jigs, and plugs.

But it is the area of flats fishing that the mutton snapper has caught on as a spectacular game fish. They are as spooky as bonefish and permit and are very difficult to approach. Anyone who has tried to catch old, wise snappers in dock areas knows how smart they become when it comes to the hook and line. The mutton snapper is shy even in moderately deep water, but on the flats it is positively intuitive, racing for deep water at the first glimpse of movement or vibration of sound.

Key West is beyond a doubt the best spot in the Florida Keys at which to try for the illusive mutton snapper on the flats, although they may be found all the way from Biscayne Bay down the entire chain of keys. I have seen them on the flats at Islamorada, Marathon, and Long Key. I have seen them tailing on the flats at Bimini, Chub Cay, Andros, and Exuma, but never had any luck with a fly rod at any of those spots.

One of the reasons more mutton snappers have been taken the last few years with a fly rod is the development of the epoxy fly. The epoxy fly has undergone some changes. Veteran guide Jose Wejebe, has added tail feathers and weed guards made from rigid plastic. Still others have learned to add weight to the hook shank so that the fly sinks to where it can be taken close to or on the bottom. Eyes have been refined on the revolutionary epoxy fly and now are made from expensive taxidermist eyes. Spun deer hair, wound grizzly hackle, and tail feathers have been added to the triangular-shaped body of the fly, and it is now able to shoulder its way through the weeds and turtle grass of the flats without getting hung up. It is this fly more than any other that has enabled fly-rod enthusiasts to take mutton snapper frequently on the bonefish flats.

The fly is not small and is difficult to cast in any kind of wind, but its action in the water makes up for its ungainly shape. The natural food of the mutton snapper is the same as bonefish and permit—small sand crabs, shrimp, and mollusks that it roots up out of the sand and coral of the flats with its snout. It also feeds on small fish and spiny lobsters.

Getting a fly to a mutton snapper is no more difficult than presenting one to a bonefish or permit—it is tough. The fly has to land close enough to the fish for it to see it, yet far enough away so that it does not spook the fish when it lands. That is a very difficult proposition when one realizes that in order to prevent the mutton snapper from cutting the filmy leader, either a wire leader or a length of tough mono is needed in front of the fly.

The mutton snapper can become educated rapidly after being hooked once or twice. I used to fish for sailfish with Captain Allen Self, who ran a sportfisherman named the *Sea Elf* out of the Ocean Reef Club at north Key Largo for many years. Allen was a student of

The epoxy fly, invented by Marathon, Florida, guide Harry Spears, is an excellent permit fly and one that occasionally works for mutton snapper.

fish as well as fishermen. We were sitting on the dock one day and he was expounding on the brains of big snappers that hung around the dock area.

"See that big mutton snapper over by those mangrove roots?" he asked, pointing a finger at the fish resting in the shade of the tree. I nodded.

"That rascal will never be caught. Every skipper and mate here has tried to catch it for years. It will take bait, but it knows every hook made and will drop it as soon as it feels the weight of the line. Watch this," he said.

He went to his boat and returned with a spinning rod and two fresh shrimp. He impaled one on a #2/0 bonefish hook and tossed it within several feet of the resting fish. Half a dozen small mangrove snappers rushed for the shrimp, but stopped short of the bait when the big snapper—one of at least twelve pounds—sped out and stopped with its nose against the shrimp.

The mutton snapper gingerly picked up the shrimp and immediately dropped it. It did this two more times before swimming slowly back to its resting place.

"See," Self said. "I told you. Now watch this."

He tossed the unhooked shrimp to the same area. The big snapper swam over, inspected the bait, picked it up carefully, and swallowed it.

"I'll be damned!" I said.

"You can spend a month on that critter," Self chuckled, "and you won't *ever* fool him!"

I didn't spend a month, but I spent a lot of hours trying to trick that fish. As far as I know, it is still there.

My favorite rod for mutton snapper is the same rod I use for permit, a 9-foot graphite capable of throwing a 9-weight, floating, weight-forward line. One needs the same good reel as for permit, one capable of holding about two hundred yards of combined fly line and twenty-pound backing. The drag—as in fishing for permit and big bonefish—is everything.

Those anglers who have caught big snappers know what a fight they put up in both shallow and deep water. But until they have caught them on the flats, they have never experienced a real battle—especially on a fly rod. The mutton snapper takes a fly in hunger and at the first bite of the hook it heads for the nearest channel or drop-off at full speed. Stopping it takes a good rod and reel and some fancy fly-rod handling. Stopped, a mutton snapper puts up a diving, zigzagging, head-shaking fight that makes a fly fisherman's day.

The fish likes movement of the fly, not one lying on the bottom. The ideal way to take one on a fly is to get the fly out in front of a feeding snapper and strip it across in front of the fish in short three- to four-inch jerks. Setting the hook is important, of course, but many times the mutton snapper will hook itself by the speed of its strike.

The ranks of mutton snapper fly-rod fishermen are swelling as word of this sporty fish spreads. The fish are not easy to find on the flats, and the best way to locate them is to hire an experienced Keys guide the first few times one goes out.

They are fairly abundant in the Bahamas, but one has to travel far from the island towns to find them. They are a much sought-after food fish in the islands and they are pretty well fished out close to towns.

As far as what the best flies are, there are a lot of opinions. Every Keys guide has his own favorite fly for mutton snappers. Many will swear by the Epoxy MOE Fly, while others prefer shrimplike patterns like Dave Whitlock's great Salt Shrimp Fly or Terry Baird's excellent

A mutton snapper taken on the flats at Guanaja, Honduras, on an epoxy fly.

Mono Shrimp. I got a good strike on Jimmy Nix's Mullet Fly off Key West, but lost the snapper to a mangrove root. I have never gotten a hit on one, but I see no reason why George Anderson's fine McCrab Fly wouldn't take mutton snappers. After all, it takes permit, and nothing is spookier than *that* fish. Jonathan Olch's Florida Shrimp Fly has taken some mutton snappers, but I think the old reliable Crazy Charlie Fly, in almost any of its variations, would be a good fly to throw at these wary snappers. I took a small one on the flats at Islamorada while fishing with Hal Chittum a few years ago, on a Chico Fernandez's Honey Shrimp Fly. It is a great fly for any fish that chases shrimp. Hal is the kind of guide who will fish for anything, any time, and is a joy to be with on the flats.

There are guides and there are guides. Some are all business and don't want to deviate from the serious business of catching fish. Then there are guides like Chittum and Rick Ruoff, who have a deep interest in the flora and fauna of a flat, and fishing with them is like taking a course in natural history. It is especially interesting when the fish are hard to find. I have had as much fun catching small fish from a snapper hole with a fly as I have had taking bonefish on an open flat. The guide can make or break a day.

10

Swimmers of the Salmon People – King and Coho

Long before the coming of the white man, the native people of the Pacific Northwest revered the salmon. Though they ate the meat of bears, moose, deer, shellfish, and berries in season, salmon was their staple food. A good salmon run meant a year of plenty. A failed run ensured starvation and death.

In the beginning words of their First Salmon Ceremony, the Native Americans chanted: "O Supernatural Ones, O Swimmers, I thank you that you are willing to come to us. Do not let your coming be bad, for you come to be food for us."

Guide Buzz Fiorini set the float plane down in an unnamed cove a few miles north of Thayer Creek, on the west side of Admiralty Island, and taxied slowly up to the rocky shore.

It is important to miss the sharp-pointed rocks that lie just beneath the surface. Even the smallest tear in the aluminum skin of a pontoon could mean disaster in this rugged land. While we could beach the plane and avoid sinking, it might be a long time before anyone could get to us for repairs.

The tips of the pontoons ground into the soft, gray sand of the beach, and Buzz flipped off the switches as I climbed from the right seat and dug a stout rope from the starboard pontoon to tie the craft to the nearest tree or snag. By the time I had the plane secured, Buzz was pulling on his chest waders, sitting on a pontoon in the bright, late-August sunlight.

"This cove is always full of coho," he grunted, heaving on his waders. "This little creek here runs up to a small lake about a mile inland. It's a pretty easy run for them up there, and the fry stay in the lake two to three years before heading down for the sea."

I looked west across the wide Chatham Strait to the hazy outlines of Baranof Island. Far out, plumes of white mist floated above the surface.

"What kind of whales are those?" I asked, sliding the rod from beneath the rear seats.

"Bowfins," Buzz said. "Beautiful big things. I had one come up under a rock shelf down the coast where I was fishing a few weeks ago. It wanted to scrape barnacles off its back. I could feel the whole shelf move!"

A hundred yards out in the cove, two glistening, black, football-size heads popped up and surveyed us.

"Seals," I said. "Will they spook the coho?"

"A little, I suppose." Buzz stood up and stamped to allow his waders to settle. "But I figure there's enough for all of us."

A light west breeze rippled the surface of the cove as we rigged up the rods. I was using a four-piece, 9-weight graphite rod and a 90-foot, 9-weight, weight-forward, floating, sinking-tip line with a ten-foot intermediate tip that sank slowly at a rate of about one and one-half inches per second. My twelve-foot leader tapered to 12-pound-test.

Buzz likes shooting heads for coho and carries a canvas stripping basket that rides on his chest. With a 9-weight graphite rod, he can shoot the thirty feet of head out 120 feet.

I slipped the aluminum fly box from the pocket of the vest and opened it in the bright sunlight.

"What do you think, Buzz?" I asked, holding up the bright yellow-and-red streamer.

The guide nodded. "Mickey Finn should work as well as anything," he said.

I tied on the fly and moved down the shore toward the mouth of the creek. The coho were not showing, but I knew they were stacked up waiting for the maturing process to tell them when to head upstream. Although they had been swimming as much as twenty-four hours a day since the urge to spawn had turned them from their feeding grounds far out in the Gulf of Alaska—hundreds of miles from the stream in which they had been hatched—when they finally reached the mouth of the creek, they had stopped to rest.

Now the eggs would ripen and separate within the females and the sperm, or milt, would form in the males. When something programmed millions of years earlier told these waiting salmon it was time to head up the creek above its mouth, they would move slowly into the headwaters as a ragged school.

I waded into the water until I was about thigh-deep and began to cast. The effort felt good after the cramped position in the small plane. I moved slowly down the shore as I cast, trying to cover as much of the water as possible just outside the drop-off. I let the fly sink slowly, then stripped it in short pulls with the left hand.

The strike, when it came, was a vicious jolt. I wasn't prepared for it after the interval of uninterrupted casting and I almost missed setting the hook. When I did, the line ripped out from the whining reel, cutting a slice through the calm surface of the cove as the fish sped for the deeper water. Then, when it felt the pull of the drag and line, it took to the air in a magnificent somersault, slapping back to the surface with a sound that echoed back from the spruces up on the bank. Buzz waved and shouted from near the plane when he heard the *whack* of the coho hitting the surface.

The fish put up a magnificent battle, running deep out to the depths of the cove and shaking its head against the strain of the rod after it had taken about 150 yards of line and backing. I kept the rod tip high and just enjoyed the tremendous strength of the fish as it alternated between breathtaking leaps and deep dives.

Buzz walked down the beach toward the end of the fight and waded out with the big aluminum net. He eased it beneath the weakening fish and, after lifting it to the surface, waded slowly ashore as I walked beside him, rod held high.

I knelt down in the shallow water as Buzz removed the bright fly from the coho's jaw. I slid both hands beneath the big silvery fish and carefully drew it out of the net. It rested limply in my hands, the late-morning sunlight reflecting off its glistening sides.

"Beautiful fish," Buzz said, staring down. "Probably go twelve to fourteen pounds."

*The author's twelve-pound coho salmon
taken on a Mickey Finn streamer.*

I nodded and righted the fish in the cold, clear water. The gills slowly worked and I pushed it toward the drop-off. It swam tiredly toward the purple depths. We both watched it disappear before going back to our fishing.

We came so close to losing this fish, I thought, as I resumed casting the bright fly toward the dark water—this fish and all our salmon.

The coho (*Oncorhynchus kisutch*) is a perfect salmon for the fly fisherman. It is also called silver salmon and silversides and will readily take a fly. When hooked, it is the most acrobatic of all the salmon, leaping and cartwheeling freely. It can be caught from Point Hope, Alaska, south to Monterey Bay, California. They can be caught in both salt water and far upstream in their home rivers. The average coho will weigh from six to twelve pounds, but twenty-pound coho are not uncommon and put up a tremendous fight on a fly rod.

In the last third of the nineteenth century the white man almost drove the entire salmon population of the Pacific Northwest into extinction. The early Americans of the west ruined the salmon runs of the great Sacramento and Rogue rivers and even the mighty Columbia. Then they turned north and—with fish traps, purse seines, gill nets, trollers, gaffs, dip nets, and sometimes dynamite—began to deplete the stocks of millions of Canadian-bred, migrating salmon of the Frazier River system.

The immigrants of one hundred years ago did not consider themselves despoilers. Most thought it was impossible to destroy the great salmon runs. Didn't a female salmon lay thousands of eggs in the gravel of her home stream? It was not realized then that only 1 percent of the eggs that matured into salmon fry ever reached maturity in the ocean.

Where once shimmering hordes of salmon swam up rivers from California to Alaska to spawn, commercial canneries sprang up along these same rivers, and canned Pacific salmon was sold in Europe and Asia for huge profits. Fishermen brought in boatloads to canneries that could not take the fish because they were already glutted with salmon. Thousands of dead chinook, coho, pink, chum, and sockeye salmon were dumped off the docks to rot in the rivers. Fishermen offered to sell their catches for as little as a quarter of a cent a pound — and that was refused.

The rotting mess was blamed for a typhoid fever outbreak on the Frazier River in 1877. The incoming tides and westerly winds held the rotting sludge in the river mouth. The banks of the Frazier River were covered with a two-foot-deep layer of fish slime and offal, which sometimes extended twenty feet up the banks. The stench could be smelled for miles, and farmers as far as eighteen miles up the Frazier pitchforked the mess onto their fields for fertilizer.

Even then it took nearly twenty years for the Canadian government to react. The first regulations against indiscriminate salmon fishing were enacted in 1889. The first hatcheries were built just prior to and after the turn of the century, and millions of salmon were planted in streams and rivers in Europe, Hawaii, Australia, New Zealand, Mexico, and South America. Only the New Zealand stockings survived in any numbers.

It was not until the war years of 1939 to 1945 that new developments in hatchery science made success possible. By the early 1950s chinook and coho salmon were being raised, in spite of diseases, in United States hatcheries. But it was not until the 1960s that fisheries biologists began to realize they could successfully raise and stock both chinook and coho salmon. It had been a long, costly, and sometimes discouraging battle.

While the raising of salmon in hatcheries has been brought to a state-of-the-art science, there was a very long road to the point where one could be sure of the salmon's fate. Times have changed a great deal from the days when the great fish were indiscriminately slaughtered. Most thinking outdoorsmen and conservationists in these enlightened times realize that mankind's very survival depends upon caring for the earth's finite resources. But there are always those who put profit before survival.

We still must worry about the damming of wild salmon rivers to provide electricity. Clear-cutting of forests and strip mining for metal still constitute a very real threat to salmon spawning beds and to the survival of eggs and fry. Pollution and development probably pose the largest threat to salmon today. The fight is far from over.

Mike Branham, son of longtime Alaskan guide and outfitter, Bud Branham, and I were having a drink at the World Hunting Congress in Las Vegas. He and Bud had just opened up a new lodge in Alaska on the Naknek River at King Salmon. We had been talking about salmon fishing with a fly rod.

"I don't know, Jack," Mike said. "We have some really big chinook coming into the Nushagak River, about eighty miles northeast of King Salmon. We fish for them far up near Ekwok and also pretty far down near the mouth. But I don't know if you can hold the big ones on a fly rod. Most of our fishermen hook them on conventional or spinning tackle and then jump into an outboard-powered boat to follow them downstream. They wear them down in the big pools with twenty- and thirty-pound line."

If I could catch roosterfish, jack crevalle, and dolphin in the twenty- to thirty-pound class, I figured I could handle king salmon of the same weight, but the answer was in the reel. It had to be saltwater tackle.

"But you're sure welcome to come up and try," Mike said. "I'd sure like to see it done."

That was in January, and it was late June before I had the chance to take him up on the offer. To my surprise, Mike's Fox Bay Lodge was only a ten-minute drive from the King Salmon jet airfield. I'd expected to take a float plane into the wilds. But with nearly everyone in Alaska owning a float plane these days, most lodges can be close to civilization.

I had brought along several 9-weight graphite fly rods and two medium-size reels for sockeye salmon and rainbow trout. One reel was the Scientific Angler System II, Model 78 that has a capacity of a little more than two hundred yards of 8-weight sinking-tip line and twenty-pound backing. The other was Billy Pate's Bonefish reel, also with a capacity of about two hundred yards. But what I had not told Mike was that I also brought one of Pate's Tarpon reels, with a capacity of four hundred yards of thirty-pound Micron backing plus a full 90-foot, 9-weight floating/sinking-tip, weight-forward fly line.

My favorite all-around four-piece traveling rod had for several years been a Deerfield 9-foot graphite rod that came with two sets of forward and tip sections. The two butt sections remained the same, but one could choose either two sections that would make up an 8- to 9-weight rod or two sections that would convert it into a 10- to 12-weight rod. It saved a lot of space while traveling. I planned to use the 9-weight tip for chinook, but with the tarpon reel.

Mike flew me and a British couple, Henry and Judy Stockdale from Northampton, England, to the huge Nushagak River on the fourth day there. We used the lodge's marvelous 500-horsepower De-haviland Beaver float plane—capable of carrying eleven people—and landed on the wide river just up from Nushagak Bay. The river was a good quarter mile wide at this point, with at least an eight-knot current and with pools twenty to thirty feet deep.

Both Henry and Judy were accomplished Atlantic salmon fly fishers and carried the traditional 15-foot, double-handed British salmon rods. They also came equipped with excellent Hardy reels, but with a capacity of no more than two hundred yards of line and backing. I had a feeling that was not going to be enough for the big kings.

In Henry's fly box there was the usual selection of Atlantic salmon flies, all in neat rows. There were Durham Rangers, Rusty Rats, Blue Charms, Lady Amhursts, Jock Scotts, all neatly arranged. I had brought along several dozen tarpon flies in #3/0 and #5/0 sizes: Stu Apte's Tarpon Fly, Winston Moore's Black/Orange, Bill Barnes's Casa Mar Special, Chico Fernandez's Burnt Orange, and John Emery's Emery Orange. I figured the brighter the better.

Nobody noticed or commented on the tarpon reel. It was not much larger than the reels carried by the other anglers. Both Henry and I began to hook chum salmon almost as soon as we began to fish, wading thigh-deep in the powerful current. The chum hit hard, but their fight did not last more than ten to fifteen minutes and they soon came to the net. Most were in the eight- to twelve-pound category, brightly splotched in pinks and dark gray colors.

But there was no mistaking the strike of a king salmon! Not only was the strike hard and quick, but the slashing leap of the hooked fish and the wild, cartwheeling jump left no doubt as to what kind of a fish it was. I lost two kings in the first hour of fishing—not because they broke my line, but because they threw the flies during the first few jumps. Some were big fish, but they moved so fast it was difficult to estimate the size.

The magnificent king salmon (*Oncorhynchus tshawytscha*) is also called the chinook salmon, spring salmon, and tyee salmon and is the biggest of the salmon. It enters rivers to spawn from California to Point Hope, Alaska, and when first entering its spawning river, is a bright silver color. It changes to a purple-and-red color the longer it stays in the river. The king salmon has only recently become a fly-rod quarry as they have been considered too large to catch on fly tackle. But with the development of saltwater fly gear, more and more long-rod anglers are trying for them. They reach a length of five feet and can weigh up to 126 pounds. The fly-rod record is held by Bill Rhoades, who caught a 63-pound whopper from the Trask River in Oregon, November 13, 1987, on a 16-pound-test tippet.

Henry hooked and landed several chum salmon, as did Judy, but the one king he hooked on a Blue Charm fly turned and went down the current until it hit the end of his two hundred yards of twenty-pound backing and the leader snapped. He slowly reeled in the line, shaking his head ruefully.

"These bloody king salmon do not act at all like Atlantic salmon," he said. "Of course, we don't have rivers this size in the British Isles either," he added.

"Maybe increase the leader strength?" I suggested.

"I'm using twelve-pound already," Henry said. I shook my head.

Almost an hour later—after netting and releasing three more chum salmon—I got a smashing strike on the bright orange Apte fly. I leaned back with the rod held high as the line tore through the water, ripping upstream. The big fish headed far out into the river, then suddenly jumped, and jumped again, and again. I could feel the throbbing power in the big rod.

"My God!" Henry said beside me, "that is a huge fish!"

With at least 150 yards of line already out, the king swung and headed down the huge river using the swift current. At about 300 yards the fish jumped again after feeling the intense pressure from all

This twenty-eight pound king salmon took a yellow-and-red tarpon fly in the Nushagak River of Alaska.

the line and the graphite rod. The three-pound drag and the big bow in the line hauled it back down to the surface with a loud splash.

"Good Lord!" Henry said, "how much bloody line do you have on that reel!"

"Close to four hundred yards plus that fly line, Henry," I said through clenched teeth. "But I'm rapidly running out of that! Thank God I'm using sixteen-pound tippet."

Disoriented by being slammed back to the surface, the big king began a stubborn, sulky battle in the current far out in the river. It kept this up for nearly half an hour as I slowly pumped line back on the big reel, gaining on the big fish a foot at a time.

The big king did not jump again, but began a series of short, fifty-yard runs back out into the river whenever I managed to get it close. It was beginning to feel the pressure from the big rod and the constant pumping. Henry had seated himself on the grassy bank to observe the battle.

It took close to an hour to wear that fish out in the heavy current. The fish knew enough to turn its side toward the pressure, and the current did the rest. It was brutal work, much like pumping in a jack crevalle or an amberjack on a fly rod.

I finally got it into the shallows where Henry and Mike, who showed up with a big aluminum net he kept in the plane, cornered the fish and netted it. There was much splashing and churning up of the sand and gravel, but we managed to get the wriggling fish up on the grassy bank. When we removed the hook and hoisted it on the brass pocket scales, it weighed a few ounces over twenty-eight pounds.

"Biggest I ever saw taken on a fly in this river," said Mike happily.

"Marvelous fish!" Henry said, beaming. "By George, I am going to get a reel like that one. What do you call it?"

"A tarpon reel, Henry—a saltwater reel. And if you ever catch a tarpon on a fly rod, you'll know why they have to use reels like this."

We released the big king after taking photos and went back to fishing. Henry lost two more kings, one to a fly coming loose and the other to running out of line. Even though he changed to a 16-pound-test tippet, the big fish ran to the end of his backing.

He and Judy, however, caught a number of good chum salmon that fought well on the long, limber 15-foot rods.

I caught another twenty-two-pound king a few hours later, just to prove the first one was not a freak accident. The second one was a bit more acrobatic, but did not take out quite as much line.

It is a marvelous way to fish, standing hip-deep in such a rushing river. One must lean backwards constantly to keep from being swept away, and at each cast one never knows what size fish will strike the fly. I lost two big fish I never saw, both turning immediately after the strike and heading down river. The fly pulled out of both. Mike said there were kings in the Nushagak that would go forty to fifty pounds. What a wonderful fight they would put up on a fly rod! I am seriously thinking of going back with my marlin reel and a 12-weight graphite rod to try for them. The Pate Marlin reel holds six hundred yards of thirty-pound backing plus a fly line, and the 12-weight graphite rods can stop huge tarpon, sailfish, and marlin. But then, all these fish—after the initial runs and jumps—fight in relatively slack water.

The June sun continued to beat down on the wide river mouth, and overhead a pair of bald eagles circled slowly. A slight salty breeze blew in from the wide expanse of Nushagak Bay, bending the bunched saw grass along the banks and sighing in the branches of the gnarled pines.

Until one has stood fishing for hours in a great river, one has never really understood the passage of time. There is something about the immensity of that huge volume of water flowing from a vast continent into an endless sea that makes one *feel* time moving. It is as if one could sense the true clock of the world, or for that matter of the universe. It is as though one could almost identify with the rate of decaying material on the riverbank, the growth rate of plants, birds, and animals. It is even possible to *feel* the rate at which these spawning salmon surge upstream to meet their death—and new life.

11

The Golden Fish —
Dolphin

It was midday and not a sailfish had come up behind the 31-foot Bertram, beating southwest ahead of a moderate following sea.

Joe Hudson and I were a competing team in a four-day sailfish tournament off Flamingo Beach, Costa Rica, and it was the third day. The fishing had been very slow—only a few fish up per team—and both Joe and I were fairly bored as the hot May sun beat down on the cockpit.

I glanced up at the skipper, Raphael, leaning out of the tower to inspect something ahead. A strip bait skipped astern on the big teaser rod and a daisy chain of plastic squid danced in the wake from the starboard outrigger. It was the first international fly tournament for billfish and the anglers had expected better fishing, but most were resigned to the ways of tournament fishing and had surrendered to the conditions.

"Dorado!" Raphael shouted, pointing to the port side.

I got up from the fighting chair and looked where he was pointing. A big wooden hatch cover was tilting in the waves about fifty feet to port. It was festooned with seaweed and barnacles, a sure sign it had been in the sea a long time. I began to climb the tower ladder when the mate, Allejandro, let out a yell.

"Aiee," he shouted, pointing from beside Raphael, "*Mucho do-rado!*"

I dropped back to the teak deck and grabbed the big 13-weight graphite fly rod from where it rested against the transom. I had been waiting for a sailfish to come up, and the 12-weight, sinking, weight-forward shooting head was ready to cast. Coils of forty-pound mono running line—fifty feet of it—were curled up in the bottom of a plastic bucket in the port corner of the cockpit.

"What about the sailfish?" Joe asked as I moved to the casting corner.

"The hell with them," I said, beginning the cast. "They haven't come up all day. I'm going to have some fun. Ever catch a dolphin on a fly?"

"Nope," Joe said. "But you're right. If we're not going to catch sailfish, we might as well catch whatever comes along."

"*Mucho, mucho, y grande!*" the mate shouted.

I had on one of my homemade popping bugs. Raphael spun the wheel to swing us to port as I dropped the white bug to the right of the wake and gave it several hard jerks to make it pop. Almost immediately, the bug disappeared in a geyser of whitewater and the big rod doubled over. I glanced at where Joe was seated in a wood-and-canvas folding chair.

"Get your fly out," I shouted as Raphael put the boat into reverse to back down on the leaping fish. "The school will stay with the hooked fish. Just get it into the water and strip it fast . . . and hang on."

The fish I had on made a long, fast run to my right and I kept the rod tip high. Joe had his white, double-hook, sailfish streamer fly in the water, and on the third strip was fast to a streaking dolphin.

"Double-header!" he shouted as his big rod bent in a throbbing arc.

Those two dolphin fought well and we finally boated both after about a ten-minute fight. The mate swung both aboard with a gaff and dropped them into the big fish box against the transom, where they continued to beat against the sides. I looked up at Raphael. He raised his shoulders and shrugged.

"Go back," I yelled up at him. "*Dos mas*—two more."

He grinned and spun the wheel to bring the boat about. Raphael is a fisherman first and a captain second. We were into two fish the moment we passed the floating hatch, and I could see the colorful green-and-gold fish shoot out from the shelter of the hatch and fight for the lures.

We caught these two—about the same size as the first two, ten to twelve pounds each—and went back for more. On the third pass I hooked into a monster that took the popper bug with a terrific smash, then headed for the horizon. While Joe brought his fish in and cast out and hooked another, I fought the big one. When I finally got it close to the transom, Raphael looked down from the bridge.

"*Grande!*" he shouted. "*Tal vez, cincuenta—sesenta!*"

I knew it was very big and I also thought it might go around fifty to sixty pounds. I had caught one off Florida years ago, when two of my sons and I were fishing off Fort Lauderdale in a 17-foot Boston Whaler. Both John and Donald were afraid to gaff it, and I had to hand the big spinning rod to John and gaff it myself. It was caught on twenty-pound mono and tore up that small boat. That fish had weighed forty-seven pounds. This one looked a lot bigger. But Allejandro, trying to get the gaff hook into the belly, cut the 16-pound-test tippet instead and the fish was gone. The mate was distraught and Raphael looked disgustedly at him, but I waved it off. The sea around us was full of big dolphin.

We took twelve good-size dolphin before both Joe and I quit because our arms were weary from fighting those bruisers on fly rods. By that time both Raphael and the mate were grinning from ear to ear. They could sell the dolphin at the docks for a good price that night. The catch, for them, more than made up for the slow day on sailfish.

My second popper bug was a battered mess, and Joe's streamer fly was a tattered remnant of its former self. We both sank into chairs and opened cold beers. It had been a ball! We went back to fishing for sailfish, but were so elated with the dolphin battle that we couldn't have cared less whether we got sailfish up or not. It was probably not the proper attitude for a couple of supposedly serious tournament anglers, but then, dolphin always do that to me.

I have taken to calling them dorado in the last few years—as do the Spanish-speaking captains and mates. The word means "gold" and it could not be more appropriate, for it is truly a golden fish, in more ways than one. I also call them dorado because I grew tired of explaining to nonanglers that I was *not* catching a relative of Flipper, the bottle-nosed dolphin mammal of TV fame.

The dolphin fish is a beautiful green, black, and gold fish that is found everywhere there are warm ocean currents. During the many

A good eating-size dorado the author caught off Cabo San Lucas on a fly-rod popper.

years I fished with big-game tackle, I caught them all over the world — in the Pacific, Atlantic, Gulf of Mexico, the Indian Ocean, and Caribbean. And even on thirty- and fifty-pound line, they put up a spectacular battle, although most big-game fishermen consider them a nuisance when seriously fishing for billfish. They should try them on saltwater fly tackle.

The average dolphin caught over most of its range weighs between eight and fifteen pounds. The largest ever caught on rod and reel was an eighty-seven-pound whopper caught at Papagallo Gulf, Costa Rica, in 1976, but they have been caught up to one hundred pounds in commercial nets and on long lines.

The first dolphin I caught on a fly was with IGFA trustee Steve Sloan as we were returning from taking part in the first Hemingway Billfish Tournament in Havana, in the late 1970s. Sloan, Ed Zern, and I fished as a team in that tournament, but did poorly. On the way back to Key West in Sloan's beautiful 31-foot Rybovich, the mate spotted a school of dolphin attacking baitfish.

We broke out a spinning rod equipped with a feather jig, and Sloan was soon fast to a dolphin that leaped beautifully. While fighting it, he remembered that he kept a fly rod rigged up and told me to go and get it from the cabin. It was rigged with a white streamer fly, and when I cast to where Steve had his dolphin hooked, I got an immediate strike. That dolphin put up such a battle on the 9-foot, 8-weight rod that I vowed to fish for dolphin only with a fly rod from then on.

It is very difficult to cast to a school of dolphin with a fly, as the school is usually moving very fast. Unless one is lucky enough to find the fish under a floating object or along a weed bed, there is little chance of getting a fly to the fish. Fortunately, there is a way of solving this problem. Dolphin will readily strike a lure trolled on conventional and spinning gear. Once the hooked fish is brought near the boat, one needs only to keep the fish close to the hull. The school will continue to stay with the hooked fish almost indefinitely. A veteran charter-boat skipper out of Islamorada told me that the reason the school stays close is that the frantic fish begins to regurgitate food as soon as it is hooked, and the other fish stick close to eat the bits of food. It makes sense.

When the school stays with the hooked fish, it is a simple task to throw flies over the circling fish, with the boat in idle. IGFA rules state—when fishing for record fish—that the boat must be in neutral, or at rest, when the fly is cast. But if an angler just wants to catch dolphin on a fly rod for fun, or food, a fly may be trolled or cast to fish while a boat is in motion.

As a matter of fact, I have had a wonderful time catching dorado off Baja, California, by trolling flies. After a day of trying to catch marlin or sailfish with a fly, I have purposely set out to catch dorado for the evening meal and have used a fly rod. The technique is simple enough. Simply troll a big #3/0 or #5/0 streamer of any bright color behind the boat. I have found that the farther back the fly is trolled, the better the chance of a strike.

Catching dorado this way is a real thrill as one can see the fish coming. Occasionally, a dorado will make a jump as much as one hundred yards off to the side before hitting the fly. And when they do hit, it is with a smashing strike. This marvelous game fish jumps like a billfish when hooked and is flat enough so that when it turns its side to the angler, the battle is nothing less than spectacular.

I started out using 7-weight rods and matching line for dolphin, but after breaking several good rods and losing a lot of flies, I got smarter. Now I use a 9-weight, 9-foot graphite rod with a reel capable of carrying two hundred yards of twenty-pound Dacron backing, plus the ninety-foot fly line. Weight-forward, floating lines are best for this type of fishing. Usually, I make my own leaders of hard Mason nylon, and for dolphin I use a three-foot, 40-pound-test butt section. I fasten that to the fly line with a nail knot and loop the other end with a double surgeon's knot.

One doesn't need long leaders for most deep-water ocean fish, as they seem to pay attention only to the lure. I take a five-foot length of whatever tippet strength I plan to use, usually 12- or 16-pound-test, and form a big loop in one end. I tie a spider hitch to hold that loop.

The IGFA stipulates that class tippet be at least fifteen inches long. There is no maximum limitation. I make double surgeon's knot loops at the ends of the large tippet section. One end goes loop-to-loop with the butt section and the other end gets tied to the shock leader with an Albright knot. The shock leader may be any pound-test, but most deep-water fly rodders use either 80- or 100-pound-test shock leader. It must be no longer than twelve inches by IGFA rules—a ruling with which I disagree. I have no objection to the twelve-inch rule except where billfishing is concerned. The mouth and bill of a sailfish or a marlin is sandpaper rough and easily frays even 100-pound-test shock leader. I think at least an eighteen-inch section or longer should be allowed in the case of billfish.

I know it will not be easy to convince the IGFA to change long-standing fly-fishing angling rules. Those anglers who set world records under the old rules would naturally object to new fly fishermen getting a break with tackle. But perhaps it might make sense to establish new rules under a whole new tippet class—say 20-pound-test tippet. That way everyone could start over again with a whole new ballgame.

The Albright knot, fastening the tippet section to the shock leader, looks like an impossible knot to tie, but it is really not that complicated once it is figured out. Named for the legendary Keys guide, Jimmie Albright, who invented it, it can be tied easily once it is practiced. The shock leader is fastened to the fly by either an Albright knot or a 3½-turn clinch knot. Those who prefer the loop to allow the fly to swing free use the former, and those who want the fly tied fast use the latter. I like the clinch knot because I believe it holds better on big fish.

The shock leader is needed for dolphin, as they have a formidable set of teeth and would cut right through a regular tippet. One of the strange things about dorado is how quickly they lose their brilliant coloring. One minute they are a glistening gold and green, and the next the colors have faded to dull black in death, which speaks volumes for releasing all of them unless they are sought for food. There is nothing more depressing to me than to see rows of black dolphin and billfish hung up on scales, drying in the sunlight. It is especially disturbing when these fish are kept only to photograph and then are dragged off to a dump. There is no excuse for depleting such a marvelous natural resource just for an ego trip. A photograph of the fish, taken just before releasing it back to the sea, should serve far better as a souvenir.

Dolphin can be caught just about anywhere in warm ocean currents. They are plentiful off the east coast of south Florida and around the Keys. The Caribbean is filled with them and they are abundant off the west coasts of South and Central America and off Mexico and Baja. The Gulf of Mexico is prime habitat for the dorado.

One of my favorite spots for them is off Cabo San Lucas, Baja, where they take flies for much of the year. A displaced Frenchman with a Dutch name, Didier Van der Veecken, fishes out of that tiny town. Didier, who grew up fly fishing in salt water off the east coast of Africa, moved to Baja because he heard the fishing was spectacular. He found the rumor to be true and began chartering his own boats to

Fighting a big dorado under the boat off Cabo San Lucas, Baja.

light-tackle fishermen—especially fly fishermen—in search of roosterfish, dorado, sailfish, and marlin.

A representative of IGFA in Cabo San Lucas, Didier is a dedicated
saltwater fly fisherman, speaks English rapidly with a strong French
accent, and looks like a sun-tanned Dudley Moore.

Some of the best areas for dorado in the spring, summer, and fall
are off Cabo San Lucas in the extreme south of Baja, around the
Gordo Banks off San Jose del Cabo and up off Punta Gorda at what is
called the East Cape. North of that, dorado are plentiful all the way up
the east coast of Baja, past Punta Arena and La Paz to Isla San Jose. In
the summer months they are plentiful off Loreto and Mulege and far
up into the Sea of Cortez.

There are public launching ramps all down the east coast of Baja,
but one should consult with local fishermen to make sure they are in
service. Permits or licenses to fish from commercially chartered fishing
boats are covered in the cost of the charter, but anyone who travels
down to Baja to fish from the shore or from a private boat must
purchase a Mexican fishing license. They can be bought ahead of time
through the Mexico West Travel Club, 2424 Newport Boulevard, Suite
T91, Costa Mesa, California 92627 or from a local fisheries office in the
various towns in Baja. But office hours are uncertain in most towns
and the cost of the license varies with the fluctuations of the Mexican
peso.

Towing one's boat down the long, nine-hundred-mile highway
from California to Cabo San Lucas requires determination and a very
good trailer. There are gas stations every one hundred miles on the
asphalt highway, so fuel is no problem. But launching ramps can be
tricky—or nonexistent. In many areas one has to launch a boat on
hard-packed sand—easy to do with a light 10- to 14-foot boat, but
tough with anything heavier.

There are only nine maintained, concrete boat-launching ramps in
Baja: Ensenada, Bahia de Los Angeles (two), Mulege (two), Puerto
Escondido, La Paz, Cabo San Lucas, and San Carlos on Magdelena
Bay. The several I know are quite good are at Bahia de Los Angeles, La
Paz, and Cabo San Lucas.

In pulling a boat down, it is very smart to get insurance. The
people are honest enough, but all sorts of accidents can befall a boat
and trailer, and one doesn't want to leave an expensive rig in some
small Mexican town to be repaired. The Mexicans offer insurance, but

I would advise one to contact their local insurance agent before leaving home to get trip insurance. Organizations like the American Automobile Association offer excellent short-term insurance on boats and trailers.

12

The Ambush Fish —
Snook

In 1972 a Chicago restaurant owner named Henry Norton called me at
Field & Stream in New York. Henry knew I was a tarpon fisherman and
asked if I had ever fished for them in the big rivers of eastern Costa
Rica. I had not and said I planned to someday. Henry said he had just
bought a tarpon camp called Isla de Pesca on the Rio Colorado and he
would be delighted if I would come down and sample the fishing.

I told him I was a fly fisherman and he said that was just fine — it
was easy to catch them on a fly rod. It turned out that not many
people were catching tarpon on a fly in those days, but that never
stopped Henry. Henry and his lawyer — whose name I have forgot-
ten — met me when my plane landed at San José late in the afternoon.
Henry instantly insisted that we have drinks at the airport bar to
celebrate my arrival. Then we had to have drinks at the San José hotel
bar while I checked in. Henry and his attorney chum picked up a
mariachi band somewhere along the line and they accompanied us to
a restaurant to serenade us while we ate. It was a long and loud
evening, and I was happy when everyone ran out of steam around
midnight.

*A*uthor holds a typical
Bahama bonefish
from Andros Island.

Whether it is wading the vastness of the bonefish flats or casting a fly from the foredeck of a flats boat, the quiet, the solitude, and the variety of marine life set the tone of this great sport. Gulls, frigate birds, terns, and myriad wading birds accompany the angler in his quest for the silvery, sleek, and lightning-quick bonefish.

A collection of typical bonefish flies.

*F*ound in the shallow water of the Texas coastal flats, the redfish will readily take small poppers. Their position in schools is usually given away by their tails protruding from the surface or by gulls hovering over them.

(Far right) Typical small redfish poppers.
(Right) An excellent fly for barracuda.

*U*nlike bonefish, which consistently takes flies on the flats, the wary permit may sometimes follow a fly up to a boat or the feet of a wading angler, but seldom actually takes a fly. Some excellent saltwater fly fishermen have cast to permit for years without hooking one of these streamlined, sickle-tailed speedsters.

Two excellent permit crab flies: a white wool-bodied permit fly (left) and a small crab fly.

When hooked, the permit puts up a mighty fight on fly tackle, making long, fast runs and turning its flat side toward the angler when pressure is applied. Those fishermen who have succeeded in taking the aristocratic permit on a fly constitute a select fraternity.

A permit Puff Fly (lower left), McCrab Fly (upper left), Mother of Epoxy (MOE) permit fly (center), and a crab fly.

The explosive silver king can be taken with flies in differing environments—the shallow and clear flats of the Florida Keys, Belize, Honduras, and similar Carribean waters and also in the muddy rivers and river mouths of such Central American countries as Costa Rica. The tarpon will regularly take a fly and provides fly-rod anglers with some of the most exciting action in all of salt-water fly rodding.

W hile fishermen can sight-cast to tarpon on the clear flats, in the murky waters of Central American rivers it is necessary to blind cast. When hooked there, the tarpon puts up the same aerial battle on the long rod.

A collection of typical tarpon flies.

*B*ack in the 1960s Dick Fisher designed the Menemsha Whaler—a trim, 17-foot, center-console and cuddy-cabin craft that predicted the future of boats for blue-water big-game fly fishermen. Today there are hundreds of similar boats roaming the reefs and dropoffs. With them fly fishermen are taking the battling roosterfish off such productive coasts as Baja California and Costa Rica.

(Far left) An excellent white double-hooked popper. (Left) Three typical blue-water flies that take roosterfish, stripers, bluefish, tarpon, dorado, and various tuna species.

 *(Far left) Successful mullet flies. (Left) Squid flies for bigeye tuna and yellowtail.*

*D*ecades ago fly rodders the caliber of Lee Cuddy, Stu Apte, Lee Wulff, Billy Pate, and the late legendary Dr. Webster Robinson began to catch sailfish off the Florida Keys, Mexico, and Ecuador. But it was not until the development of modern graphite fly rods, corrosion-resistant lines, and anodized, large-capacity fly reels that the spectacular sailfish was captured in any numbers.

Probably the first successful general-purpose billfish fly, developed by Billy Pate: a double-hooked, white saddle-hackle fly with a small Styrofoam attractor that slides down the 100-pound shock leader ahead of the lead hook.

*T*oday a legion of billfish fly rodders seeks the acrobatic sailfish on the long rods — with considerable success.

A single-hooked billfish fly in two sizes (top and bottom) and pink and red single-hooked billfish flies.

W hile sailfish have traditionally been taken in good numbers off Palm Beach and the Florida Keys, the fishing pressure has resulted in fewer and smaller fish over the years. Fly rodders have turned to newer areas, such as the Virgin Islands, Venezuela, Brazil, and the Gulf Coast states.

A selection of excellent sailfish poppers.

*I*n the late decade sailfish have been found in large numbers off the west coast of Mexico—notably in the Mazatlan area—and off the west coast of Costa Rica. Northern Costa Rica is productive from May to December; the central coastal area near Quepos down to Golfito in the south is excellent from December to June.

*A*lthough the first striped marlin was taken on a fly at Cabo San Lucas by the late "Doc" Robinson—on a cork-bodied popper in 1965—only recently have marlin consistently been taken on flies. The weight record goes to Lee Wulff's 148-pound striped marlin taken at Salinas, Ecuador in 1967.

(Far left) Two excellent "Muddler head" double-hooked billfish flies. (Left) Billfish poppers.

*B*illy Pate was the first to take all four marlin species on a fly: an 80-pound white marlin from Venezuela in 1975; a 146-pound striped marlin off Ecuador in 1970; a 96-pound Atlantic blue marlin off Cuba in 1978; and several Pacific black marlin, including the world record 46-pound, 4-ounce black marlin on 8-pound tippet off Cairns, Australia in 1972.

A colorful double-hooked streamer fly for billfish.

*T*here are no areas in the world where one may be certain of catching a marlin on a fly, but the chances are certainly better in some places than others. For instance, Venezuela is noted for its numbers of fly-rod-size white marlin in October and November, Brazil in December. Small black marlin may be caught regularly off Queensland, Australia from August to December each year.

An excellent all-around sailfish and marlin double-hooked fly.

I got my revenge in the early morning, however, as the desk clerk woke us up about 4:00 A.M. to catch a very early twin-engined plane for the twenty-five-minute hop over the mountains to the Rio Colorado. Neither Henry nor his lawyer pal enjoyed the flight very much.

Isla de Pesca was a nice tarpon camp built right on the bank of the Rio Colorado. The main lodge and the surrounding cabins were built up on stilts and were very comfortable. The aluminum johnboats belonging to the lodge were all painted yellow, making them easy to distinguish from the turquoise-colored boats of Casa Mar, about a mile upstream. Pete McGhee was the manager of the camp and ran the operation like the former Navy gunnery mate he was.

All of the guests at the camp were either spin fishermen or used big level-winding reels and stout boat rods. The favorite lure for tarpon was a strange-looking, heavy, cast-iron monstrosity called a Sea Hawk—I think. One threw it out and let it sink to the bottom, where it was jigged until a tarpon struck it. Nobody carried a fly rod nor knew how to use one for either tarpon or snook.

Fortunately, the owner of Casa Mar was Bill Barnes, an excellent fly fisherman, and I went up to see him that first night in one of the camp boats. He was kind enough to show me the right flies to use for both tarpon and snook and gave me some of each. There was one other fly fisher at his camp, a Japanese woman who was very good and who had caught several tarpon on a fly rod.

The next two days saw me catch four or five nice tarpon on Bill's Casa Mar Special flies. They were not big fish, most were in the forty-five- to sixty-pound category. It was not very exciting fishing—at least compared to tarpon fishing in the Florida Keys. One simply cast the fly across and downstream and stripped it in the muddy water until a tarpon struck. After the strike, however, the fish put up a fine battle in the strong current, jumping and twisting in the air.

On the third day the guide suggested we try for snook. I had taken a number of small snook on a fly from the Florida backcountry around Fort Myers and down near Flamingo. There I used both yellow-and-white streamer flies and small bass poppers. Here, the guide said, I should use a big Whistler-type fly that Barnes had given me. He had given me two—a white-and-red and a yellow-and-red—both tied on #3/0 hooks. They were big flies with bead-chain eyes that made them sink quite rapidly.

The guide ran us a long way to a big canal that emptied into the ocean on the east end. The banks were lined with trees, their exposed roots jutting into the water.

"Get the fly back into the roots," said the guide, shutting down the 25-horsepower motor and grabbing a wooden paddle.

I cast the big fly into roots for several miles while the April sun broiled me and the humidity caused me to wipe the sweat from my eyes after each cast. Bill had advised me to use an 80-pound-test shock leader ahead of the fly, as the gill plates of the snook would easily cut through the 16-pound-test tippet. He should know. He had been fishing for big snook there all year and had taken a number of large ones from both the river and outside in the ocean. It was his first year as manager of Casa Mar, and he had moved there from Florida, where he had been fly fishing the flats of the Keys for years. Eight years later he was to catch a huge, twenty-six-pound snook off the sandbars at the mouth of the Rio Colorado on a 16-pound-test tippet while he was fly casting for tarpon. It turned out to be a world record and, as of a decade later, still is.

Snook in the mangrove islands of the Florida Keys are the ultimate predators, lying in wait far back in the roots and slashing out at baitfish that approach too closely. They are taken from the canals along the east coast by anglers fishing live bait off the bridges, and casting plugs and flies up against the walls of canal locks and in the mouths of rivers. They are a great game fish—both wary and strong.

In the Flamingo area I had caught several good snook while fly fishing for both tarpon and redfish on the flats. They hid in the mangrove roots of small islands that we passed. While the guide poled quietly close to the trees, I dropped small poppers close to the roots. One had to let the bug lie still to about the count of ten, then twitch it several times. The snook usually struck it on the second or third twitch. They immediately turned and dug for the safety of the roots, and it took a good fly rod to get them turned before they tangled the line in the maze of mangroves. They also leaped like tarpon when first hooked and put up a spectacular fight.

They grow big in Florida, but Costa Rica is the home of really big snook. The world all-tackle record was set there in 1978 when Gilbert Ponzi caught one that weighed fifty-three pounds ten ounces.

"Snook," said the guide as I was retrieving the big fly from beneath a cutbank.

A nice twelve-pound snook that took a whistler-type fly.

I looked at him. "You sure?" I asked.

"I saw the flash deep under the fly when it first moved," he said. "Try him again, but let it sink a little first."

I was fishing with a doctor from Denver who was jigging one of those iron lures on the bottom as we moved down the shore. He had wanted to come along and I figured he wouldn't be in the way of my casting. So far he had not gotten any strikes.

I was using a 10-weight rod and throwing a 10-weight, floating, weight-forward line with an intermediate sink-tip. While I used a sinking line for tarpon, I didn't want to go through the agony of trying to get that sinking line out of the water each time for a backcast. I cast the big white-and-red fly back to the same spot, letting it sink for a few seconds on the edge of the clay-coated roots.

When I could no longer see it, I started the strip. On the second strip there was a bright flash of gold deep down and a sudden jolt as a fish took the fly. I struck quickly with the big graphite rod and the fish veered away as it darted for the sanctuary of the roots. It made a quick run downstream and I stopped it short of a fallen tree below us. When it felt the pressure of the big rod and the 16-pound-test tippet, it took to the air in a series of spectacular leaps.

"Wow!" shouted the doctor.

"Good fish," grunted the guide, back-paddling us away from the bank and its obstacles.

The snook used the strong current to help it and ran a good way down the muddy river before it decided to fight it out in the depths. The river couldn't have been more than twenty feet deep at that spot so it was no trouble to hold it in the river current.

When we finally got it in and the guide gaffed it, we estimated its weight at about twelve pounds—my biggest snook on a fly.

I took two smaller snook later in the day on small poppers before the heat and humidity drove us off the canal and out to the surf where there was a light breeze. The snook were not in the surf that day, though I cast from both the anchored boat and the sandy beach for hours. It seemed hard to believe snook would lie in that fast water and rip, but the guide assured me they not only stay in that chopped-up water, but feed voraciously when hungry. They spend part of the year in the rip and off the sandbars of the big, muddy rivers, and the rest of the year in the fresh water of the rivers.

While it is fun to catch big snook in the surf and at the river mouths, the most fun is catching small ones far up the tributary rivers of eastern Costa Rica. I first noticed them a few years ago while fishing for guapote with a fly rod. Guapote is a sort of bream—a chunky and strong fighter—that inhabits the streams and lagoons of the tributary rivers. They, and another fish called the machaca, are fun to catch on small flies in these quiet jungle ponds.

The guapote lie under sunken trees and, like sunfish, will come out for small poppers—smashing them on the surface and diving for the shelter of the underwater logs. The machaca like fruit that falls from trees and they lie under them. A popper that is left to float quietly will take them regularly. They are fairly small and streamlined, but fight like small tigers on a light rod.

While fishing for these two fish far up some of the tributary streams a few years ago, I occasionally got a vicious strike from a fish and generally missed it. When I asked what it was, the guide shrugged and said it was robalo—snook.

"How big?" I asked.

The guide shrugged and held up two hands about a foot apart. "Not big," he said, "but hit hard. You strike too quick. Wait a little before you strike."

I did what he said and began to hook the small snook, some up to

*Veteran saltwater fly rodder Bill Barnes,
owner of Casa Mar, with his world-record
Pacific snook of twenty-six pounds, taken on
a fly at the mouth of the Rio Colorado in
eastern Costa Rica. The big fish was taken
on 16-pound-test tippet and was caught
October 19, 1980.*

five pounds, but most in the three- to four-pound class. They put up a great fight on a light, 6-weight fly rod.

I went back to Casa Mar in the fall of 1989 with my son Jim, who lives in Delray Beach, Florida, and is a good fly fisherman. We got caught in the first few days of the rainy season and it rained sheets of water most of the day. But we fished these jungle lagoons with Lefty, one of the veteran guides of Casa Mar. Lefty showed us some great sunken trees and a spot where clear river water pours into a murky lagoon. The snook was there.

The snook inhabited a sunken tree by the dozens and slashed upwards at a fly-rod popper from the murky depths like small torpe-does. A yellow streamer or a yellow wooden popper worked best, and the snook hit most readily very early in the morning or late in the afternoon.

It was marvelous fishing. We were draped in raincoats and wearing wide hats to keep the rain from our eyes. The jungle was silent all about us and the occasional echoing roar of a howler monkey or the call of a bird sounded far louder than they were. Now and then we would spot an iguana lizard on the bole of a tree or a bright green lizard resting on lily pads. The little snook were all good eating size, and we kept most for dinner that night.

The only other spots I found to compare with Costa Rica for snook was one spot on the east coast of Baja and another on the west coast of Mexico. Ray Cannon said he saw snook in excess of seventy pounds near the village of Mulege on the Baja coast of California. He caught one on a level-winding reel and twelve-pound line that weighed forty-eight pounds and was three feet five inches long while fishing with Frank Dufresne. But he said he saw one harpooned that was five feet seven inches long and must have weighed at least seventy pounds!

Those were the black snook, and I went down in the mid-1980s to try for them with a fly rod, but caught only a few small two- to three-pound snook from the Rio Mulege. I was told by natives that spearing and netting had depleted the river of big snook in the 1960s. Ray and Frank were fishing for theirs in 1955.

The other spot where I found snook was in a mangrove swamp a few miles south of San Carlos on the northern coast of Mexico, near Guaymas. They were not large, but there were quite a few of them in the shallow bays and one could catch them by casting small spinning lures and flies into the mangrove roots. The native fishermen, who spent most of their time netting mullet or fishing for yellowtail off-shore, didn't seem to know the snook were there, or care much. They also did not know they had bonefish in the area. The bonefish were very small and were found more in semideep water close to the shore, rather than on the flats.

13

The Awesome Jack Crevalle

I was casting a white streamer fly from the northern point of Cat Cay, trying to interest some cerro mackerel in taking the fly as they streamed through the cut between Cat Cay and Gun Cay. I had put on a short piano-wire leader because mackerel have a mean set of teeth.

The construction crews had decided that the north end of the island would make a good dump for all sorts of scrap—rusted cars, scrap lumber, old cement mixers, and corrugated roofing sheets. The discarded refuse had been rusting in the shallow water just off the rocky point for months and had attracted considerable numbers of fish. Barracuda patrolled the edges of the rusting piles, waiting for small fish to venture away from the shelter. Triggerfish lurked in the hollows of the dump and schools of small jacks swam close by.

I had cast for perhaps half an hour and was about to quit when there was a swirl behind my streamer. I struck too quickly and missed the fish. It had come out of deep water, so I cast far out and let the white fly sink slowly before retrieving it in short jerks.

The fly was just coming up from the blue depths when there was a flash of color and the rod tip slammed down. I reared back on the 10-weight fly rod and the big Pfleuger saltwater reel screamed as the line was ripped off. I had about four hundred yards of thirty-pound braided Dacron backing on the battered reel so I wasn't worried too much that I might lose whatever fish had taken the fly.

I should have been worried. That fish went straight across the deep cut between the two islands—never slowing down. It was about 150 yards across the cut. When the fish reached the far shore it turned left and headed west out into the Gulf Stream. At about 300 yards out it slowed, but by then it must have been nearly 100 feet deep. Doug Gifford, the young engineer who was supervising the construction of the island, was perched on a large coral slab behind me.

"That must be a big shark," he said.

I shook my head. "A shark doesn't move that way," I said. "A shark doesn't streak off at that speed. And when it goes down it tends to circle. This fish just keeps boring away like a tuna, but it's too shallow here for a tuna."

That fish put up the most stubborn fight I had ever had on a fly rod up until that time, and it was nearly an hour before I got it close to the shore. Both the fish and I were exhausted by the time it was circling slowly in the clear depths below us.

"What is it?" Gifford asked, staring down.

"A big jack," I said. "It's got yellow on the sides and the pectoral fins are real long—a jack crevalle, I think."

"It must weigh thirty to forty pounds," Gifford said. "How are we going to get it in?"

"I don't know," I answered, leaning back on the 9-foot fiberglass fly rod. "I'll try to get it up close and you grab it by that narrow place just ahead of the forked tail."

Doug had been a college football player and probably weighed 220 pounds at that time. He inched down the face of the rocks and carefully reached down into the shallow water. He grasped the tired fish by the tail. There was an explosion of water and Gifford was yanked face down in the shallows. The jack sped off into the depths, leaving my parted leader as a reminder never to grab a big jack by the tail when off balance.

That was my first introduction to the strength of the jack crevalle—at least a big one—until years later in Costa Rica.

"There goes Bill Barnes's world record!" said my son Jim as the big graphite fly rod doubled over and the tarpon reel whined its big-fish song.

My fly-rod popper had just disappeared in a huge boil of water in the waves, and the fish was tearing off fly line and backing as though the big fly reel had no drag. We had been fly casting all day for snook in the murky surf of the Caribbean, just off the mouth of the Rio Colorado, and this was the first strike. It was mid-October and the snook were supposed to be in. The fishing for them had been excellent the week before—a condition all anglers know well.

"It hasn't jumped," I said, gripping the bucking 9-foot graphite fly rod. "Funny for a snook."

"Not necessarily," said Lefty, our Casa Mar guide, that premier tarpon camp on Costa Rica's jungle-shrouded east coast. "Like Bill Barnes's record," Lefty observed, "that big fish just took the fly right here on the sandbars at the mouth of the river. Fought the whole time underwater. Bill thought he had a big tarpon for a while."

Barnes, who was fishing down the shore from us while his German shorthair pointer, Spook, chased shorebirds, caught the big snook in 1980.

The big tarpon reel, holding the ninety feet of 9-weight, floating, weight-forward fly line and four hundred yards of thirty-pound backing, sang as the big fish headed out to sea. More than two hundred yards of backing had already left the reel, and there was no sign the fish intended to slow down.

"Big jack crevalle," said the guide from the middle boat seat.

"You think so, Lefty?" I said dubiously.

"Sure," he said. "No snook fight that hard. Gotta be a big jack crevalle."

Thirty minutes later, with my right arm nearly dead, Lefty lip-gaffed the big, green-and-yellow fish as it wallowed in the foamy water close to the gunwale. It weighed twenty-eight pounds on the brass pocket scales, not enough to break the current world record of thirty-three pounds twelve ounces on 12-pound-test tippet set in 1972 at Sebastion Inlet, Florida.

"Close," said Lefty.

"But no cigar," I added as we released the big fish to the surf. It didn't matter. It was a hell of a fish and it may well give another saltwater fly rodder the same terrific battle it gave me.

Lefty was right. No snook fights like a jack crevalle, as great a game fish as it is. Nor does any other fish, except perhaps roosterfish, for that matter. It is an awesome fighter—especially on fly gear.

I have been catching jack crevalle for years off the Florida Keys, the Bahamas, the Caribbean, Central America, and Baja, and no other fish I know tries to pull my arms out of their sockets the way this fish does. Even the relatively small ones can put up a tremendous fight. I threw a white streamer fly into the cone of light off a rock jetty in Guanaja, Honduras, one night while fishing with John Uhr, and a fish almost yanked me off the rocks when it struck. After a twenty-minute battle, I finally brought in a fifteen-pound jack crevalle that had taken more than two hundred yards of my twenty-pound backing out onto the flats in the darkness.

Most light-tackle fishermen I know, particularly the fly rodders, hope the strike they get is *not* a jack crevalle. They are just too much work for the size of them!

I have never caught any really big ones on conventional tackle, but I can imagine what a brutal fight they must put up when they get large. The world record for conventional saltwater fishing tackle was set in Angola, Africa, March 30, 1988, by one Jose Borge—a whopping fifty-two pounds seven ounces! But it was closely followed by another giant fifty-one-pound-eight-ounce fish taken June 3, 1982, at Grande Isle, Louisiana, by Glenn Templet. The record was taken on thirty-pound line and the runner-up on fifty-pound line, and I'll bet both anglers wished they were using eighty-pound line by the time those battles ended. While forty- to fifty-pound jack crevalle are often taken by angling in the Florida area, some up to seventy pounds have been taken in commercial nets.

What makes the jack crevalle such a vicious fighter? Well, it is a member of the family Carangidae, which includes some other spectacular battlers: amberjack and pompano. And it is cousin to the horse-eye jack, another slugger of note. It is equipped with a huge sickle tail, much like its cousin the Atlantic and Pacific permit, and anyone who has been fortunate enough to catch one of these great game fish on light tackle knows what a war they wage.

The fish has a lot of local names on the Pacific Coast—cavally and cavalla from Peru on up through Central America—and I suspect the reason it is called horse crevalle is because the local people know it pulls like a horse. It is common off the east coast of Baja California, from La Paz down to Cabo San Lucas, and there it is called *toro*— the bull!

The jack crevalle is usually a schooling fish, but the larger ones

The author and his big twenty-eight-pound jack crevalle that hit a white popper in the Costa Rica surf.

seem to be solitary. I have seen schools of them off Baja in the spring, within a few yards of the surf line, where the schools number in the hundreds of fish. The guides say they are spawning then and show no interest in any artificial lures—particularly flies. One can drop a popper or a streamer right in the schools streaming by rapidly, and the fish will pay no attention to it. Guides say they will occasionally take a sardine or small mullet bait while the fish are moving this way.

But the individual fish will certainly smash artificial lures, whether on the flats or over reefs. It is difficult to get them to hit streamer flies unless one moves the fly fast. When a jack crevalle strikes at a fly, the secret is to move it in a series of very fast strips. The jack won't hit a fly or lure that has slowed down. For that reason I prefer big poppers for these fish. The popper seems to excite them with its splashing action and by the sound it creates.

I also think the bigger poppers attract bigger fish. I have become somewhat of a popper freak the past few years after taking big jacks, sailfish, marlin, and roosterfish on them consistently, when other flies fail.

Jack crevalle are eaten over much of their range, but I have observed that the meat of the larger individuals is dark and strong and most native people would prefer something else. Most guides don't argue when I suggest releasing them.

For the light-tackle devotee out for sport, the jack crevalle is just the ticket. Beginning fly fishermen would do well to use nothing smaller than a 9-weight rod and matching floating line. The reel should be capable of holding at least two hundred yards of twenty-pound backing, but one holding four hundred yards would be a lot more practical.

This great game fish is found all over the world in tropical and subtropical waters. It can show up anywhere—just off river mouths and jetties, in the surf, inhabiting reefs, and over sunken wrecks. Since its primary food is small baitfish, almost any sort of fast-moving floating or sinking fly will cause it to strike. Watching for the frantic baitfish schools is one good way of locating them. They will herd bait into tight schools and then slash through them like marauding wolves. A fly cast into such a school is almost sure to be struck by a rampaging jack crevalle.

14

The Silver Wolf— Barracuda

The first barracuda I caught on a fly was a complete accident—not that it wasn't a great battle.

I was bonefishing at Treasure Cay in the Bahamas and I had quit for lunch. A couple of friends and I were lolling about in a flats boat, having finished off some excellent sandwiches and cold St. Pauli Girl beer. Just before lunch I had spotted a big horse-eyed jack in a pocket of a narrow creek that emptied out on the flats. Though I had tried interesting it in a popping bug, the big jack moved back into the mangrove roots and sulked there. I had given up and decided lunch was more interesting than the stubborn fish.

But with lunch over and a feeling of well-being setting in, I let the popping bug gently ride the current of the small creek. It gradually floated out on the wide flat and I continued to feed the fly line out, giving it a chance to finally drift at least one hundred yards away. More from habit than anything else, I gave the bug a couple of slight jerks that made it duck and gurgle on the calm surface.

The surface of the flat erupted in a boil of water and I was jerked upright on the boat seat as a huge barracuda—popping bug stuck in the side of its mouth—went greyhounding across the shallow flat. Fortunately, I had on a big saltwater reel with at least two hundred yards of twenty-pound braided Dacron backing so I was in little danger of being stripped. The only reason that big barracuda did not cut the 12-pound-test leader was that the big, cork-bodied bug held the fish's teeth apart.

As it was, that fish put up an epic battle, and it was some time before I could get it near the boat where a guide finally netted it. The length was just over five feet and the girth was as thick as my thigh. We had no scales with which to measure the big barracuda so we released it, but not before taking a photograph. I was amazed that it took the popping bug at the time, but since then I have taken a number of them on a fly rod with surface poppers.

Saltwater anglers who have never hooked a barracuda on fly tackle in shallow water have missed one of the most spectacular saltwater game fish around.

The great barracuda—found from Florida to South America and the Caribbean—outruns bonefish, leaps like a billfish, and tears up tackle like no other flats fish except a tarpon.

Most anglers consider the barracuda a nuisance and don't fish for it in shallow water. It is frequently caught by fishermen angling for bigger fish in deep water and does not put up much of a fight on heavy tackle. For that reason it is dismissed as a game fish. Nothing could be farther from the truth.

Barracuda taken on flies, light-spinning, or level-winding tackle in shallow water will give anglers the fight of their lives!

And the barracuda is no lightweight. On the flats of the Bahamas, Caribbean, and the Florida Keys, it can and does often reach weights in excess of fifty and sixty pounds and grows from five to six feet in length. The all-tackle record is eighty-three pounds, caught in Lagos, Nigeria, in 1952 on fifty-pound line. But a number of anglers in the Keys and Bahamas have taken big thirty- to forty-pound barracuda on light gear such as two-, four-, six-, and eight-pound mono. Jim Anson—just to show it could be done—took a twenty-nine-pound-twelve-ounce barracuda at Key West in 1985 on 2-pound-test mono!

While not a whole lot of saltwater fly rodders stalk barracuda with the long rods, enough do now to make it a growing sport. The fly-rod record was set at Key West in 1978 by Joe Machiorlatti, who took a thirty-seven-pound-twelve-ounce monster on a 12-pound-test tippet.

Fly fishing for barracuda is like fishing for permit and bonefish. It is a combination of hunting and fishing. One needs sharp eyes and polarized sunglasses to see these wary fish. They tend to lie just off

The great barracuda—a terrific fighter on fly tackle.

banks on incoming tides, against the roots of mangrove islands, and far out on the sunlit flats where they are nearly invisible when motionless. They are seldom spotted while resting, but the moment they move they can be distinguished by the black spots found near the tail, and the black tail itself.

Just off the mouths of tiny creeks that run into the flats are excellent places to fly cast for these big pikelike predators. I was fishing on the west side of Andros Island with Rupert Leadon. It was a windy day, and we had run out through the Middle Bight to get into the lee of the big island. We had taken a number of nice bonefish using a Crazy Charlie Fly on a #14 hook and were watching a school of bonefish feeding just inside the mouth of Mangrove Creek.

The fish were herded up there and seemed reluctant to come out. Rupert nodded toward a dark shadow just off the mouth. "Good reason," he said. "Big 'cuda waiting for them."

I was using an 8-foot graphite rod and throwing an 8-weight, floating, weight-forward line. I had on a long, nine-foot leader that tapered down to 8-pound-test. It was about a sixty-foot cast and I dropped the little fly about three feet from the barracuda. At the second strip the big fish turned slowly to face the fly and on the next strip was after it. I never expected to hook the big fish and figured if I did, it would pop me right off.

When I struck, the little hook sunk in, and that barracuda headed directly west toward the Florida Keys, rapidly emptying my reel of line and backing. For some strange reason, the hook was in the outer edge of the fish's mouth and it was not able to cut the leader with its sharp teeth. I led the fish in a circle for what seemed like an hour until it finally tired and we got it to the boat. It was nearly five feet long and a toothy old fish. We let it go after retrieving the fly. A Crazy Charlie is a valuable fly in the Bahamas!

That was the day Rupert took me to Pot Cay, just north of the Middle Bight, and showed me the ruins of what may have been the very first bonefish resort in the Bahamas owned by foreigners. The houses were made from coral rocks and were impressive structures: a main lodge, a freshwater swimming pool close to the main lodge, and another saltwater pool down close to the water's edge. There were houses for the servants' quarters and another big house that had a laundry and repair shops. I took photographs of the ruins while standing in the hot sunlight and thinking what a grand place it once must have been.

The jungle vines and shrubbery had taken over what had been lawns and a garden area. The roofs of the rock buildings had long ago fallen in, and the big swimming pool had several feet of amber-colored rain water in the bottom, dyed from rotting palm fronds.

"Used to be called the Bang Bang Club back in the days just before World War Two," Rupert said as we walked beside the pool. "The old people around here say it was owned by an American colonel—don't remember his name. He used to fly all kinds of sports and their women over from the States. The bonefishing was great in those days, they say. And there is a freshwater pond over there on Pine Cay where they did a lot of duck hunting and pigeon shooting. It must have been something," he said, shaking his head slowly.

I looked at the high stone walls. Remnants of wooden frames were still sagging in window openings. Half a century had gone by since those days. I closed my eyes and tried to see the place as it must have been. I wondered what it must be like to come over here on a moonlit night and sit quietly on the old stone steps of the club and try to see if the ghosts would come back—ghosts of men who loved to fish the bonefish flats as much as I do.

The barracuda eats almost anything that moves on the flats. It is particularly fond of mullet, but I have seen it take puffers, needlefish, and lots of bonefish. Barracuda occasionally school in small packs on the flats and surround and harass bonefish schools. I have seen hundreds of frantic bonefish cornered in a cove with no way out except through several waiting barracuda at the cove's mouth. These lean killers often streak in and neatly slice a bonefish or permit in half while the fish is struggling against the rod and reel.

One of the most interesting sights to be seen on the flats is that of barracuda actively feeding on a bonefish school. The bonefish take to the air in schools when the barracuda slice through their midst. The sound is like someone ripping a large piece of canvas.

But while the barracuda is nonselective about its live meals, it is very choosy when it comes to hitting artificial lures. Although I have had several hit trolled spoons in shallow water, they seldom hit them when cast. A spoon needs to be moved very rapidly in order to excite a barracuda, and it tends to hang up in weeds and turtle grass. A fly, particularly one with lots of tinsel and long hackle, will take these great predators, but it needs to be cast long distances and stripped rapidly. It is difficult to cast a heavy fly very far, especially with a short length of wire ahead of the fly. Wire leader, or a length of heavy mono, is a necessity ahead of all light-tackle lures and flies, as a barracuda has a mouthful of razor-sharp teeth.

It is great fun to take big barracuda on a streamer fly trolled fast behind a boat around the mangrove islands in the Bahamas, but this isn't cricket if one is trying for record catches recognized by the IGFA. Nevertheless, it is a challenge fighting one of these big 'cuda on a fly rod as the fish streaks across the shallow-water flats. It is necessary to have a fly reel capable of holding at least two hundred yards of backing, as these savage fighters take out a lot of line before slowing down!

But perhaps the best and sportiest way to hook these big pikelike carnivores is by casting a surface popping bug a dozen feet from where one of the big predators is lying, then chugging the popper rapidly to make a big commotion. The resulting strike and fight will be spectacular!

It is difficult to move a fly fast enough—especially on a fly rod—to evade the strike of a barracuda. Their speed is simply astounding. I have seen them overtake a greyhounding needlefish on a flat, and there are few fish that can move faster than those pencil-thin speedsters.

There again, one needs a reel capable of holding lots of line in order to control these strong fish. They can be taken with 8- to 12-pound-test tippets easily, as long as there is plenty of line on the reel and there are not too many obstacles like coral heads and mangrove roots around to cut the leader.

Of all the lures that have proven successful on barracuda, none have caught more of these great fighting fish on the flats than the Tube Lure, either in red or chartreuse green surgical tubing. It has been

This huge five-foot-long barracuda was caught on a flat near Treasure Cay in the Bahamas.

used on conventional and spinning gear for years. The barracuda apparently think it is one of their favorite foods, the needlefish.

Any fly, however small, that imitates these fish has a good chance of enticing the big predators. But barracuda will strike any fly that imitates baitfish and is moved properly. That fine northeast-coast fly fisherman, Lou Tabory, makes a fly he calls Tabory's Surf Board Foam Fly for stripers, but it works on barracuda as well. Another fly that causes barracuda to strike well is Bobby Popovics's Bob's Bunker Fly, another striper lure. I have had barracuda smash at Jimmy Nix's Mullet Fly too, as mullet are a large part of a barracuda's diet on the flats.

There is not much interest in eating barracuda on the part of Florida anglers, but the Bahamians eat them regularly. In the Caribbean they are considered a so-so meal, but the toxic poisons they ingest from eating small, toxic food fish that inhabit coral reefs and heads make them a risky meal. I knew a bartender on Cat Cay who ate them all the time. He said they caused his hair to fall out one time—indeed, he was as bald as a billiard ball—but he said he didn't care. They were too good to give up for such a minor luxury as hair.

I return all my barracuda to the flats to fight again. I am sure some of the bonefish and permit guides would prefer that I kill them, but I have to respect such a game fighter. Besides, I figure they are all a part of the great scheme of things.

15

Trevally and Queenfish of the Barrier Reef

Out beyond the Great Barrier Reef the seas were running twelve to fifteen feet high and enormous combers were smashing against the vertical wall of rock. In the bright morning sunlight the white plumes of waves thrown high into the air looked opal-colored as the sun filtered through them.

On the bridge of the sportfisherman *Reef Hunter*, Captain Geoff Ferguson looked dubiously at the seas outside the narrow passage. "I don't know," he said. "We'll go if you like, but it's going to be bloody awful out there today."

Beside him, I shrugged. Yesterday I had done what I came to Australia to do—catch a one-thousand-pound black marlin. I had battled three hours and forty-five minutes on 80-pound line, and we had tagged and released the huge fish to fight another day. I had nothing more to prove. That huge fish capped a thirty-year, big-game-fishing career that included all the big billfish of the world—all caught on heavy tackle. Today was to have been only another day of fighting billfish just for the sport of it. But the weather forecast had been for very high seas and strong winds. Geoff had wanted to come out to the narrow Cook's Passage to check for himself. Now we knew.

"Well," I said, "I suppose we could all use a quiet day on the beach after this week. Unless you have any other ideas, Skip."

"Well, I can't say Lizard Island is exactly a hazard area," Geoff said, smiling, "but if you'd like some real sport fishing, we could run over to the lee of Whale Island and try for trevally on light tackle."

I watched him turn the boat in the narrow passage and again marveled that England's great navigator, Captain James Cook, had taken a wooden sailing ship through this tiny slot in August of 1770 to escape from behind the massive reef. Cook had sailed one thousand miles north in the shallows inside the reef before finding a way out through the huge wall a few miles east of Lizard Island. Once out, he almost lost his tiny ship against the reef in huge seas. Looking at the thundering seas hurled skyward against the reef face, I marveled again at his courage and seamanship on that day more than two hundred years ago.

"Trevally," I said to Geoff as he increased the power to the sleek sportfisherman for the approximately fifteen-minute run back to the island. "They're a lot like our jack crevalle in the States. I wonder if they'll take flies." I had brought a big 10-weight rod along with the thought of taking some dolphin with it if the marlin fishing slacked off.

"I expect so," Geoff said above the roar of the twin engines. "I've never used flies in salt water, but trevally take spinning lures with a vengeance."

We dropped two crewmen off at the beach in front of the luxurious lodge and picked up an aluminum skiff powered by a 15-horsepower outboard motor, which we towed behind as we headed for the low silhouette of Whale Island only a few miles away. I rigged up the big fly rod as we went, and rummaged through a small fly box to see what sort of flies would attract trevally. Geoff said they liked shiny, reflector-type lures, so I chose a Lefty's Deceiver fly tied on a #2/0 hook. Remembering the tough mouths of the jack crevalle, I tied it on 16-pound-test tippet material. I had a big saltwater Pfleuger reel loaded with 10-weight, floating, weight-forward line and two hundred yards of twenty-pound Dacron backing.

Leaving Johnny, the wireman, aboard to watch the *Reef Hunter*, Geoff and I climbed into the skiff with the rods and headed for the white sand beach fifty yards away. Away from the sea and slightly in the lee of Lizard Island, the wind was hardly more than a breeze. Leaving the skiff anchored in shallow water a few yards offshore, we waded toward the sand. The beach was studded with black coral rocks close to the water's edge.

"Mind you," Geoff said, hefting his spinning rod, "keep a sharp eye out for trevally just on the edge of the drop-off. They are school fish and will be cruising for baitfish. If you are lucky, you'll see them attacking bait schools. Throw the fly right into the school."

I sloshed down the beach in ankle-deep water, being careful to avoid the sharp coral outcroppings, keeping an eye out for signs of fish. There were a number of small baitfish flashing in the shallow water out ahead of me, but I could see no larger fish.

I walked down the beach for several hundred yards, the November sun warm on my face. I was inspecting the bottom at my feet when I saw a fleeting movement out of the corner of my eye. Looking up, I saw a pod of about eight to ten fish curving in toward shallow water near me. A school of baitfish was flickering in the very shallow water near the beach.

I stripped out line frantically and began a backcast, the rod loading up as I cast. I dropped the white fly a good twenty-five feet ahead of the streaking lead fish and began to strip the fly in short jerks. I had made about three strips when there was a boil in about two feet of water and the reel screeched as I raised the rod tip.

The entire school of fish churned up the sandy bottom as it headed for the drop-off about fifty yards out. The hooked fish gradually moved off to the left of the school as it felt the weight of the line and the pressure of the bent rod. It was a powerful fish and I simply raised the rod tip and let the rod and reel do the work.

I could see Geoff running toward me from up the beach as I slowly backed up toward dry land. The fish was in deeper water now and already had a little more than sixty yards of line and backing out.

"What is it?" Geoff asked as he splashed up behind me.

"I guess it's a trevally," I said, holding the rod high. "The school looked like big jacks."

"Strong fish," Geoff said. "It will be a while before it tires."

I knew he was right. From the jack crevalle I had caught on a fly rod, I knew them to be the strongest fish for their size I had caught.

The fish finally tired in the deeper water and I led it, little by little, back up on the shallow flat where it continued to circle in water not much more than two feet deep.

"We won't need a net," Geoff said, "if we can get it close. It's easy to grab them by the tail."

I managed to slide the fish into the shallow water close to the water's edge and Geoff grabbed it by the slender, bony section just ahead of the sickle tail. The sunlight glinted on the soft blue-and-silver body marked with tiny black spots on the side. There was one spine just ahead of the prominent dorsal fin and the large pectoral fins were yellow. The fish looked as though it might weigh five to six pounds.

"Small bluefin trevally," Geoff observed. "Lovely fish—fight like hell and are very good to eat."

"If you want to keep it we will," I offered.

"No, let it go," Geoff said. "It's fairly small and perhaps you'll catch a larger one later."

We eased the fish into the shallow water and watched it dart away in a trail of churned-up sand.

"We've got three kinds here," Geoff explained, "the bigeye trevally, this fellow, and the giant trevally. The giant trevally can get up to a hundred pounds or more. These bluefins grow to weigh perhaps twenty to thirty pounds. The bigeye gets to about the same size but feeds mostly at night. Somebody told me it is the same fish you call the horse-eye jack in America."

"I know the fish," I said. "I caught one on a fly rod at Treasure Cay in the Bahamas once."

Geoff went back up the beach to continue his fishing, and I moved on down the shore looking for more trevally. Half an hour later I decided to begin blind casting out into the deeper water instead of waiting for the fish to come into shallow water.

I had been casting for several minutes when I saw a small school of baitfish move into the shallows to my right. There were several shadows flitting back and forth in deeper water just out from the moving school and I decided to drop a fly there in case they were trevally.

The fly had no sooner hit the water and moved several inches when there was an explosion of water and a long, silver fish took to the air with the fly stuck in its mouth. I struck as the fish did a flip in midair and the line went slack. The fish went tail walking across the surface until it disappeared in deeper water.

Reeling in, I inspected the leader and found it neatly cut just ahead of where the fly had been. There was no sign of fraying so I knew the fish must have a sharp set of teeth, or perhaps sharp gill plates like a snook.

A nice trevally taken on a streamer fly cast to the edge of a drop-off.

I carry a small coil of #2 piano wire in a fly box. It has a breaking strength of about twenty-four pounds and can be made into a thin leader in front of a fly when toothy fish are sought. It will easily pass through the eye of a small fly, whereas bulky shock mono will not. It can be twisted into a short fly leader if the twisting is done properly. I made up a leader of about twelve inches and cast another Lefty's Deceiver fly back in the same area.

I had made about a dozen casts and was about to move on down the beach when I saw a quick flash behind the fly. I struck at the same time as the fish did and felt a sudden jar as the speeding fish hit the end of the taut leader. When the hook bit in, the fish came out of the water like a tarpon and did a complete somersault in the bright sunlight. My first impression was that it was a big ladyfish, which jumps the same way and is a bright silver color.

The subsequent run was long and fast, much like a jack, but it ended with a series of aerial flips and cartwheels that left me wondering about my reel capacity.

I heard Geoff shout encouragement as I began backing up, but the fight was just beginning. The fish ran down the beach a good seventy-five yards before heading out for deep water. I have never had a hooked fish go any faster underwater. It streaked like a bonefish or permit, but took to the air at the end of each run and did some spectacular acrobatics before coming back to the surface.

I heard Geoff slide to a stop behind me as I tried to keep the speeding fish away from some coral rocks down the shore.

"You've hooked into the loveliest fish in Australia," he said.

"Queenfish. I only hope it doesn't get off. On light tackle there is nothing like it for a bloody battle!"

"I had a feeling it was no trevally! That first jump must have been six or seven feet high!"

"Oh, they will really jump," Geoff said, "and dive, and tail walk, and pull like hell. One would think they were twice the size they are. Pete Goadby, the old dean of fishing in this country and the bloke who wrote *Big Fish and Blue Water*, wrote that Zane Grey compared it to the great fighting roosterfish of Central and South America. He also said if it grew to two hundred or three hundred pounds, it would be impossible to beat with any tackle!"

The queenfish took another quarter of an hour to subdue and we finally slid it into shallow water at the sand's edge. Geoff managed to scoop it up onto the dry sand by using his hands and feet. We both fell on the twisting fish. It would have weighed perhaps eight to ten pounds and was a cross between a sierra mackerel and a permit—my first impression. It was a steel blue above and silvery below. It had an undershot jaw, the tail was a powerful V-shape, and it was obviously a member of the jack family.

"My God!" I said when we finally held it up for photographs, "the damn thing never quits fighting!"

"They are really beauties," said Geoff, "but they are only fair to eat. The silvery skin is very tough and it is used sometimes for strip baits for billfish. Might as well turn this rascal loose if you have no reason to keep it."

"None," I said, slipping the fish into the shallows where it took off like a thrown javelin. "The photos are enough."

We didn't have a scale with us, and I forgot about the great fighting fish until I was back in the States a few weeks later. Then I looked it up in the IGFA record book.

Only two had ever been entered for fly-rod records: one, a nine-pound fourteen-ounce fish caught by Nick Currey at Vernon Island, Australia, on 12-pound-test tippet in May 1986, and the second, an eight-pound-thirteen-ounce fish caught by Peter Fooks at Veronica Island, Australia, in August 1986 on 16-pound-test tippet.

I wouldn't want to wager any money on it, but I'll bet that fish of mine on 16-pound-test tippet would have weighed a little more than the world record! So much for not carrying pocket scales. Sometimes I wonder if I ever learn anything from experience.

16

Like a Streak of Lightning — Wahoo

When we were rebuilding the island of Cat Cay I had a lot of fun with my 17-foot Menemsha Boston Whaler. There were no boats on the island except a few work boats, used to cart supplies from incoming barges, and supply boats. The few fishing boats there were big 38- to 45-foot sportfishermen belonging to club members who never came over anymore. They had been battered by the 1965 hurricane, Betsy, and most were awaiting marine mechanics from Fort Lauderdale or Miami to come over and make them right—a long wait.

The bonefish flats had not been fished since 1965. There were schools of bonefish everywhere, endangered by pods of large barracuda that circled them constantly. I tried to buy or rent a flats boat from Bimini, but boats earn a man a livelihood in the Bahamas and there were no spares around.

I had purchased the Whaler in New Jersey a few years earlier and had trailered it down to Fort Lauderdale where it was being used constantly by my sons. It finally dawned on me that I had just the boat for the waters around Cat Cay. It was powered by an 85-horsepower Johnson outboard and I had rigged it with fifteen-foot collapsible outriggers. I had an 80-pound and a 30-pound big-game rod and reel stowed in the top of the cuddy cabin, and half a dozen spinning rods and reels with line from eight to twenty pounds on the reels.

In addition, I had two fly rods: an 8-foot, 7-weight rod for the bonefish flats, and a 9½-foot, 10-weight I used for bigger stuff—mostly tarpon. On the larger rod I had an old Pfleuger saltwater reel loaded with 10-weight floating line and about two hundred yards of thirty-pound braided Dacron backing. I had used the bonefish rig a lot, but the big rod had hung idle in its overhead rack for quite a while. I kept it oiled against the ravages of salt water.

My oldest son, John, who was thirteen at the time, and I decided to run the whaler over to Cat Cay for the Christmas holidays. John had several weeks vacation and it seemed like an adventure to him. I tried in vain to find someone who would tow the whaler over to Cat for a fee, but everyone seemed intent on fishing. As the departure date arrived, it became clear we would have to run the little boat across the Gulf Stream ourselves. The trip seemed like a great idea to John, but I had been across the Stream a dozen times in Chalk Airways planes and big boats and knew how rough it could get with a west or north wind.

However, the day we were scheduled to leave dawned clear and calm. Fortunately, I took the two standard six-gallon tanks that were stowed beneath the transom and the twelve-gallon tank that was beneath the center-console seat. In addition, I carried two more six-gallon tanks filled with gas up front in the cuddy cabin. I was not fearful about running out of gas. It was just that gasoline at Cat Cay cost about three times what it did in Florida.

We left Fort Lauderdale at 9:00 A.M. on a warm, clear morning in December and I took a heading for Cat Cay. There was about a three-foot sea running, and the little boat bounced along fine, shedding water like a porpoise over its clamshell hatches on the bow. It was to be a trip of fifty miles, and with the outboard pushing us along at a fuel-saving, conservative ten to fifteen knots, I figured we should hit Cat Cay at around 2:30 or 3:00 P.M.

The high-rises and office buildings of Fort Lauderdale and Miami dropped below the horizon about 10:00 A.M., and I noticed the seas were a bit higher out in the Stream. At noon the wind swung suddenly from the southeast to the west, and I throttled back as the seas began to come over the bow. With the bow high, I was able to take the bigger swells.

The rest of the afternoon was a nightmare. The wind swung around to the north, and anyone who has run the Stream knows what *that* meant. It was the beginning of a northeaster, and since I was already in the middle of the Stream, I thought I might as well keep heading for the island.

We switched the two empty six-gallon tanks to the two new ones and ran on them until they were empty. With the bow high in the air, we were using gas like a thirsty camel and making very little speed. A wind of about thirty knots was slamming us southward and the Stream was running north at about eight knots. I had to guess where we were and maintain a constant heading. Having been a navigator in the Air Corps in China during World War II, I knew my dead reckoning would not be too far off, but I was worried about the weather and the gas.

When it grew dark and there still was no sight of land, I grew worried about the boy. I knew we could throw out a sea anchor and ride it out if the gas gave out—since the whaler was almost unsinkable—but I didn't relish a night on the pitching Stream.

At about 7:00 P.M. I heard surf breaking on rocks and we hit Riding Rocks about ten miles south of Cat Cay. With my heart in my mouth and running low on gas, I headed north into the teeth of the gale; we finally sighted South Cat Cay an hour later. Battered, wet, cold, and running on gas fumes, we swept through the cut between North Cat Cay and Gun Cay and eased into the tiny harbor, the outboard muttering in the darkness. It was almost 8:00 P.M.—eleven hours after leaving Fort Lauderdale.

The huge dockmaster, Jimmie, waddled down the new concrete dock, flashlight in hand. He watched us as I tied the whaler.

"Mister Jack, mon," he said, shaking his head slowly from side to side, "you must be a religious man!"

A stupid one was more like it.

John and I fished the flats with the whaler for ten days and cut a swath through the barracuda by trolling big red-and-white Daredevil spoons through shallow water. I caught some by trolling big white streamer flies on the big fly rod, and a couple of the barracuda we caught measured five feet in length.

John went back to Florida by Chalk Airways when his vacation was up, and I continued to spend all my spare time in the whaler. A young engineer named Doug Gifford was an amateur fisherman, and we spent a lot of time running the small boat out in the Stream during the next few months, catching white marlin, yellowfin tuna, small blue marlin, dolphin, and wahoo on trolled cerro mackerel and mullet.

By spring, I began to use the big fly rod for dolphin, catching them first on conventional tackle and shoving the rod in a gunwale holder to make the school stay around the boat. Then I threw streamer flies, mostly Lefty Kreh's bucktails, tied on #2/0 hooks. The dolphin put up a wonderful fight on the limber rod and were marvelous to eat.

One of the cooks for the construction workers was a native Bahamian named Curly for his shiny bald head. Curly loved fresh fish and volunteered to cook any fish we brought in. Doug Gifford became more and more busy as the construction drew to a close, and Curly and I spent more time fishing together. He was an Andros Island man and knew all sorts of interesting things about fish. We would anchor the whaler out over a sunken boat, one hundred yards or so to the east of North Cat Cay, and fish for small Spanish mackerel. He used a light spinning rod and shrimp and I jigged weighted flies in the depths.

But his favorite sport was fishing for dolphin out in the Stream when the weather was fairly calm. We towed lead-headed Japanese feathers on the spinning rods, and then I caught some on the big fly rod. We were trolling along one sunny February afternoon—Curly half asleep in a folding chair and me with a leg thrown over the back of the console seat—when a pair of wahoo came out of nowhere.

The first thing I saw were two shapes, traveling at tremendous speed, shooting straight up into the air. At the top of the arc, which must have been at least fifteen feet high, the two torpedo-shaped fish dove straight down on the trolled feathers. I shouted as they came down, and Curly jerked awake just as his spinning rod doubled over.

That was a terrific battle. We finally managed to get both those wahoo in, after getting both twelve-pound mono lines tangled several times and nearly losing one fish at the boat. Curly was delighted, and that night we had a feast of wahoo broiled over charcoal and treated with garlic, melted butter, and lime juice. It not only made me want to catch more wahoo, but it started me thinking about trying to catch one on the big fly rod.

Curly said he thought it might be done, but added he didn't think I could do it with anything less than 15-pound-test leader because the

Sage Rod Company's Les Eichhorn caught this monster wahoo on a fly off Cairns, Australia, using a 16-pound-test tippet and a Sage RPL rod.

fish went so fast they would break anything else because of the resistance of the thick fly line. So, for the rest of February and March we tried to catch one on a big white streamer fly.

We caught wahoo on trolled feathers and on trolled dead baits, but we couldn't get the schools of fish to stay around the boat long enough for me to cast a fly to them. The schools would make a quick circle of the hooked fish, then depart—unlike dolphin, which stayed with a hooked fish.

Curly figured the problem was that we couldn't horse in the hooked wahoo fast enough on the light spinning gear to get schools to stay around. He devised his own way of solving the problem. He reasoned that if the speeding fish struck a trolled bait on the elastic thirty-pound mono we had on a Penn International, he could put some pressure on it. Then, he said, when the freshly hooked wahoo and its mate—or the rest of the school—got close to the boat, I could cast to them.

He hooked several wahoo this way, but the rest of the school never got close enough for me to cast, or when I did, they ignored the fly. I never ceased to be amazed at the speed with which these slim fish struck a lure, appearing out of nowhere and flashing away with it in their mouths.

By the end of March, I had about decided to give it up as a bad job. There were plenty of wahoo off Cat Cay, but although I was doing fine with the fly rod on dolphin, barracuda, Spanish mackerel, snappers, and bonefish—wahoo didn't seem like a practical fly-rod fish.

Curly and I were cruising in the whaler along the drop-off just west of Gun Cay when I saw a boil of water far back by his trolled mullet bait. Curly jumped up, picked his 30-pound rod from the starboard gunwale holder, and struck. A big wahoo slanted from the water with the bait hanging from the corner of its mouth—tearing a white-water path across the surface. When it began a long, underwater run, Curly leaned back on the big rod and turned to me.

"I see a lot of fish with it," he grunted. "Get ready."

I stripped off some line from the old Pfleuger reel and flipped the white streamer fly into the water behind the transom. I had about a twelve-inch piano-wire leader ahead of the fly. Curly was really leaning into the big rod, and the wahoo was being dragged in, fighting wildly in the depths.

When he got the struggling fish angled toward the wake, I cast the big white fly about thirty feet back and began stripping it. It never occurred to me to take the rumbling outboard out of gear. We were only moving ahead at about four knots.

On the third or fourth strip there was a terrific strike and the fly rod was almost jerked from my grasp. I had the good sense to let go of the line with my left hand and raise the rod tip. The line at my feet whipped out through the guides in a flash and the old reel shrieked as a wahoo headed east toward Gun Cay.

"You got one!" Curly yelled, frantically cranking the big Penn International to get his fish out of the water. My line was peeling off the fly reel at an alarming rate and I figured I had already lost at least 150 yards of backing. I was thanking my lucky stars I was using a 15-pound-test leader as I leaned back and let the big rod do the work.

The fish began a turn just shy of the two-hundred-yard mark, and Curly reached down and slammed a gaff into his thrashing wahoo. Hoisting it into the cockpit, he quickly jammed his rod butt into the gunwale holder and grabbed for the wheel. Heading the bow at the streaking fish, he gradually increased the speed.

"Get in as much line as you can," he shouted, angling the bow so he could see my slanting line.

We fought that fish for twenty minutes until we could see it gleaming in the depths. Curly let the engine idle as I stood in the stern, rod bent into a bow. The wahoo slowly circled below us as I pumped it upward. It made an occasional high-speed run outward for forty to fifty yards before the big fly rod slowed it down.

We finally got it up within a few feet of the transom and Curly reached for the gaff. I had the rod tip underwater by then, trying to get the zigzagging wahoo away from the idling prop. It finally quit struggling and Curly reached out and took the leader. He gently led it close to the transom and then, raising his right arm, struck with the gaff.

The gaff hit the taut leader, popping it with a pinging sound. The fish was gone. We both stared at the spot in the royal-blue water.

"Well," Curly said lamely, "I had the leader. It was a release. Fish probably go fifteen, twenty pounds—at least."

I would rather have had the fish.

That was my one and only experience hooking a wahoo with a fly. I have cast to a few that were rocketing behind the boat off Baja and once off Costa Rica, but none ever came close to taking my fly again. I was pleased to find out from Stu Apte a few years later that he and Jim Chapralis had a similar experience off Panama.

Instead of using the stretchable thirty-pound mono the way Curly had done, they had trolled a heavy jig attached to a wire leader. That wire was in turn attached to quarter-inch nylon rope. The rope was tied to a boat cleat and the jig run about sixty feet behind the boat. They figured that when a wahoo struck, the rope would keep the fish within casting distance.

The trouble was, Stu said, that when the streaking fish hit, they were going so fast they would simply tear the lures from their mouths. Stu and Jim solved that by tying a couple feet of elastic bungee cord between the wire and the rope to cushion the shock of that first lightninglike strike. They said they lost the first few fish, but that it finally worked. Stu went on to catch a number of wahoo this way, including several world records.

Their successful gear was made up of a 10-weight fly rod, a reel with two hundred yards of twenty-pound backing, a sinking shooting head, a nine-foot leader with 12- and 15-pound-test tippet, and a twelve-inch, 27-pound-test wire shock leader.

There is no doubt wahoo can be successfully taken on fly rods if one uses the proper technique and tackle. Les Eichorn took a world record wahoo in Australia in September 1988 on a Sage III fly rod, a Pate reel, and 16-pound-test tippet. He told me it put up a tremendous battle, but that he finally landed it in heavy seas off Cairns. The monster wahoo weighed forty-six pounds four ounces!

17

The Prehistoric Fish — Alligator Gar

I was out on the drop-off off Guanaja, Honduras, with "Little John" Uhr and Dave Gower, looking for small blue marlin and white marlin on a fly rod, when John brought up the subject of alligator gar.

We had been catching some nice little blackfin tuna on flies, casting into schools of them from the 29-foot Rampone, center-console sportfisherman. The marlin and sailfish had been scarce, but we knew they were there. John had taken two sailfish the day before outside the one-hundred-fathom curve, along with some nice wahoo.

"You wouldn't believe it, Jack," John said, steering from the remote wheel in the tower. "Alligator gar are as good a big-game fish as a marlin or sail on medium tackle. When hooked they can jump like a billfish and they fight like hell."

"Alligator gar!" I said.

"That's right," he replied. "We got lots of them off the south Texas coast. They spend the winter far up inland creeks, but come down to the bays in the spring and spend all summer out in big holes in salt water. All you got to do is drop a mullet in there on a treble hook and let it sit a spell. They'll pick it up directly, and when you set the hook, they really fight."

"What kind of tackle?" I asked.

"Oh, fairly heavy stuff," said John. "I use a fifty-pound big-game rod and a Penn Thirty International. Thirty-pound mono is about right. Some of these gar run over one hundred pounds!"

"Jesus!" I said. "I guess that rules out a fly rod."

"I honestly don't know," John admitted. "They pick up mullet real quick, but I don't know what kind of a fly they'd go for. They eat small fish and I guess crabs and the like. I've caught small ones up the creeks on spinning rods and little surface plugs."

"I caught a spotted gar on a fly rod in the Tamiami Canal just outside of Miami," I said, "on a popping bug. I was fishing for bass and the little critter grabbed it on the surface. Ugly little thing—about three pounds."

"There ain't nothin' about these critters that's pretty," John said. "They look about a million years old and the teeth can give you nightmares. Gotta be real careful about getting them in the boat or they're liable to chew off an arm or a leg."

"Well," I said thoughtfully, "maybe they would take a fly of some sort—maybe a big popper on the surface."

"Come on down and try it," urged John. "Hell, I've seen you catch everything else on a fly—permit, bonefish, jack crevalle, blackfin tuna, mutton snapper. Why not? At least you can watch me catch them."

I made a note to see John do this, but it was July before I got a chance to fly down to Rockport, Texas, where John lives. Rockport is a lovely town on the Texas Gulf Coast and is famous for its redfish and sea trout, but apparently only John and a couple of close cronies realize alligator gar can be caught there regularly.

John builds small flats-type boats, and he took me out in one he had just finished, which was bought by a friend of his, Robert. It was a 21-foot, aluminum-hull craft that sported an upswept bow and drew only about eight inches of water. It was run from a center console and was powered by a 250-horsepower outboard. It would navigate the tricky shallows around Rockport and still have a shallow enough draft to get up inland creeks.

John insisted we try going up some of the shallow creeks that empty into St. Charles Bay—Twin Creek, Salt Creek, and Cavasso Creek—to see if the gar were there. The sleek boat thundered across the bay and zipped into the mouth of the first creek, scattering shore birds and waterfowl like confetti ahead of us.

"Watch the banks for big wild pigs," John shouted over the roar of the engine. "We shoot them with bows and arrows in the fall months.

Some of them weigh three or four hundred pounds and are meaner than snakes."

We ran the boat aground far up the creek and Robert snubbed it to an old mesquite tree. It was hotter than the hinges of hell—close to 100 degrees—and there was very little breeze. I could feel the sweat oozing from my pores and running down my body under the light shirt.

The two men rigged up #5/0 treble hooks with small, dead mullet and tossed them into the center of the creek. We were anchored at the head of a long one-hundred-yard pool. The water was hot and sluggish and the current barely moved. Every now and then the water would explode as something thrashed to the surface.

"Gar," John said matter-of-factly. "They ain't eatin' nothin'. Maybe just getting oxygen."

Green horseflies buzzed about, and now and then landed on us. They bit like hot coals.

"You get used to them," John said reassuringly. I doubted it.

It was at least twenty minutes before anything bit, besides the flies. Then Robert's line slowly began to move downstream. He carefully picked up the big rod and free spooled the reel. The line went a good one hundred yards downstream before it stopped.

"Want to make sure he swallows the mullet," Robert said, holding the rod aloft. After a few more minutes he suddenly struck. The big rod doubled over and the reel screamed as the fish headed downstream.

It was a long, stubborn battle. Robert finally led the fish upstream where it sulked beneath the boat for a while. When he finally pumped it to the surface, John reached down with a big gaff and sunk the point into the belly of the fish. There was an explosion of white water and the fish thrashed against the metal hull, the blows echoing in the stillness of the morning.

When the fish's struggles finally died down, John slid its head over the gunwale and eased the big fish onto the deck. I backed up into the stern.

"My God," I said, "that is one ugly fish!"

The gar had a head very much like an alligator, with rows of formidable teeth. It had a long, greenish white, heavily scaled body with a single dorsal fin far back on its back, just ahead of a blunt paddle tail. It somewhat resembled a northern pike, but a great deal bigger—perhaps fifty to sixty pounds.

"How big do they get?" I asked.

"I've seen them well over a hundred pounds down here," Robert replied, "but I hear they get up around three hundred."

"They good for anything?"

"They're pretty good eatin'," John said, "when they're fried up good. The meat's white and dry, but I hear tell the roe will kill people."

They stowed the dead gar in a big metal fish box and prepared to fish again. A few small gar swam by the boat on the surface, finning lazily.

"Let me try a popper on those little guys," I said. "They are about the same size as the one I caught in Florida."

Robert made room for me in the bow, and I began to cast a small, cork bass bug at the cruising gar. I cast for at least half an hour, but none of the gar gave the bug a glance. It was growing hotter the higher the sun rose. I finally reeled in the bug.

"Boys," I said, "these gar are not the least bit interested in this bug. Got any other ideas?"

"Well," John remarked, "it ain't going to get any cooler here. Let's run out into the bay and we'll show you where these fellas like to lay up in the big holes. At least we'll get some cooler breezes out there."

The wind quickly dried the sweat from our bodies as the stream-lined boat sped down the narrow, winding creek and slammed out into the choppy waters of Aransas Bay.

"Nobody knows why," John shouted over the motor noise, "but these gar come down out of the tidal creeks and get together out here in the bay. They find a hole—maybe fifteen to twenty feet deep—and hundreds of them will lay up in there in the summer. I don't know what they eat—small fish I guess. Anyway, we catch 'em on mullet."

We thundered across the shallow bay for half an hour until Robert found the spot he wanted and cut the motor. The boat skidded to a gradual stop and John went forward and slid a big anchor from a forward locker. He threw it over the side and played out the anchor rope. The water around us looked no different from the rest of the bay, which stretched for miles.

"What makes this place so special?" I asked.

"You can't tell unless you know it's here," John said. "But there's a big shallow hole right here. Me and Robert found it by accident while we was fishing for redfish. There must be hundreds of gar laying on the bottom here. Watch."

John impaled a large mullet on his treble hook and heaved it over the side, where it landed with a splash about twenty feet from the boat. There was a slight current running and his line slanted away from us to the south. Robert baited his hook and threw it over the side a moment later.

It was only a few minutes until John's line began to run out. He free spooled his reel and watched as the thirty-pound mono ran out quickly. The fish ran about fifty yards, then stopped. John waited a few minutes, then struck. His line became taut and suddenly a gar thrashed to the surface. It came half out of the water, shook its head savagely, and dove for the bottom. John's boat rod doubled over and he began to battle the fish.

It was a long and tough fight. The fish finally began to come in, but it was at least a half hour before the big fish was drawn to the boat. When Robert gaffed it, the struggle was titanic. Water splashed over all of us as the big fish fought the steel gaff. I was surprised at its size when it was finally subdued.

"This fish will go over a hundred easy," John said as the two lifted it into the bow. It was a huge, scaly monster, its paddle-shaped tail feebly beating on the carpeted deck.

"We'll release this one," John said. "It's not badly hurt from the gaff and they heal up pretty good." The two men dumped the big fish over the side where it slowly sank into the depths.

"I'm going to try a big popper," I said. "I sure as hell don't see any gar rising for anything, but a popper makes a hellacious racket and maybe I can get one to come to the surface."

I rigged a big, cork, concave-faced white popper on a 100-pound-test shock leader. It was mounted on a #5/0 stainless-steel hook and had a tuft of white feathers jutting out the rear of the body. The current was running fairly steadily to the south, and I cast the big popper as far as I could from the boat, then let the current carry it away. I stripped the line until it was all gone from the reel and the backing began to run out. When the bug was about thirty to forty yards from the boat, I began jerking it toward us.

While the two men tossed out their rigged mullet baits and began catching gar in earnest, I continued to chug the big popper in the current. The breeze felt good after the sweltering swamp, and the sun was high in the Texas sky. John had brought a cooler full of Lone Star beer, and we all agreed the sun was over the yardarm enough to try some.

I finally decided trying to catch an alligator gar was a waste of time on a fly rod and brought in the big popper. By that time John and

Robert had caught half a dozen gar, several in the one-hundred-pound class. Some had leaped from the surface when hooked and all had put up a tremendous struggle. I was convinced the gar was a good game fish.

John had caught two gafftopsail catfish on his mullet baits; both fish were about four to five pounds. They are excellent eating and John kept both. I knew they were bottom feeders and would take crabs and small fish on occasion. I had caught several on light spinning rods and knew them to be good fighters. I decided to see if they would take a fly fished slowly along the bottom. I dug in my fly box and came up with a weighted, black Whistler-type fly with big metal eyes. It was a #3/0 hook. I tied it to the same shock leader, more because I was too lazy to change the leader than I was afraid a catfish would break the mono. I cast it as far from the boat as I could and let the current carry it down and away. When I thought it was about forty yards from the boat, I began to strip it slowly. I could feel it digging into the bottom occasionally.

John and I were on our third beer and discussing the best methods of catching redfish on a fly when I raised the rod tip. The fly had become stuck on the bottom, I thought.

"What you got?" John asked.

"Bottom I think," I said, yanking on the rod. I had on a 16-pound-test tippet and was not afraid it would break.

"Your bottom's moving," Robert observed.

I suddenly jumped to the platform in the stern and raised the rod tip high. Whatever it was, was going away rapidly. I leaned back on the 9-weight graphite rod.

"This is no catfish," I said excitedly. "This is a big fish!"

"Bring in your line, Robert," John replied, rapidly reeling in his own. "We don't want to get it fouled up."

The fish went straight away for at least 150 yards before slowing down. I had a Pate Bonefish reel on the rod and knew I had at least 200 yards of twenty-pound backing. When the fish stopped, I began putting pressure on it. The fish began shaking its head but it did not take out any more line. It slowly began to swim in an immense circle around the boat.

"You know what?" John grinned. "You got a gar—the first gar in the world caught on a fly rod."

"Not yet it's not caught." I said grimly. "And I'm sure a lot of people have caught gar on a fly rod."

"Little John" Uhr holds up the big gar caught by the author.

"Not this size," John said.

He was right. It was a big fish and put up a long, hard fight. I couldn't put a great deal of pressure on it with the fairly light rod. If I had brought my 12-weight tarpon rod, I could have leaned into it, but I simply had to wear it down.

John and Robert drank beer and gave me considerable advice while the fish swam in ever-decreasing concentric circles around the boat. It must have taken at least forty-five minutes before it finally tired and came to the boat. When it stuck its snout above water, John swiftly gaffed it and hung on. The gar thrashed noisily against the boat hull, but finally gave up.

"I estimate this fish will weigh at least sixty pounds." John said, holding it up by the gaff so that Robert could take a photo. "What's the world record on a fly rod?"

"I'll be damned if I know," I laughed, "but this sure as hell is no fly-rod record. I don't really think you could call that bottom jigging fly casting!"

"Maybe not," John said, easing the gar onto the deck. "But for my money, it's the first alligator gar caught on a fly rod in my neck of the woods, and it's going to be a record down here, that's for damn sure!"

18

The Offbeat Fish

There is a huge, cement-hulled ship sunken on the flats just to the east of Gun Cay in the Bahamas. I used to hear all sorts of stories as to how it got there. One version was that it was sunk by the Coast Guard back in prohibition days when it was apprehended carrying booze from Nassau to Miami. The other was that it was towed there and used as a naval target in World War II.

While nobody in Bimini seemed sure how it got there, every fisherman knew it was a great place to fish. Chunks had fallen from the hull and the sea had grown a garden of vegetation on the rest of it. All sorts of sea creatures lived in, around, and under it. Predator fish preyed upon all sorts of baitfish that lived off the rotting hulk.

I used to run the Menemsha Whaler to it from Cat Cay, and it was a grand place to catch cerro mackerel, Nassau grouper, barracuda, jack crevalle, blue runners, bar jacks, permit, mutton snapper, red snapper, and all sorts of fish that love wrecks. Curly and I would catch a batch of pilchard and balao from the Cat Cay docks with a cast net and carry them in buckets to the wreck.

There we would cut the fish up as chum and toss them overboard near the towering hull. Curly liked to fish with a big boat rod and twenty-pound mono and I would use the fly rod. He would use cut-up pilchards as bait and I would use weighted #2/0 white streamer flies and Hi-D sinking fly line. We could see the fish coming up from the depths as the chum sank, and it was a real thrill to get a bait or a weighted fly down to them as they began to feed in a frenzy.

Curly caught a lot more big fish than I did—big grouper and amberjacks—because he could haul back on the stout fiberglass boat rod and set the drag on his level-winding reel. He also caught some nice permit that put up a mighty struggle in the depths. I would catch a lot of medium-size stuff on the fly rod, but I think I had a lot more fun than Curly did. I used a 10-weight rod and a reel with two hundred yards of twenty-pound backing and 16-pound-test tippets. Usually, I used an 80-pound-test shock leader because most of the fish I was hooking were toothy critters.

I never landed an amberjack on a fly rod because they were either just too big or strong for my tackle. I hooked a couple, but they went straight down. If I had had a 15-weight fly rod and some of the excellent big-game fly reels I have today, I might have been able to stop them. I also hooked some big grouper I never saw again.

But I did hook some small sharks near the wreck and on the flats that I was able to subdue with that 10-weight rod. Most of them were small nurse sharks, but I did catch a couple of little lemon sharks and a small blue shark on popper bugs. I tried to catch a mako out in the Stream, but although I did get a couple to come up for trolled teaser baits just offshore, I could never get them interested in a big white streamer fly. My hope was to do just what Billy Pate did in 1984 in New Zealand—catch a mako (thirty-seven pounds seven ounces) on a fly.

One bright morning in June, Curly and I were busy baiting fish with chum on the north side of the wreck. We had taken a nice mess of cerro mackerel, and I had fought and landed a big jack crevalle that had come zooming up through the chum to whack my white streamer. Curly had devised a great system of getting fish to come up from the depths. He would dump a bunch of chum over the side, then grab a long cane pole he carried just for the task. He had a blue runner hooked through the back, and he lowered this fish over the side and let it tear around on the surface. The splashing and noise that runner made would bring all sorts of interesting predator fish up from the deep blue depths.

The world fly-rod record for mako shark on 8-pound tippet is held by Billy Pate with this thirty-seven-pound-seven-ounce mako caught in 1984 in New Zealand. He also holds the record for the biggest mako caught on a fly rod: a sixty-five-pound mako caught on 16-pound tippet in New Zealand the same year.

I had just missed a permit that came slanting up and had jerked the fly from the water when I saw a dark brown shadow flash up from beneath the boat and just barely miss the thrashing blue runner.

"What the hell was that?" I yelled, casting the fly back into the water.

"Cobia!" Curly shouted, flipping the blue runner back into the water. "Great eating fish. See if he won't take that fly."

As soon as the fly had sunk, and I had given it several strips, a dark shape appeared from the depths and took the fly in a flashing swirl. The rod doubled over and the reel screeched as the fish dove deep. The cobia ran down to the base of the hull and then made a straight run out from the wreck, taking line as it went.

I couldn't remember fighting a stronger fish on a fly rod. That cobia never jumped, but it did come to the surface several times and thrashed there before diving again. I have no idea why that fish did not get off. I did everything wrong, letting it get close to the wreck and dive deeply, but it stayed on. When it tired, I brought it close and Curly gaffed it. He said it would weigh about twelve to fifteen pounds. We had no scales with us and seldom did we weigh anything anyway in those days. There were so many fish around in the Bahamas that nobody was concerned with weight. If a fish was good eating, it was kept. If it wasn't, one let it go.

I remember that cobia was dark brown on the top and had dark bronze and silver stripes on the lighter sides. It had a flat head and a strange set of spines ahead of the dorsal. It looked more like a shark than anything else, but it was a hell of a fighter. Curly broiled it over charcoal that night and it was a marvelous fish to eat. We tried for months to catch another at the wreck, but never did, even though Curly said it was a school fish. I learned later that cobia grow to large sizes and that the all-tackle record is held by a guy from Australia who caught one weighing over 135 pounds. The fly-rod record is held by Jim Anson, who caught an 83-pound 4-ounce monster on a fly rod at Key West in January 1986.

I have tried for a number of years to catch cobia on a fly in the Florida Keys, but with no success. I have tried for them along the edge of the flats in the spring, when they are supposed to be migrating north, and I have looked for them along the east coast of that state where they are caught regularly from jetties and piers. They are a difficult fish to find, and when you find one, it does not always take lures. There is a big cobia fishery along the northwest coast of Florida, but not a big fly-rod following.

I have not had a great deal of luck surf fishing with a fly. I caught some stripers and blues off the surf in New Jersey and in New England, but it was tough fishing and I never really enjoyed it that much. If there was any kind of surf, the fly line kept getting tangled up and the surf battered one considerably. I can see why it is really a sport for the spinning-rod and level-winding-reel enthusiast.

When we were fishing in the International Billfish Fly Tournament at Flamingo Bay, Costa Rica, in 1989, most of the anglers would head for the big hotel swimming pool on returning each day. The hotel was right on the sandy beach and the surf looked fishy. I would go down in the evening with a fly rod, but I never really caught much. I caught a small roosterfish and several little pompano, but the waves were strong and there was a considerable undertow.

Nick Curcione, that excellent California fly fisherman, was with me. He tried the surf on several nights and caught some small stuff. Nick knows the surf and uses sinking lines for certain conditions— something I should learn. He fishes the southern California surf and down into Ensenada, Mexico, regularly taking corbina, pargo, calico bass, croaker, and barred perch. In the deeper water he has a wonderful time with bonito and yellowfin tuna—fish not everybody catches on a fly rod. I asked him how he handled the problem of the fly line getting tangled in the surf.

"Surf fishing poses some unique conditions for the fly rodder, so certain modifications are necessary," he said. "One of the most important is the use of a stripping basket. I realize that some anglers try to avoid one whenever possible, but for most surfing applications they are a virtual necessity. About the only time you might get by without one in California is early-morning corbina fishing on a calm day when the wind factor is nil. Corbina tend to hug the shore, searching for sand crabs and other small crustaceans literally within a few feet of the water's edge. Because they spook easily if they detect your presence, it's best to make your casts from up on the beach. Here at least you can let your line fall on the dry sand without too much bother from snarls or snags. However, for most other occasions where some wading is involved, a stripping basket is the only way to go."

Nick said he used the commercial stripping baskets for a while, but found them too shallow in strong winds. When a fly rodder bent over in the surf to pick up fish, the line would either fall out or blow out and become tangled in the water. He finally settled on a soft plastic container that was designed as a waste basket. It was small enough to carry on a belt, but deep enough to keep the line inside.

He fishes for barred perch from late fall to early spring and corbina from late spring to early fall. The beaches of Baja, however, provide good surf fishing year round. Because the surf conditions, wind, and weather differ for various locations and different seasons, Nick uses three specialized fly-rod combinations.

For the smaller species in the two- to five-pound class, such as barred perch, corbina, yellowfin croaker, pargo, and the various kinds of rockfish and bass, he uses an 8½- to 9-foot fly rod designed for an 8- to 9-weight line. Sometimes when the surf is running high, he switches to a 9½-foot rod because it gives him better line control.

When the winds are down and the waters calm, he may switch to a light fly rod designed for a 6- to 7-weight line. It is used for corbina close to the water's edge and for small fish in the shallows. He uses this rod mostly with a floating line.

The third outfit is strictly for heavy duty and consists of a 11- to 12-weight rod and matching line and reel. He uses these rods when fishing from high ledges that jut far above the water. The height—combined with the powerful backwash created by the waves smashing into the rocks—means a strong rod is necessary to play fish in turbulence.

"Of course," Nick said, "the size of your flies will also play a part in the type of rod you use. Fishing for corbina under conditions of clear, shallow water can be a fairly delicate affair. This means you don't want a big, bulky fly tearing up the surface with each cast. Besides, corbina don't have large mouths, so small bonefish-type flies tied on #4 and #6 hooks work well. With barred perch it is a completely different type of proposition. They are nowhere near as wary as corbina and waste no time smacking a fly. However, you don't take them on the clear, calm sand flats that corbina like to prowl. Barred perch like the violent water, so the churning froth is where you want to fish. Due to this type of habitat and the perch's fierce feeding habits, the fly patterns are larger than those I normally use for corbina."

Nick said barred perch also have fairly large mouths, making it easy for them to take flies tied on #2 and even #1/0 hooks. He said the calico bass have even larger mouths and he likes to throw big flies— #2/0 to #5/0—at them. With flies that large and the strong winds coming in off the sea, it is not hard to see why 11- and 12-weight rods are sometimes needed.

"The flies themselves," he said, "are quite simple. For barred perch and corbina I tie a pattern that closely resembles the Comet series. Attractor color combinations seem to work best with bright reds, oranges, and yellow bringing the most action. In the case of calico bass and other rock dwellers, I tie heavily dressed versions of south Florida tarpon-fly patterns. Only on a few occasions do I try to match the hatch. For example, practically all the halibut I have taken in the surf have fallen for white Lefty's Deceivers. I believe the reason is that between the months of March and July, when barred perch give birth to their live young, halibut come in close to the beach and gorge themselves on the small, silver-colored fry, which average between one and one-half to two and one-half inches in length. Apparently, the small Deceiver patterns bear a close resemblance to these fry, because it has been the only fly that has produced good results when halibut have been in the area."

Regardless of the pattern used, Nick said, there are two basic requirements that should be noted when tying flies for the surf. They should be both durable and nonfouling. Fragile creations may look great mounted in a case, but they will soon be torn apart in a churning surf. As far as materials are concerned, Nick uses hackle and bucktail, but is using more artificial substitutes like Fishair each year. He said he uses only stainless-steel hooks, as regular hooks rust out quickly in the salt water.

"Of course," he said, "the best fly ever tied will never realize its

Nick Curcione, a dedicated California fly rodder, catches innumerable surf species plus bonito and yellowtail, like this one, on fly rods.

full potential if it isn't fished on the proper line. And by far, with the exception of shallow-water corbina fishing, lead core is the most practical line for the surf. Seldom do you encounter depths of more than fifteen feet, but with the strong currents, lead core will get the fly down quicker than most conventional sinking lines. Lead-core shooting heads are not only easier to cast directly into the wind, but more importantly, their stiffness makes them lay out better in the water compared to conventional lines, which have a tendency to tangle in the turbulence."

Nick said he prefers the uncoated, lead-core shooting heads over the coated variety because the coated lines tend to become worn easily in the sandy surf and that makes them more difficult to cast. He said lead-core shooting heads that weigh about 17 grains per foot seem to handle best in the surf. For his 8- to 9-weight rods he uses shooting heads of approximately twenty-six feet and for his 11- to 12-weight rods he goes to thirty-foot shooting heads.

"The leader setup for the medium and heavy outfits," he said, "is roughly the same, and I try to keep them short to avoid tangling. Besides, with the exception of corbina, most species are not overly selective so long leaders are not necessary. I tie most of mine between two and one-half and three feet in length. So I can change them quickly, I put a loop in the end of the shooting head and fasten the ten- to fifteen-pound-test class tippet via a loop-to-loop connection. First tie a Bimini twist in both ends of the tippet. Double one end of the loop over itself and tie a surgeon's knot. This is formed to slip inside the loop of the shooting head. The double line at the other end of the class tippet is used to tie to a twelve-inch section of the shock leader, which generally consists of from thirty- to fifty-pound mono."

Nick said that like most other saltwater fly rodders, he owns some expensive anodized, saltwater reels, but that he does not use them in the surf. He says most surf species do not make long, lightning-quick runs the way some flats fish do, so there is no need for reels with sophisticated drags. Sand also gets into the surf reels and it is best if they have a quick take-apart feature.

But he does use his more expensive and bigger reels with smooth drags for his excursions into deeper water for bonito and yellowfin tuna. He has found, in the heavily populated area around Los Angeles, that there is a great fly-rod fishery for Pacific bonito right in his own back yard.

"This bullet-shaped, souped-up junior version of the bigger tuna—also known as bones or boneheads—takes flies readily and is known for long, scorching runs when it feels the hook," he explained.

"They're one of the fastest swimmers in the ocean. That's something to think about when you are gearing up for them. Because of this constant movement, the bonito's energy requirements are very high. That doesn't mean they will eat anything that's thrown at them. In fact, at times they can get satiated and become downright selective, but a pod of bonito in a feeding frenzy is an awesome sight. I've seen bonito herd small schools of anchovies against sea walls at Kings Harbor in Redondo Beach, one of the top bonito fisheries in the world. Then they pick them off one by one. It is so methodical you'd swear they'd planned the whole course of attack."

The anchovy is the main food of the bonito, Nick says, and it is best to imitate the anchovy when tying flies for bonito. He suggests tying the flies on the small side, from 1¼ to 3 inches in length. Albacore, skipjack, yellowfin, and bonito respond better to the smaller patterns, he says.

"A second relevant factor," he pointed out, "is that with smaller flies you can more effectively simulate the movements of injured baitfish. A relatively slow jerk and a pause as a stripping motion causes the fly to accelerate, dart, and then settle briefly in the water. This is the typical reaction of baitfish when tuna start attacking a school. Tying in bead chain or lead eyes immediately behind the hook eye will give the fly the desired effect."

He advised me that two excellent fly-tying hooks for bonito are the Eagle Claw 254SS and the Mustad 3407, with the largest size a #1/0 hook. He likes to use Lefty's Deceiver, a small version of Dan Blanton's Whistler series, and his own Tonic Tuna flies that he developed a few years back. He thinks white is the most productive color to use in tying, in combination with yellow, red, green, and blue.

He uses his bonito leaders in the same fashion as the ones he uses for surf fishing, but likes to omit the butt section. Instead, he ties class tippet directly to the fly line. He says it eliminates a bow in the leader as it sinks, allowing him to lift it out of the water easier when using sinking lines. He also says it turns over the fly better. Even though bonito have a strong set of needlelike teeth, Nick says one can forgo the use of a shock leader, as the class tippet will slide between the teeth and not be cut.

Throwing chum into the water will bring bonito up, and Nick says it is best to use lines like Hi-D or a 400-grain Deep Water Express line to get them down deep in heavy currents. He uses a 10-weight rod most of the time for bonito. His reels are of good quality, like the Pate and Abel reels, and he uses a thirty-foot shooting head, one hundred feet of twenty-five- to thirty-pound running line, and at least 150 yards of twenty- to thirty-pound Micron or Dacron backing.

While bonito may travel in huge schools and hug the bays and inlets of the coastline, their cousins, the yellowfin, are generally found offshore.

The yellowfin are so strong and burn up so much energy, Nick says, that eventually they grow to such huge proportions that their nourishment demands outstrip their ability to feed themselves. That is why there are so few yellowfin over four hundred pounds. They simply die when they get to that size and age.

"First of all," Nick explained, "you can roam offshore and look for telltale signs of feeding activity. One of the most obvious signs is bird activity. Diving, screeching gulls are a sure sign that smaller baitfish like anchovies are being pushed to the surface by marauding schools of predator fish.

"In the absence of bird activity," he said, "another good feeding sign to look for is referred to as 'nervous water,' or the 'wedge.' When tuna move in on a school of bait they generally do so in a wedge-shaped formation. A watchful angler can detect this kind of feeding action by watching the water. Another age-old sign known to tuna fishermen is the presence of schools of porpoise. The two often travel together."

Nick says the yellowfin is one of the strongest fish in the ocean, and having battled the giants on heavy tackle, he should know.

"And when you nail one on fly gear," he said, "about the only way I can describe the experience is to use a phrase from popular language: *it is awesome!* They do not effect the stunning aerial acrobatics of tarpon, sailfish, or dorado, but none of these species can match the sustained runs and sheer staying power of yellowfin. When they inhale the fly and feel the sting of the hook, it seems they will never stop running. For that reason, even on school-size yellowfin in the fifteen-to thirty-pound class, I like to use a reel that holds at least three hundred and fifty yards of thirty-pound backing."

There again, live anchovies are the best bait for bringing yellowfin to a boat where flies can be cast to the feeding school. The difference between fishing for yellowfin and bonito is the size of the tackle. Nick uses a 12-weight fly rod and a heavy-duty, well-designed reel with a large line capacity and a smooth drag for these larger tuna. On yellowfin, Nick uses a shock leader of 40- to 60-pound-test. As for flies, he uses the smaller patterns and basically the same flies that he uses for bonito.

Not every fly fisherman goes out for tuna. It is an offbeat sort of fish for the long rodders, and one needs a boat, except when fly fishing for some shore-hugging bonito. My tuna experience is limited to fishing for them while out looking for billfish, wahoo, or dolphin with a fly rod. I have caught bonito, albacore, and small blackfin tuna so far, but that is about all. But I am still trying.

The blackfin were caught with John Uhr and Dave Gower off Guanaja, Honduras. We were trolling teasers for sailfish and blue marlin when we ran into schools of blackfin feeding on baitfish. We cut across in front of the schools and cut the engine. When the tuna surfaced around us, I threw big streamers at them. They hit hard and fought hard, and though a lot of them were cut in half by predator fish following the schools, we landed a few. I expect the predator fish were either wahoo or barracuda, but we never saw them. I lost half of a big

Inveterate saltwater fly rodder Mike Sakamoto of Hawaii caught this huge 135-pound yellowfin tuna on a fly rod. Because it was taken by trolling a popper, Mike did not turn it in for an IGFA record. It took him one hour and forty-five minutes to land the fish.

albacore I hooked off Key West to sharks. It was too bad, as it was a very big albacore, and it took a big Lefty's Deceiver fly I cast into the chum line.

But the all-time champs of tuna fishing are a couple of avid fly-rod fishermen from Hawaii, Mike Sakamoto and Terry Baird. These two guys have been experimenting with flies, fly rods, lines, and leaders for a decade or so, and while not trying to set IGFA records, they have caught a lot of interesting fish on flies.

Mike caught a 206-pound Pacific blue marlin on a fly rod—the first man to do so. While the gear he used prevented him from qualifying for an IGFA record, it was a hell of a battle and a hell of a fish to land on fly tackle. He trolled a fly he had designed himself, one the local fishermen now call the Sakamoto Special or the Bag Lady. It is made from the foam of a surfboard or bodyboard and is decorated with plastic strips from a garbage bag. It takes fish—as his marlin can attest to.

Mike used about four hundred yards of thirty-pound Dacron backing, knotted to one hundred yards of fifty-pound mono, tied to fifteen feet of 80-pound-test mono. That section was connected by a ball-bearing swivel and a crimped sleeve to fifteen feet of 400-pound-test mono shock leader. His Bag Lady fly carried a #10/0 Mustad hook.

His reel was a #4 Fin-Nor, and he used one of Tim Grennan's experimental 8-foot, 14-weight Fenwick Iron Feather rods (IF #8014-2). This great marlin and tuna fly rod has fifty-seven million graphite modules, big ceramic stripping guides, and a large tip guide that can withstand the strain of big fish. Also, it has a backbone that can lift huge fish from the depths. Grennan is a true pioneer in the big fly-rod arena, and I expect to see some more excellent rods from him in the future.

Now before any purists start complaining that Sakamoto's terminal tackle does not comply to the IGFA standards for record fish, let me say that I am not in complete disagreement with Mike's theory that a long shock leader should be used on billfish. They have a tough, rough, thorny bill and can easily wear through the presently required twelve-inch shock leader. There is a movement under way to have that shock leader lengthened for billfish and I thoroughly support that effort. Two of the last three striped marlin I lost at the boat were because the 100-pound-test shock leader was worn through. Sakamoto was not trying for IGFA records, but was trying to find out if he could catch a blue marlin on a fly rod. Naturally, his fifty-pound running line and 80-pound-test mono section were far above the 16-pound-test tippet limitation. But it is guys like Sakamoto who are doing the

Terry Baird of Hawaii strains to raise a bigeye tuna from the depths with a fly rod.

Terry Baird's world record nine-pound bigeye tuna taken on a fly rod with 8-pound tippet off Hawaii on January 2, 1982.

experimenting with big fly rods and are paving the way for some interesting developments to come.

Terry Baird has done some pioneer work in the Pacific on saltwater flies and has also caught some spectacular fish on the fly rod. He holds the world record for a nine-pound, bigeye tuna he took off Kailua-Kona on an 8-pound-test tippet. Fishing with Mike Sakamoto and Warren Osako on January 2, 1982, Terry used a 10-weight rod and a twenty-foot lead-core shooting head. He used one hundred yards of mono running line and thirty-pound Dacron backing on a Pate reel. His fly was a white streamer he had designed himself.

They would go out to a buoy in a boat and cast the sinking shooting heads as close to the buoy as they could. The bigeye tuna were feeding deep and close to the buoy, chasing small baitfish that had congregated around the buoy chain. Letting the shooting head sink, he began stripping it up toward the surface. He finally got a terrific strike and the tuna dove for the deep. It took half his 450 yards on the reel before he could stop it.

After an hour and forty-five minutes, Terry finally got the bigeye close to the boat where Warren gaffed it. It was the first bigeye tuna taken on a fly, and it still remains a record on 8-pound-test tippet. It was not until May 1987, when Mike Sakamoto took a 9-pound-8-ounce bigeye tuna on 12-pound-test tippet, that another was taken on a fly rod. Mike later went on to take a 135-pound yellowfin tuna on a fly rod, but it was not an IGFA record because Mike was trolling a big popper when the big fish hit. Terry has designed some interesting tuna and marlin poppers made from foam squares and with two hooks set back in white-and-blue hackles. He sent me several and I am just waiting to see them take big fish.

In 1990, while fly fishing for sailfish strip bait at Bahia Pez Vela in Costa Rica, I caught a twelve- to fifteen-pound bigeye tuna. I was fishing with Skipper Kaleen, and we cut up the tuna for bait. We photographed it, however. It would not have been an IGFA record, because the boat was in gear when I cast the streamer fly.

Mike Sakamoto is the kind of fisherman who has always fasci- nated me. He will try anything new to catch fish. He caught a giant trevally, an African pompano, and an amberjack—all on a flyrod. But what makes his catches so interesting is his system of hooking them. These fish were all hooked at a depth of 350 to 400 feet!

Mike used what he calls his Hawaiian "drop-stone" leader sys- tem. I asked him about it.

"Granted," he said, "you wouldn't be fly casting in the true sense of fly fishing, and any fish caught this way would be disqualified from being an IGFA catch. But the objective was to catch big, deep-water game fish on a fly rod and have fun doing it. And the idea was to open the door to catching other kinds of fish that would be normally out of the reach of the fly fisher.

"The drop-stone idea consisted of taking a stone, wrapping some cotton cord around it, and leaving a loop to tie on a breakaway line. I tied eight to ten inches of four-pound mono as a breakaway line and tied a loop in this that would be looped over the bend in the fly."

His fly consisted of two parts: a metal tube fly that glistened and sparkled when he moved it through the water, followed by a plain white streamer fly on a #1/0 hook. He used one of Tim Grennan's 14-weight graphite fly rods, a Fin-Nor #4 reel, and his line-leader combination went from thirty-pound Dacron backing to fifteen feet of forty-five-pound lead core, and a two-foot section of 60-pound-test shock leader.

"Once all the components were assembled," he said, "I took the streamer fly and hooked it to the four-pound loop, which was tied to the stone. I then gently lowered the stone over the side and fed line

Mike Sakamoto shows off a big amberjack he took on a fly rod using his unique "drop stone" technique.

from the reel, allowing the stone to take the streamer fly down to the bottom, which lay sixty fathoms below. Once the stone and fly hit the bottom, I tightened the line and gave the rod a quick jerk. This immediately broke the four-pound loop and the fly was free. Once this was accomplished, I began working the fly up from the bottom with short, quick strips of the backing line. The amberjack and trevally prey on anything that ventures into their territory, so once the fly was free to spin and pulsate, the amberjacks attacked the streamer with a vengeance."

IGFA record? Of course not, but I can't imagine a better way to catch these deep-dwelling fish on a fly rod. Or—for that matter—a better way to have fun.

19

The Spectacular
Sailfish

The May sun was high overhead. It was hot—somewhere in the nineties—and the humidity made it suffocating.

The 31-foot Bertram, the *Marlin Azul,* wallowed in a following sea of three- to four-foot waves and it was difficult to stay awake. Joe Hudson, asleep in the fighting chair, made no pretense of trying to. The combination of heat, the rolling boat, very slow fishing, and an ice chest full of Costa Rica's Imperial Beer made it hard to concentrate on the trolled strip bait skipping astern.

We were about twenty miles out of Flamingo Beach on Costa Rica's west coast and it was the fourth and last day of the First International Invitational Billfish Fly Tournament. The first big international fly-fishing contest was being sponsored by Billy Pate and George Hommell of World Wide Sportsman of Islamorada, Florida.

The fishing for both sailfish and marlin had been terrible. The gods of angling had decided to be fickle, as they do on most occasions. In 1988 the months of April and May had been great for billfish—the sailfish in particular. So when Pate had decided to hold the big tournament in Costa Rica for the year 1989 he picked May as the month, giving himself a month's cushion.

By about the end of April it was apparent to everyone concerned that the billfish were late in arriving off Costa Rica's northern coast. But the thirty-two anglers from all over the world had made their plans months before and there was no possibility of changing the dates. Billy decided to stonewall and hope for the best. The best was late in arriving.

The first three days had seen very few sailfish come up for the trolled hookless strip baits that had been specially flown in from Florida for the competition. A dozen of the sixteen teams had fish come up and perhaps eight teams had taken one sailfish per team. Even such consummate pros as Pate, Bill Barnes, Steve Sloan, and longtime Florida Keys guide Lee Baker had lost fish, although most had caught one sailfish.

My partner was Joe Hudson, veteran saltwater fly fisherman from Islamorada, who at one time had held the world record for tarpon on a fly. Joe and I had hunted and fished together over half the world and were old friends. Although we were both experienced saltwater fly rodders, neither of us were under any illusion we could defeat the likes of Pate and Barnes, who were fishing as a team.

By the last day we had seen only three sailfish. One had taken Joe's double-hook streamer fly with a Styrofoam attractor ahead of it, but the fly had come off on the first jump. The other two sails were

A fly-hooked billfish leaps from the water off Costa Rica.

not interested in the flies. I had not had a strike as the final day approached and had decided I was definitely snake bitten as far as this tournament was concerned.

The only other fly tournament of this kind I had ever seen was the first fly sailfish contest held in the early 1970s off Islamorada. I had been with Pate on that one and the weather had been horrible. There was only one sailfish caught in that tourney and it was caught by Rip McIntosh of Palm Beach. People in those early days were not exactly falling over themselves to enter billfish fly tournaments. In fact, most people thought we were all a little goofy to be trying it.

Nevertheless, here we were—on the second try—but this time we were also out for marlin. Each sailfish was worth one hundred points—marlin five hundred points. Naturally, everyone was hoping for a marlin, not only because of the number of points, but because nobody had ever caught a Pacific blue marlin on a fly under IGFA rules. Mike Sakamoto of Hawaii had taken a Pacific blue of more than two hundred pounds by trolling a popper bug on a fly rod, but he had not cast a fly to one, so it didn't count. As far as I am concerned, IGFA rules or not, Mike is the first man to catch a Pacific blue on a fly rod. It was some feat—casting or not. After all, Doc Robinson doesn't appear in the IGFA record books either, but he was sure the pioneer of the sport.

The morning of the final day dawned bright, but very windy. Raphael, captain of the *Marlin Azul*, had run up the coast, hoping to hit a fresh area and find some sails. All we found in the early morning was high seas offshore of the Nicaraguan border. Finally turning south, we rode a following sea down the coast, hoping against hope to find the elusive sails. Deedee Harkins of Austin, Texas, a veteran big-game fishing angler, had come along the last day hoping to get some photographs.

We were all caught completely by surprise when about 10:00 A.M. a sailfish surfaced behind the strip bait. It was my turn on the big teaser rod and I leaped to the left side of the cockpit where the rod was in a gunwale holder.

The sail was hungry and behaved just right, pursuing the strip bait as I reeled it just ahead of the bill tip. Joe cast his fly perfectly and hooked the sail in the side of the mouth as it made a turn and took the fly. The fish made several spectacular jumps and made a long run when Joe set the hook.

Handling the boat beautifully, Raphael threw the Bertram into reverse and backed down on the battling fish in high seas. The mate, Alejandro, perched on the transom, waiting to spot the leader. The fish took about twenty minutes to subdue and the mate carefully led it by the 16-pound-test leader to the transom and hauled it aboard by the bill. It was a fish of about seventy-five pounds and there was much backslapping and handshaking at the victory.

As we went back to the fishing, there was still no elation or thought of winning as half a dozen teams had already caught one fish, and there was a very good chance those teams would catch at least one—if not several more—during the day.

Here it was, about 2:45 P.M. in the heat and humidity, and we had not seen another fish all day. We were to take the trolled bait from the water at 4:00 P.M., as it was necessary to be back at the dock by 5:00 P.M. under tournament rules. For some strange reason known only to the gods of fishing, I had changed from a streamer fly to one of my homemade cork poppers an hour earlier. I just had a feeling I would do better with the big white popper mounted on a #5/0 stainless-steel hook, rather than the #3/0 streamers most anglers were using. A second #5/0 hook was rigged trailing behind.

I was already thinking about the fresh fish we would have at the final banquet that night, and I had just started to get up to get another cold beer when I heard a shout from the bridge.

"Pez vela!" I heard Raphael scream.

I looked back to see a sailfish bill slashing at the strip bait. Joe woke at the same instant and jumped for the teaser rod. I had my rod leaning in the right-hand corner of the cockpit with the tip on the transom. There was about a dozen feet of the twenty-eight-foot shooting head, the leader and the popper resting on the deck. The rest of the shooting head and about twenty yards of thirty-pound Micron backing were coiled in the bottom of a dry plastic bucket in the corner.

Joe was doing a masterful job of bringing the sailfish close to the boat, and as it slashed wildly at the bait, Joe lifted the bait away from the fish and I cast the big, white popper over the fish and to its side. As I stripped in the bug in a chugging motion, the fish whirled and took the popper in a wide-open-mouthed lunge. I set the hook and the sail made two towering leaps and was off across the surface.

"I got both those jumps!" Deedee yelled from behind, camera in hand.

The mate grabs the 16-pound leader after a twenty-minute battle and gently leads the fish toward the transom. Notice the white popper stuck in the sailfish's jaw.

That battle lasted about fifteen to twenty minutes. Nobody was watching the time very carefully. When Alejandro gingerly led the fish to the transom and grasped the bill, everyone aboard went wild. He lifted the fish high for photographs, the big white popper jutting from the corner of its jaw. *Both* #5/0 hooks were sunk in the tough cartilage of its mouth.

Even after the elation of the catch had started to fade, neither Joe nor I had a suspicion we had won. We knew we had done well for that day, but we were certain we were far behind the rest.

It was not until 4:00 P.M. — time to take out the bait — that I got on the ship's radio and called the tournament boat. It was the 42-foot *Barbarella*, captained by Tom Bradwell.

"Jack Samson, Tom," I said. "How many fish caught today?"

There was a long silence, then Tom's voice, half broken up by the static.

"You guys won it. First team to take two fish. The Japanese team caught two, but after you did."

I was stunned. When I told Joe, he was amazed. When I told the crew, they were delirious — it meant a lot of money to them!

So that last sailfish had been the winner in the First International Billfish Fly Tournament. If I never do anything else, fishing-wise, I will go down in the record books for that. Talk about luck!

Just a few years back the very idea of trying to catch billfish on a fly rod would have been laughable. Only a handful of anglers had even attempted it — Dr. Webster Robinson, Lee Wulff, Stu Apte, and Billy Pate. Today, with the exploding technology of high-tech tackle and equipment, literally hundreds of saltwater fly rodders are pursuing both sailfish and marlin over much of the world.

The late Doc Robinson and his wife, Helen, pioneered fly fishing for sailfish and marlin in the 1950s. When Robinson began his experiments off the Florida Keys, his rods were either split bamboo or the first heavy fiberglass rods built. The only reels available for big saltwater fish in those days were the venerable Fin-Nor or Seamaster models. Doc had to make his own lures by fashioning large flat-bottomed corks into poppers decked with saddle hackle feathers and with a #7/0 hook riding point upward.

With this relatively primitive tackle Doc — with Helen handling a teaser rod and trolling sewn strip baits without hooks in them — began fishing for sailfish off Florida. It was not until 1962 that he caught his first Atlantic sailfish — one of 74½ pounds — on a fly. In the next few years he was to catch more than a dozen sailfish, plus five striped marlin off Cabo San Lucas, Baja, California, the largest being a brute weighing 145 pounds — the first marlin ever caught on a fly. Robinson never entered any of his catches for IGFA records, probably because he was using leaders in the 20-pound-test class for marlin, when the maximum pound-test allowed in those days for records was 15-

pound-test. (It later became 16-pound-test.) But he used 12-pound-test tippets for sailfish.

The first marlin entered for record was credited to Lee Wulff in May 1967 on 12-pound-test tippet. It was a striped marlin caught off Salinas, Ecuador, and it weighed 148 pounds. Two years later Billy Pate caught one in the same place, on 16-pound-test tippet, that weighed 146 pounds.

The first Atlantic sailfish to be entered for a record was one caught by Billy Pate off Venezuela on September 18, 1975. It weighed 75 pounds and was taken on 16-pound-test tippet, but the *first* sail to be caught on a fly, according to Lefty Kreh—and he certainly should know—was a 47-pound Atlantic sailfish caught by Lee Cuddy on June 4, 1964. Lee was a legendary, early saltwater fly fisherman and a close friend of Doc Robinson. His guide was Captain Bucky Stark.

The next on a fly was a Pacific sail of 136 pounds, caught by Stu Apte on 12-pound-test tippet at Pinas Bay, Panama, June 26, 1965. Pate was later to set the 8-pound-test-tippet record of 78 pounds 8 ounces while fishing with me at Flamingo Beach, Costa Rica, in 1988. The 16-pound-test tippet-class world record is held by Eizo Maruhashi, with a 124-pound Pacific sail caught off Costa Rica on July 21, 1989. Maruhashi, an excellent saltwater fly fisherman, came in second in the 1989 International Billfish Fly Tournament at Flamingo Beach.

Let's face it. All these records are doomed to fall. Fly-rod records—more than any others—are made to be broken. And with the rapid development of better rods, reels, leaders, lines, and boats, it is only a matter of time before these records go the way of all others. But that is the way it should be. Nothing is more natural than to have a whole new generation of saltwater fly rodders eagerly pursuing billfish on the long rods.

The sailfish is a natural for the fly fisherman. It chases bait well, charges right up to the transom following a trolled bait, and readily takes a fly—sometimes a number of times before being hooked. When hooked, it fights a spectacular leaping battle and can usually be brought up successfully by a fly rod after sounding. And it does not grow to such weights that it cannot be handled on a fly rod—like marlin.

Lots of fly fishermen today have taken sailfish on a fly. I remember fishing with Billy Pate off Islamorada, Florida, in the late 1960s when it was really an achievement to take a sailfish on a fly rod. One could count on the fingers of one hand the number of anglers who had.

Veteran guide Chuck Rizuto battles a big sailfish on a fly rod off Bahia Pez Vela in Costa Rica.

Today, thanks mainly to better rods and reels, it is far simpler to do it, but it is still quite a challenge. It is the technique that needs practicing, for it is a far cry from the standard trolling method done with conventional gear. But thanks again to expanding technology, it also is not necessary to use big, expensive, gas-consuming sport-fishermen to fly fish for sailfish.

Any good open-style, center-console boat can be used for the sport. The main feature is to have space in which to cast a fly. The advantage of such a boat, besides being less fuel consuming, is that it can get you out and back to the fishing grounds quickly. I have taken both sailfish and marlin from open, 20-foot *pangas* off Baja, and they are nothing more than open, wooden rowboats powered by an out-board motor. Needless to say, they are considerably cheaper than chartering a sportfisherman here in the States!

This is not to say you cannot take billfish with a fly rod from a sportfisherman. Certainly, a large, stable platform is easier to fish from, and it is far easier to keep your footing while fighting a billfish with a fly rod. But it is necessary to remove one of the outriggers if you are to have backcast room. Which outrigger depends on whether you are left- or right-handed.

I think training a crew, or your fishing partners, to catch billfish on a fly is the most difficult part of the sport. IGFA rules for billfish records do not permit trolling a fly, so it is necessary to *cast* a fly to your sailfish. In addition, when a sailfish comes after the teaser bait, the boat must be taken out of gear when the fly is cast. This calls for some fancy cooperation between the person handling the teaser rod, the skipper, and the angler.

The person handling the teaser rod can make all the difference. The teaser bait must be kept barely ahead of the sailfish, just enough to let the fish taste the bait (even grabbing it sometimes), but not letting the fish have it. The one holding the teaser rod must know exactly when to lift the bait out of the water—when the sailfish is ready to hit the fly.

Billy Pate likes to leave the teaser bait—whether a whole fish or a strip bait cut from the belly of another fish—in the water until the last minute. It is his theory that letting the hungry fish eat the bait close to the boat and then yanking it out of the fish's mouth makes the fish even more ready to take a fly. I am sure he is right, but letting the fish have the bait sometimes can cause problems. He let a small blue marlin have the bait while we were fishing together out of Quepos, Costa Rica, in April 1990, and when he went to yank the bait away from the fish, the 30-pound teaser rod line parted, leaving the marlin with the bait. The same line parted again on a sailfish, so we switched to a fifty-foot section of far heavier line. As a result of that trip, I always use fifty-pound mono on my teaser rod. Once a billfish swallows the bait, it can be very difficult to pull it away.

In addition to knowing how and when to take the boat out of gear for the cast, a skipper who has done a lot of fly fishing for billfish must know how to handle the boat while the fight is on. A captain who is experienced in backing down and maneuvering a boat while a fly fisherman is battling a sailfish can be the difference between success and failure.

Presentation of the big sailfish fly is all-important. It is not necessary to cast great distances in billfish fly fishing, but placement is vital. A good thirty- to forty-foot cast should be enough on most occasions, but the fly should land off to one side of the fish so that it will turn and take it in the corner of the mouth.

It is not generally necessary to set the hook with hard strikes, as the speed of the strike usually sets the hook, but pressure from the fingers of the left hand helps set the hook solidly as the fish turns and

A big sailfish comes alongside the Cubero *off Bahia Pez Vela.*

makes the first run. When the fish jumps, try to lower the rod tip to give it as much slack as possible.

Refinement in technique over the past decade has made it more likely that the tippets will hold under the strain of speeding and jumping sailfish. At one time we all used the standard ninety-foot, floating fly line, but lost fish over the years taught a lot of us to go to fast-sinking shooting heads, cut down to twenty-five to thirty feet in length. They offer far less resistance to the water. Fly rods in 12-weight and 13-weight sizes are used for billfish, and a weight-forward, 12- to 13-weight, fast-sinking shooting head should be used.

Most saltwater fly rodders now have pretty much settled on the ideal rig for billfish, although there is some disagreement on certain lengths of running line, mono, strength of backing, and some knots. I will tell you what I have found to be the best for me.

I use a 12-weight graphite rod, either two-piece or four-piece. There are excellent rods made in each length, but I have begun using four-piece rods because careless airline baggage handlers have broken a number of two-piece rods, even in sturdy rod cases. Probably the best two-piece, big-game rods today are made by Sage Rod Company of Bainbridge Island, Washington; Fenwick Rod Company of Hunnington Beach, California; Graphite USA of San Diego; and Deerfield

Rod Company of Hackensack, New Jersey. The best four-piece break-down or travel rods being manufactured today, in my opinion, are by Joe Fisher of Carson City, Nevada.

In the field of reels for big fish, there are not many. In the past the Fin-Nor and Seamaster reels were all there were, but as good as they are, they have limited capacity for *big* billfish—marlin. With a capacity of about four hundred yards of thirty-pound Micron or Dacron back-ing, they can be used for sailfish, as can the Abel #4 reel, 3M's excel-lent System 111 (Model 1112), and Billy Pate's Tarpon reel. But I feel much more comfortable when fishing for big billfish if I use the Pate Marlin reel, with a capacity of six hundred yards of thirty-pound backing, or Steve Abel's #5 big-game reel, with the awesome capacity of nine hundred yards of thirty-pound backing, plus a fly line.

One never knows when a really big billfish will strike. I caught a 105-pound Pacific sail in Costa Rica in 1989 that took out nearly five hundred yards of line on the first run. I was lucky I was using the Pate Marlin reel. Nick Curcione was fishing with us on that same trip and hooked a 350-pound Pacific blue marlin, which he had on for more than three hours before losing it. Imagine what he would have done with a reel with only a four-hundred-yard capacity!

As far as fly lines are concerned, it is a toss-up between Cortland and Scientific Anglers as to who makes the best big-game saltwater lines. Both have done considerable research in this field and both put out excellent products. I use Ande leader material for running line and shock leader, but I have found that Mason leader material is by far the hardest and resists cuts and nicks. I think it makes the best tippet material.

There is ample room for a difference of opinion on what are the best knots for saltwater big-game fly fishing, but here is my sugges-tion: fasten the backing to about one hundred feet of soft, shock-absorbing, thirty-five- to forty-pound mono line with Albright knots. (For years I was a devotee of the nail knot, but even though they are bulkier, the Albright knots are stronger.) This runs through the fingers when the short twenty-five- to thirty-foot shooting head has passed out through the guides.

The butt end of the leader—about three feet of 30- to 40-pound-test—should be fastened to the shooting head with the same knot. The loop on the class tippet can be formed by using a spider hitch. I prefer the spider hitch, or five-times-around knot, because of the ease in tying it. The class tippet must, by IGFA rules, be at least fifteen inches long, measured from the connecting knots. I usually make mine eighteen to twenty inches long.

The leader section is connected to the shock leader—usually 100-pound-test in the case of billfish—by an Albright knot. This knot is not easy to tie, but I don't know of any substitute I like as well. This shock leader must be no longer than twelve inches by IGFA regulations—a rule I think needs changing. Billfish tend to get the fly far back in the mouth and the shock leader takes terrible punishment from the tough, thorny bill. I would hope the rule would, in the future, allow at least eighteen inches, or more.

Tying the 100-pound-test shock leader to the fly can be a chore and pliers can be a help. There are three options: a tight-loop knot, a free-loop knot, or something I now use most of the time, a crimped connector sleeve, which forms a loop.

I use a 3½-turn clinch knot for a snug fit, and a double surgeon's loop when I want a free-swinging fly. But for the fastest-tied loop and the strongest hold, I crimp the 100-pound-test shock leader to the eye of the fly with .098 nickel or black Berkley connector sleeve. I use a pair of point-opposing crimping pliers. Mark Sosin, an expert on almost anything having to do with saltwater fishing, taught me that trick. For small- to medium-size saltwater fish, one connector sleeve will do, but he and I both use two sleeves to crimp the heavy shock leaders for billfish. This method utilizes round sleeves only, but some big-game fishermen use the heavier-walled oval sleeves, and in that case one needs to use a stronger cup-opposing pair of crimping pliers.

Every billfish fly rodder has a favorite fly. Billy Pate and a lot of other experts prefer the double-hook, white streamer fly with tandem-rigged (one up and one down) stainless-steel #4/0 hooks. They like to mount a round, white Styrofoam block just ahead of the fly to act as a popper. I have used this fly with considerable success for years, but I have switched to bigger poppers lately—made either by me, Edge-water Fly Company of Clearfield, Utah, or the Fly Factory of Belle-glade, Florida. Like Doc Robinson, I think billfish prefer a noisy popper.

For a lot of saltwater fly rodders, the sailfish is the ultimate chal-lenge. They don't plan to go on to try for marlin. Sailfish are quite plentiful and fairly easy to find, while marlin require a lot of time, money, and effort to locate. Besides, a sailfish is a billfish, and anyone who has taken a billfish on a fly rod belongs to a select group of saltwater fly fishermen.

Sailfish may be found in a great many places, but there are places that are really well suited to taking sailfish on a fly. I would choose the area around Mazatlan, Mexico, from May to December if I wanted to catch a lot of sailfish close to home. Mazatlan is only a two-hour jet flight from such cities as Phoenix and Los Angeles.

By far the best country in which to catch sailfish is Costa Rica, all the way from Flamingo Beach and Bahia Pez Vela on the north to Quepos and Golfito on the south.

Nestling like small jewels in an aquamarine sea off the northeast coast of Honduras, the tiny Bay Islands may offer big-game fishermen a new and fertile fishing ground for marlin and sailfish.

The fish are there. John Uhr of Rockport, Texas, and I found both sailfish and blue marlin just outside the drop-off on the northeast coast of Guanaja, the easternmost of the three small islands that make up the Bay chain. John had brought down a 29-foot Rampone, center-console sportfisherman in the early spring of 1988 for the sole purpose of finding out what kind of billfish cruised the drop-off. Reefs circle the small island on all sides, and the wall is not more than a mile or so offshore. There the water drops from two hundred to three hundred feet on the edge to a deep canyon. The curve is so similar to the contours around Cozumel—a mere 150 or so miles to the north—that both John and I knew there had to be the same fine billfishing. I had been invited to come down and find out where the fish were and to try for them with some light spinning and fly tackle.

It is easy to reach the islands. The Honduran airline, Tan Sasha, serves the nearby mainland airport of La Cieba with daily jet flights from Miami, New Orleans, and Houston. It is a quick two-hour hop from all three cities. From La Cieba, one takes a thirty-minute ride in a vintage DC-3 to Guanaja. The other two islands, Roatan and Utila, are only a few miles to the west of Guanaja. A jet strip has been constructed on Roatan that now makes it possible to take direct flights to the island from the States.

A quick boat ride from the airport on Guanaja took me to La Posada del Sol, the posh hotel and marina on the island. The marina held several sportfisherman and a number of big diving boats used to take scuba divers out to the nearby reef. A number of flats boats were tied up to the dock in front of the hotel. They were for the use of the many permit fishermen who come down on a regular basis. While not a prime bonefishing area, Guanaja may be the premier permit fishing spot of the Caribbean. I have fished for them there with fly rods, and nowhere else—including Key West and Belize—have I seen so many permit that will take a fly.

A spectacularly beautiful island, Guanaja was the spot at which Columbus landed on his fourth and last voyage in 1502, and he found people living there. Archaeologists later proved that the mountainous island had been populated for thousands of years.

Many of the natives on the island were enslaved by the early Spaniards between 1516 and 1526 before the Spanish finally abolished slavery in the Bay Islands in 1530. The island was to serve later as a haven for buccaneers in the early 1700s and was a base from which they plundered the Spanish galleons.

The British initiated trade with the islands in 1742, but there were no English settlers there until 1796 when white settlers began arriving from the Cayman Islands. Britain annexed the Bay Islands as a colony in 1850, but the United States invoked the Monroe Doctrine, forcing Britain to cede the islands to Honduras. In 1859 the Bay Islands gained limited sovereignty, and for the last one hundred years the islands, for all practical purposes, have remained politically and economically independent. Honduras has shown little interest in them and the Bay Islanders have thrived on fish, shrimp, and lobsters that they sell commercially.

John Uhr, Dave Gower, and I were up at sunrise and out through the cut between George's Cay and North East Cay, a few miles north of the hotel. It was a beautiful April day and the seas were moderately calm in the prevailing easterly wind. We decided to experiment by catching our own fresh bait and trying some Kona heads the first few hours.

Along the drop-off we had no trouble taking all the small bonito and blackfin tuna we wanted with the fly rod and light spinning rods. The early-morning sea was alive with tuna schools, and although a number of the little tuna came in with only a head remaining from barracuda and wahoo strikes, we managed to get enough for marlin bait. The day before I arrived, John had been using a small blackfin tuna for bait and had been stripped of his fifty-pound mono by a big yellowfin tuna that had taken him into the depths off the reef. He was eager to repeat the battle.

The skipper, Arturo (left), slides the big 105-pound sailfish over the transom for the author who caught it in 1988 using a fly tied by John Barr of Boulder, Colorado.

One sailfish and a small blue marlin surfaced behind the baits in the morning before we decided to run in through the reef and up to the white beach at Michael's Rock for lunch. Neither fish had been hungry. A swim in the clear water of the beach before lunch was just what we needed after a morning in the hot sun.

In the afternoon we rerigged our baits, running a blackfin off the starboard outrigger for marlin, a daisy chain of squid off the port outrigger for sailfish, and both Kona heads and strip bait off the stern, or flat lines, for whatever came up.

In midafternoon three sails came up as we followed the ten-fathom curve to the north of the island. Dave and I yanked in the blackfin and the flat lines as John hooked one of the sails on the squid, which had been splashing behind on the twenty-pound line. The strong fish tail-walked across the surface until it tired and we pulled it alongside and released it. The other two sails did not come back up, and again we continued our quest.

It was about 3:30 P.M. when the blue marlin smashed the skipping blackfin bait. The line fell to the surface and the thirty-pound mono whipped off the reel as John made a dive for the rod. The blue was a nice, strong fish and greyhounded off to the starboard side as John shoved the rod butt into his fighting belt. When the blue was finally subdued, we estimated his weight at about 250 pounds before releasing the fine fish to fight again.

It was late in the afternoon when the sailfish came up again, and I finally managed to get the fly to one that was infuriated at not being able to eat the rubber squid Dave was pulling from its bill. The fish put up a great fight as the sun was sinking against the western horizon. That was the only billfish I took on the fly, but I caught a number of small tuna and some good dolphin before the next few days were over. John took another good marlin and two more sails. Wahoo were scarce on top, but were definitely there. The scuba divers each night reported they had seen them cruising the reef.

There are plenty of billfish on the drop-off to the east and north of Guanaja. We did not have time to circle the entire island. It is possible there are better grounds to the west and south. A deep tongue of the ocean cuts in a few miles north of the three Bay Islands and the billfishing should be excellent. All that needs to be done is to have a number of sport-fishing boats explore the area.

But the fact remains, it is unspoiled, virgin billfish water. The local fishermen do a lot of reef fishing, and some of the bigger boats go out for days of fishing for wahoo, which are sold commercially. But no one in the region except a few Americans with small sportfishermen ever try for the billfish. It is not an easy run to the area. Boats that have tried it have come over from Miami. They have made the long run to the north of Cuba to Cozumel off Yucatan. There, it is a straight run south to Guanaja.

Once in Guanaja, there are plenty of berths for big sportfishermen, and the accommodations at La Posada del Sol are luxurious, to say the least. Fuel is plentiful and bait is available locally. Radiotelephone connection to the States is available at the hotel, and charter of several big-game boats at the hotel is simple. There are tennis courts, a huge swimming pool, and white sand beaches close to the hotel.

For those who, like me, would rather fish than loaf, there is excellent night fishing off the piers and docks near the hotel for horse-eye jacks and jack crevalle. I startled the hotel manager the first night there by catching a fifteen-pound jack on the first cast of a fly. The hotel turns on big flood lights at the outer ends of the jetties at night and predator fish hang around the lights waiting for baitfish to swarm. Day or night, in deep water or on the flats, it is a fly fisherman's paradise.

20

The Ultimate Challenge — Marlin

I was watching my wife, Victoria, and her sister Jackie vegetate by the pool in the big house Jackie had rented for the winter in Jamaica.

It was not that the company or the surroundings were not pleasant, but I am a fisherman — not a sunworshipper. Jackie had asked us down to spend a week or ten days in January, and it was nice getting away from the cold weather up north. I had packed a four-piece fly rod just in case there were dolphin offshore or permit flats, but so far nobody I had talked to knew anything about fishing — of any kind. The house was near Round Hill up above Montego Bay and the coast seemed rocky and the water deep. Search as I did, I could find no flats.

One local "guide" assured me he knew a river where there were lots of tarpon. He took me up there in a dugout canoe, but all I could see in the shallow stream were a few catfish in one deep pool. Equipped with snorkle gear, I swam out to a small reef about one hundred yards from the house, but did not even see any bar jacks. The area seemed fished out. I was even more convinced this was so the following day when two boats appeared in front of the house and a dozen men spread what looked like half a mile of purse seine along the beach. I watched them pull it in after a couple of hours, but all they hauled in were a few pilchard and small pompano.

I was about to give up on the project and settle down to enjoy the excellent local rum, when the cook said her cousin knew a man who had a boat down the shore who caught *lots* of fish. She said she would have him come around.

Sure enough, that night a small man, wearing a multicolored golfing cap, showed up at the house. Yes, he had a fine boat. Yes, he would take me out (for $300) to catch many yellowfin tuna, wahoo, and dolphin, or dorado as they are called in his native Spanish. His English was fair and we agreed that I would go the following morning.

I had brought a travel rod made by Deerfield that had interchangeable top sections. One two-piece section made a 9- to 10-weight, graphite fly rod and the other two-piece section provided an 11- to 12-weight rod. I planned to catch some big dolphin on the rod so I rigged the 11- to 12-weight sections with 12-weight, thirty-foot shooting head fly line and put on a Billy Pate Tarpon reel with four hundred yards of thirty-pound Micron backing. I put a big, white cork popping bug, mounted on a stainless-steel #5/0 hook, on 100-pound-test shock mono and used a 16-pound-test tippet.

Jose came to get me the following morning in a battered Ford pickup truck and we rattled down the road to where his boat was docked. It was a 26-foot, blue-painted wooden boat with a tattered canvas top, no outriggers, and a single rusty diesel engine of ancient vintage. There were two old fiberglass rods stuck in rear gunwale rod holders, holding a couple of corroded 9/0 Penn Senator reels filled

One of the first—if not the first—marlin to be caught on a fly was taken by Dr. Webster Robinson off Cabo San Lucas, Baja, in the early 1960s. It weighed 145 pounds but was not entered for an IGFA record.

with what looked like thirty-pound-test mono. Jose's mate was named Porfirio—Porfi for short. He was twice the size of the skipper.

The one-lunged diesel chugged us out to the blue water in about an hour, making a steady eight to ten knots against a fairly high sea. The sun was bright and the wind blew from the northeast.

Porfi began rigging up two big mullet baits, sewing a #7/0 hook into the belly of each one with heavy twine. It took me nearly fifteen minutes, with my abysmal Spanish, to convince both men that I wanted to troll only one hooked mullet, and when a dorado hit it, to bring the fish in close to the boat and leave it there so I could cast the big popper at the fish that would stay with the hooked baitfish. Also, I wanted to troll the other mullet with no hooks in it so I could use it as a teaser for any fish that came along.

No hooks in it! This gringo is mad! What the hell, anybody crazy enough to pay us $300 per day for this tub can't be too dangerous. Do what he wants.

They rigged both mullet on their flat lines and we began trolling. We trolled for about three hours without seeing anything. No birds showed up on the horizon; no barracuda, no small tuna, and no dolphin bothered our baits. Porfi was asleep on top of a fish box near the wheel and Jose was steering half awake in the midday sunshine. I had about given up on any kind of fish when I suddenly saw the bill come up behind the port-side bait. My feet hitting the deck woke both men. I grabbed the old rod and began rapidly reeling in the bait with the hook. I had caught enough sailfish on a fly to know the proper method. I wanted the fish to follow the hookless teaser.

"No, No!" yelled Jose. "Leave the hook in the water!"

I reeled as fast as I could and flipped the hooked mullet into the boat.

"Porfi," I shouted, pointing to the other rod and shoving the one I had into a holder, "reel that one in."

Porfirio must have been used to taking orders because he leaped to take the other rod and began reeling.

"No, No," screamed Jose from behind the wheel, unable to comprehend what we were doing.

The small billfish was as confused as Jose. It saw one bait leave the water and, as it turned to the other, it too speeded up. It followed—all lighted up with anger. As I grabbed for the fly rod, my subconscious mind was telling me it was a marlin and not a sailfish, as I had thought it was at first sight. No sail broke the surface. From its tiny size I simply assumed it was a sailfish.

"Alto!" I yelled at Jose, trying to get him to put the diesel into neutral. He had no idea what I was shouting about and kept on at his four- to five-knot speed. I made one backcast and let the big popper fly go. It hit about ten feet on the other side of the small marlin just as Porfi pulled the bait from the water. By this time the marlin was so angry it would have struck at anything that came into sight.

At the second chugging, gurgling movement of the popper, the marlin whirled and smashed the lure in a vicious strike, its shoulders coming clear out of the water. I struck sidewise, to my right, and felt the hook take hold. I only had about twenty feet of line outside the top guide and had no time to let out any more. There was no slack line anywhere and the marlin was directly on the reel. I let go of the line with my left hand and raised the rod tip.

Feeling the bite of the hook, the small marlin — which I suddenly saw now was a blue — went straight up into the air.

"Aieee!" shouted Porfirio, throwing his arms up, "marleen!"

That little fish threw itself upward, twisting and turning in the bright sunlight until I thought it would never stop. When it came down and landed close to the stern, it threw water all over us. Then it took off across the surface, leaping toward the horizon.

"Reel, reel," yelled Jose, *now* getting into the act!

I had no intention of reeling. The Pate reel was set on about four-pound drag and it was going to do all the work with that little fish. I wasn't worried at the moment, for I had caught half a dozen sailfish by that time, some of them Pacific sails off Mexico, weighing close to one hundred pounds. I knew this fish couldn't weigh much more than fifty pounds.

We ran in a circle after the little marlin settled down some, and although it made several more jumps, the marlin tired in about twenty-five minutes, and I slowly began bringing it in. For the first time — when the small blue got close to the transom — I began to worry. I suddenly remembered that very few people had ever caught an Atlantic blue marlin on a fly. I knew Billy had the world record and that it was ninety-six pounds, but it wasn't a record I was worrying about. I just wanted to land that fish. I needn't have worried.

Porfirio suddenly appeared with a big rusty gaff and sank it completely through that little marlin before I could tell him not to mutilate it. With a mighty heave, he hauled it into the cockpit, and just to make sure it didn't flip out into the sea, repeatedly bashed it on the head with a big wooden club. I took a photograph of it before he decided to gut it then and there.

It was then that I realized these men had no idea we had done anything unusual. It was just another fish to them, caught on just another rod and reel.

"*Bueno*," I said to Porfirio, grinning. He shrugged.

"*Muy pequeno*," he grunted, stowing away the bloody gaff.

I sat down in one of the battered white wooden chairs with the plastic straps across the back and looked at the little, battered marlin lying on the bloody deck. You may be *muy pequeno*—very little—to that character, I thought, but you are a winner to me, little guy. And you are going to live forever if I have anything to do with it.

We didn't catch any more fish that day off Round Hill, Jamaica, even though we trolled for four more hours. The wind came up strong later in the day and we quit about 3:00 P.M. I took a photo of Jose holding that little marlin on the dock and Victoria took a picture of Jose and me posing with the fish in the yard of Jackie's rental house. Jose wanted to keep the fish to eat, he said, and I sure didn't want to have it mounted—as small as it was. It weighed forty-three pounds on the garage scale.

The cook told me later that Jose skinned it out and carried it, wrapped in banana leaves, up to the big hotel at Round Hill. There, he sold it to the kitchen to make smoked marlin for hors d'oeuvres. The cook said I should try them. They are very good, she said.

Not likely. It would be like eating one of my brothers.

If there is one spot on the globe where saltwater fly rodders could be reasonably sure of catching a striped marlin on a fly, it would be the fishing port of Cabo San Lucas in lower Baja California.

Fishermen there bring in between fifty and eighty striped marlin a day. Most of them weigh from 75 to 120 pounds and most are caught by drifting live green mackerel in about thirty to forty feet of water. I go there to hook billfish on a fly—and do so, occasionally—but Didier Van der Veecken *regularly* hooks striped marlin on the fly, as do some of his clients who come down to fish with the long rods.

Didier, in spite of the Dutch name, is a Frenchman, born in Paris. He moved to Africa at the age of sixteen and there developed a love of fly fishing. He moved from freshwater to saltwater fly fishing while living on the Seychelle Islands in the Indian Ocean for seven years. Now, about forty years old, he has lived in Cabo San Lucas for nine years and runs a charter boat business. Although most of the clients who charter his two 30-foot, diesel-powered sportfishermen fish with conventional gear, Didier himself prefers to fish with a fly rod. As a result, he has attracted a number of saltwater fly fishermen to the area to fish with him. A representative of the International Game Fish Association, Didier is rapidly making a name for himself in the saltwater fly-fishing field. He takes his fly-fishing clients out in a center-console boat, far better adapted than the sportfishermen for fly rods.

Van der Veecken holds all the listed world records for fly-caught California halibut. He took them during a trip to Magdalena Bay on the west coast of Baja in 1982. While he regularly hooks striped marlin on a fly, his favorite quarry is roosterfish that inhabit the shallow water close to the surf line.

Although he has set no world marlin records himself with the long rod, several of his clients have come close. An eighty-eight-pound striped marlin, caught by Ed Rice of California, has been submitted to the IGFA for consideration as a world-record fly-caught

The first black marlin taken on a fly was caught by Billy Pate on September 8, 1972, off Cairns, Australia, on a 15-pound tippet. The fish weighed forty-two pounds eight ounces.

marlin. Rice caught the fish in December 1985 while fishing with Didier.

That was quite a fishing trip, according to Didier. In a five-day period, Rice hooked thirty-two striped marlin in an area called the Jamie Bank, about twenty miles west of Cabo. Of those fish hooked, nineteen of them got away when the 8-pound-test mono tippets broke. Twelve more escaped when hooks broke under the strain of the fight. Didier fought another fish for more than four hours before having to break it off because of darkness.

Marlin fishing is never a certain thing under the best of circumstances, as all big-game fishermen know, but fishing for them with a fly rod is a chancy business. There are only five tippet classes: 2-, 4-, 8-, 12-, and 16-pound-test tippets. Several of these tippet classes are likely to remain vacant for decades, such as the 2- and 4-pound-test categories. One would have to hook a pretty small marlin to land it on 2-pound-test tippet.

Even in the higher tippet categories there are a lot of vacant tippet catches. Only five black marlin have ever been caught on a fly and qualified for records. All five were caught in Australia, two by Billy Pate and one by Andrew A. MacGrath. Two were caught by Californian Ray Beadle. My 50- to 60-pound black marlin, caught on 16-pound tippet at Cape Bowling Green, Australia, in August 1990, would not have qualified as an IGFA record because my fly rod broke, but I didn't care. I just wanted to catch one on a fly. No Pacific blue marlin have ever qualified for records on a fly rod in any tippet class. Hawaii's Mike Sakamoto caught a Pacific blue marlin of more than 200 pounds by trolling a popper fly on a fly rod—no mean feat even if it did not qualify for an IGFA record.

Billy Pate caught the only Atlantic blue marlin that ever qualified: a marlin of 96 pounds, caught off Havana, Cuba, in 1978. My little 43-pound Atlantic blue was caught on 16-pound-test leader, as was Billy's, but it was far down the weight scale, and the Jamaican skipper I had did not take the boat out of gear when I cast that popper. Islamorada fly rodder Jim Gray caught two Atlantic blue marlin on a fly in 1990 at Saint Thomas in the Virgin Islands. One was a 151-pound fish on 16-pound tippet and the other was smaller, approximately 100 pounds on 12-pound tippet. Both have been submitted to the IGFA as possible new records.

Lee Wulff still holds the 12-pound-tippet record on one of the only two striped marlin listed so far, a fish of 148 pounds caught in 1967 off

Salinas, Ecuador. Pate caught the second biggest at the same place in 1970, a 146-pound striped marlin on a 16-pound tippet. Denton Mill of Paradise, California, hooked and landed a 174-pound striped marlin on a fly, using 16-pound tippet, at El Ocotal, Costa Rica, in the summer of 1990, but the IGFA disallowed his catch because the crew used a flying gaff instead of a conventional gaff. The detachable head had been tied down with wire and cord, but rules are rules. No flying gaffs are allowed in saltwater fly-fishing competition. It was nevertheless an epic battle, and the fish would have shattered Billy Pate's longstanding record. My 131-pound striped marlin, caught on a fly off Mazatlan in February 1990, was too far short of Billy's 16-pound-tippet record to qualify as a record fish.

Three men have caught record white marlin on a fly so far. Pate holds the 16-pound-test tippet-class record with an eighty-pound white caught off Venezuela in 1975. Dave Chermanski holds the 12-pound-test-tippet-class record with a sixty-eight-pound white caught in 1972 off Fort Pierce, Florida. Pat Ford holds the 8-pound-test-tippet-class record with a seventy-three-pound white caught off Venezuela in 1984.

So many variables enter into the quest for marlin on a fly that it makes the sport very "iffy." First of all, one has to be fairly well off to even entertain the idea of setting many marlin records on a fly rod. We all know what it costs to run marlin boats these days. Even on conventional tackle—in line classes all the way from 12- and 20-pound-test line up to 80- and 130-pound-test—marlin get off. I have lost them all over the world on 80-pound-test—even under the best of conditions. And over the years, as I went down in line class, the chances of losing them grew even greater. Now that I fish for them with a fly rod, I don't expect to land many.

Fly-rod tackle of the quality required for marlin is not cheap. A good 9- to 9½-foot graphite, boron, or even fiberglass fly rod strong enough to handle marlin and capable of throwing 11- and 12-weight, weight-forward fly line will cost in excess of $300. The type of reel capable of holding six hundred yards of thirty-pound Dacron or Micron backing plus thirty feet of fly line—with a drag smooth enough to withstand the run of a marlin—would cost anywhere from $500 to $1,200.

Handling such a rod and line while fastened to a leaping and sounding marlin requires that one be in pretty good physical shape. It is not necessary to throw a big marlin fly one hundred feet—as in the case of some other saltwater game-fish species—but it is necessary to get it thirty to forty feet from the boat and into the path of a marlin that has just charged a teaser bait. One must be able to cast a heavy fly and a heavy line in all sorts of wind conditions.

Didier and I spent three days one February trying to lure striped marlin up to a big teaser and to a spot where we could throw a fly to one. The trouble was that on those three days the marlin showed absolutely no interest in the teaser. The wind blew a gale the whole time and the seas were monstrous. It would have taken a high-wire expert to keep his footing on the deck while fighting a marlin on a fly rod in those seas. I was actually relieved at times that the marlin did not strike. It would have meant fighting one from a chair with a fly rod.

But on one day marlin were on the surface all around us, slicing through the face of waves and following alongside the boat. Bait fishermen took them easily, but they were not interested in anything on the surface—at least not to eat.

For the beginner there are plenty of excellent rods, reels, and lines to choose from. One can have a custom rod made, but first-class billfish fly rods are being made today by Fisher, Graphite USA, Sage, and Fenwick—to name a few. By far the best saltwater marlin fly reels made today are those by Pate and Steve Abel of California. Remember that to handle two-hundred-pound marlin, a reel must have a capacity of at least six hundred yards of line and backing.

In Cabo San Lucas many of the blue and black marlin come in during the late spring, summer, and fall, some running seven hundred to eight hundred pounds. Didier says there is not much of a chance that the fly fishermen will do well with these big fish, but he adds that small blues come in during December and some are small enough to be taken on a fly rod.

There are a few rules to saltwater fly fishing that need to be kept in mind if one intends to try for marlin. Any type of fly line and backing may be used and leaders must conform to generally accepted fly-fishing customs. That is, a leader includes a class tippet and, optionally, a shock tippet. A butt section between the fly line and the class tippet is considered a part of the leader. There are no limits on its length, material, or strength.

A class tippet must be made of nonmetallic material and either attached directly to the fly or to the shock tippet. The class tippet must be at least fifteen inches long, but there is no maximum length limitation. The shock tippet, which may be made of wire or heavy mono, must be no longer than twelve inches. The only restrictions on fly rods are that they can be no shorter than six feet. No electric or electronically operated reels may be used.

As far as hooks are concerned, a conventional fly may be dressed on a single or double hook or two single hooks in tandem. The second hook in any tandem must not extend beyond the wing material, and the eyes of the hooks should be no farther than six inches apart. Treble hooks are not allowed.

The lure used in saltwater fly fishing must be a recognized type of artificial fly, that is: streamer, bucktail, tube fly, wet fly, dry fly, nymph, popper, or bug. As regards other gear, gaffs and nets used to land fish must not be longer than eight feet. The use of a flying gaff in fly fishing is not permitted.

Unlike conventional fishing, trolling a fly is not permitted and the craft must be completely out of gear during the time the fly is cast and during the retrieve. Outside of that, pretty much the same rules apply as in conventional saltwater fishing.

The technique used by Didier to bring up marlin within casting distance of a fly is much the same as that used by most saltwater marlin and sailfish fishermen. He uses a multicolored teaser that is run in the wake of the boat on a line. When the marlin charges that teaser, it is hauled in by hand until the fly is cast to the fish, and then the teaser is flipped into the boat. The theory is that the fish, excited by the teaser, will now take the fly. I have had marlin take the fly as soon as it hit the water. Sometimes it is not necessary to move it at all. Other times no amount of action will interest a billfish.

I have fished with crews off the Florida Keys and in the Bahamas where rigged baits—mullet, mackerel, or bonefish—are run behind the boat without hooks in them on spinning tackle. When billfish surface, these rigged baits are quickly hauled in so a fly can be thrown. The outriggers on most sportfishermen are placed so that they are in the way of a backcast. Usually, the outrigger on the side the angler intends to cast the fly is removed.

One of the biggest problems with setting a hook into the boney mouth of a billfish is the hardness of the bone and gristle and the dullness of a hook. A hook should literally be sharpened to razor sharpness and should hang up on the surface of a fingernail. I have

Billy Pate with the first white marlin ever taken on a fly, from Venezuela in 1975. The tippet was 15 pounds and the fish weighed eighty pounds.

lost most of my billfish takes because I fail to set the hook on the strike. Didier gave me some invaluable advice on that problem. Rather than strike when the marlin hits, Didier lets the fish take the fly in its mouth and run with it. He gradually increases pressure on the line by squeezing with the fingers of his left hand until the hook point sinks in at some soft spot. It apparently works for him!

Billfishing with a fly rod is a sport still in its infancy, but a lot of anglers are showing interest in it. Fishermen like Didier Van der Veecken are leading the way, and he certainly is in the right place for it. I expect to see a number of striped marlin fly-rod records show up in his area in the next few years.

The other area that should see marlin caught on a fly is Salinas, Ecuador. There, striped marlin in the 150- to 200-pound class are common and it is not unusual to see a dozen a day basking on the surface. I have fished for them in March and there are plenty of fish around. It is about a fifteen- to twenty-mile run to the marlin grounds.

Costa Rica has some fine marlin waters—the northern portion from April to December and the southern region from December to March. High winds hit the northern section in the winter months, but I don't know of a better spot to fish for both marlin and sailfish with a fly rod than the small resort of Bahia Pez Vela, just north of San José.

For the winter months, I would go south to Golfito Sailfish Rancho. The waters are calm in the south in winter months and there are plenty of billfish around. Perhaps the best all-around spot in Costa Rica is the port of Quepos. The weather is good there most of the time, there is a good port, and it is only about a half-hour run out to blue water.

For white marlin there are no better spots than Venezuela in the fall and Cozumel in the spring.

I really once thought the *only* place in Mexico where one could expect to catch striped marlin regularly in the winter months was Cabo San Lucas. That small town on the extreme tip of Baja California has been, for me, a refuge for billfish when the snows of the north start me thinking of blue water and white beaches.

In the winter of 1990, I received a phone call from Jerry Jergens, who runs a fishing operation in the big resort city of Mazatlan, almost directly across the Gulf of California from Cabo San Lucas on the west coast of Mexico. Mazatlan Sportsman is Jerry's company and he handles thousands of sport fishermen a year who come to his tropical city in search of marlin, sailfish, dolphin, wahoo, broadbill swordfish, yellowtail, and all sorts of reef fish.

I don't know why, but Mazatlan was a complete and pleasant surprise to me. For some sort of silly reason I expected the city to be

Mike Sakamoto of Hawaii and his 206-pound Pacific blue marlin—the only one ever caught on a fly rod. Because his leaders were far above IGFA limits and because he trolled a fly, he did not enter it for a fly-rod record, but it is still a tremendous feat.

one big resort full of zonked-out yuppies spending their days on the beaches and their nights dancing on the tables of discos. Not that there weren't a few of those around, but what I found was a lot of *fishermen* from all parts of the world. There were knowledgeable anglers from British Columbia, eastern Canada, and from much of the United States—all happy to be away from the winter weather and all seeking good fishing.

While I was prepared for big resort hotels, I was still thoroughly impressed when Jerry put me up in the El Cid with 1,100 rooms, fourteen restaurants and lounges, an eighteen-hole golf course, seventeen tennis courts, and six heated swimming pools—all on nine hundred acres. Some fishing camp!

The last time I fished Mazatlan was in the 1970s, and at that time the resort was a sleepy Mexican city sporting a few good hotels and a battered fishing fleet. I had been there in the summer, and although the sailfishing had been good, it was hotter than the hinges of Hades. I had fished with a crew that was not overly concerned with boating safety, and I remember that the mate insisted in setting the hook on every sailfish. He and the skipper wanted to make sure those sails reached shore, where they were sold on the dock for food. So I was still prepared for some second-rate boats and crews, regardless of hotel accommodations.

I met Jerry in the lobby at 6:00 A.M. and we took a taxi for the ten-minute ride to the marina at the southern edge of the city of nearly six hundred thousand people. I had told Jerry I was a saltwater fly fisherman and that he probably would have trouble finding a crew that understood the peculiar requirements of the sport.

"Don't worry," Jergens said as we climbed out of the cab at the marina. "Jorge Lujan specializes in fly fishing." So far so good.

Bill Heimpel's Star Fleet, comprised of fifteen boats, is the oldest and biggest in Mazatlan. Bill began his fleet with one boat in the early 1960s and gradually increased it by building his own boats, plus a marine railway. Most of his boats are from 36 to 43 feet long and all sport diesel engines.

"A diesel is by far the best engine for a sport-fishing fleet," he told me as we sat in his office. "We had one accident back in the early days with a gasoline engine on one of our boats and I switched to all diesels right after that. Diesel fuel will burn, sure, if you try and make it burn, but not like gasoline. With all those fumes, gasoline is an explosion waiting to happen."

Jorge, the skipper, and Jesus, the mate, were ready to go aboard the big, wide, 43-foot sportfisherman. The port outrigger had been removed and there was plenty of room in the big, clean cockpit. A dozen big mullet were already rigged for trolling—hookless. I looked at Jerry. He laughed.

"I told him you were right-handed last night. He took the 'rigger off this morning."

The sun was just touching the jagged rocks surrounding the harbor as we nosed out from the marina.

"What's out there today?" I asked Jorge.

"Mostly striped marlin and some broadbill at this time of the year," he said. "A lot of sailfish came in last week. We saw pods of several hundred a couple of days ago, but they weren't hitting baits. Too many sardines for them and they are a little early. Some dorado, but mostly marlin in December, January, February, and March. Lots of sailfish and striped marlin April through November—with some big blue and black marlin then too."

"When's the best time for dolphin—dorado?"

"April to December. Lots of fish. Right now there are some big wahoo farther out—along with some yellowfin tuna and yellowtail."

"We run for about an hour," Jerry said. "The marlin can be found from fifteen to twenty-five miles out this time of year. I believe an angler has a better chance of catching a billfish here than anywhere else in the world. Our water is far warmer in the winter than at Cabo and the marlin stay here. Then the sails come in early in the spring and stay here until late fall. It's not unusual to see boats flying anywhere from five to twenty billfish flags a day in the peak of the season. On several months last year there were more than twelve hundred billfish caught here."

"What are your biggest?"

"Our biggest blue weighed nine hundred eighty-eight and we had a black that weighed thirteen fifty. Our sails run big here too. We had one caught that weighed one hundred and ninety-eight pounds. Most of the stripes are good fly-rod size—one hundred to one hundred fifty average."

"Any trouble with catch-and-release?"

"We did at first," Jerry said. "The people here need the protein. The crews get about thirty dollars per fish at the dock so, naturally, they want to keep them. But we encourage the anglers that want to release fish to tip the crews fifty dollars and that way they make money whether the fish are released or not, and they don't mind now if they are released."

Jorge suddenly increased power and swung the boat to starboard.

"Broadbill!" he shouted, and I slid down the ladder to the cockpit—Jerry right behind me. I grabbed the 12-weight fly rod with the big Pate Marlin reel on it. It was rigged with 16-pound-test tippet and a cork popper mounted on a double #5/0 hook fastened to 100-pound-test shock leader. The other, a 13-weight rod, held a large Abel #5 reel and was rigged with a #3/0 double-hook, white streamer fly at the end of 16-pound-test tippet.

The broadbill was resting on the surface, its tail and dorsal fin out of water. Jorge eased back on the throttle and the boat slowed down. It was a fish of about two hundred pounds. I felt my heart begin to hammer in my chest. A broadbill has never been caught on a fly.

The skipper began a circle and I cast the big white popper as he slipped the boat into neutral. The sportfisherman glided in a curve past the resting fish. The popper passed within a dozen feet of the fish as I frantically stripped the line. The big lure chugged as I jerked it and the broadbill suddenly lashed its tail and shot up to within a few feet of the bobbing lure.

"He's going to take it!" Jerry screamed, and I braced myself for the strike. At that, the big fish suddenly swirled and sounded. I leaned against the gunwale, breathing hard.

"My God!" Jerry said, collapsing into a chair. "That could have been the first swordfish ever taken on a fly rod. What would you have done if he'd taken it?"

"Fainted dead away," I said, retrieving the popper slowly.

That was just the beginning of a great day. We had been fishing only about thirty minutes when a striped marlin came up behind a mullet trolled on a flat line on the edge of the wake. Jerry handled the teaser bait perfectly, keeping it just ahead of the bill tip as the marlin frantically tried to grab the bait. When he jerked it from the water not more than twenty feet from the transom, I cast the big white popper to the far side of the searching fish. It turned and took the popper in a classic strike and I set the hook in the corner of its mouth.

When it felt the hook, the striped marlin took to the air in a series of greyhounding jumps that took it out at least three hundred yards before it finally ceased. The thirty feet of 12-weight, sinking, weight-forward shooting head and one hundred feet of thirty-five-pound soft mono running line had whipped out through the guides like a flash, and the fish was taking out the thirty-pound Micron backing as if it were not there.

That was a great marlin, and it took almost an hour to bring it to the boat. I thought it might be big enough to be a threat to Billy Pate's 146-pound world record striped marlin on 16-pound-test tippet, but I was kidding myself. It looked that big or bigger, but it turned out to weigh 131 pounds—still a very respectable fish on a fly.

Jerry hooked a slightly smaller marlin an hour later and lost it close to the boat when the hook pulled out. He is an excellent fly rodder, having taken almost everything but marlin on a fly. I hooked another after two more fish came up to the bait but refused to fly. That last fish popped the leader as it jumped a number of times far out from the boat. But I cannot remember another day when that many marlin came up for a trolled teaser bait. Hooking three striped marlin in one day on a fly is good enough for me any time!

For the saltwater fly rodder interested in taking striped marlin on a fly in the winter months, I cannot think of a better place to try for them than Mazatlan. And for the same fly fishermen wanting to take sailfish, I would certainly suggest trying this fine port city from May to December. Mazatlan is only an hour-and-forty-five-minute nonstop jet flight from Phoenix and a two-hour nonstop flight from

The author with his 131-pound striped marlin.

Los Angeles. Delta, plus a number of Mexican airlines, serve the city several times a day.

There is only one spot in the world where one can be sure of seeing a number of small black marlin—off the Queensland Coast of northeast Australia. That is where I caught my black marlin on a fly in August 1990.

The 40-foot sportfisherman *Seaducer,* with veteran captain Calvin Tilley at the wheel, was wallowing in a following sea about ten miles northeast of Cape Bowling Green, Australia, when the small black marlin surfaced behind the hookless port teaser bait.

"Billfish!" Calvin screamed into the face of a fifteen-knot wind, and mate Alan Zavodny scrambled to bring in both the starboard teaser and the Kona-head lures skipping off the outrigger.

The black, fluorescent with anger in the royal blue depths, zig-zagged back and forth in the wake as it searched for the bouncing, elusive baits.

Standing in the port-side corner of the cockpit, I picked up the 9-foot graphite fly rod and dropped the double-hooked streamer fly into the foamy wake just aft of the transom, letting it run back a dozen feet on the surface. The black was not twenty feet away; its dark shape flitted from side to side in the wake.

Glancing up at Calvin, I pointed the rod tip at the fly and began the backcast.

"Okay," I shouted as the fly zipped back over my right shoulder and Calvin slipped the controls into neutral. The blue-and-white fly landed about six feet to the left of the marlin, and with a lightninglike lunge the billfish came half out of water and took the lure. Seeing it go from my right to left, I dropped the rod tip to the right and struck sideways. The hook bit into the soft corner of the mouth, and with the bite of the front #3/0 stainless-steel hook the marlin went wild.

As it always does with hooked marlin on a fly rod, everything went into slow motion. I could hear the shouts from the skipper and mate and from fellow anglers Ian Miller and Steve Starling as the black began a series of greyhounding leaps across the surface of the sea. The big, golden fly reel sang as the twenty-five feet of 12-weight fast-sinking shooting head, the 100 feet of forty-pound mono running line and thirty-pound backing whipped off the spool.

Several hundred yards out, the black made a towering leap into the bright morning sunlight, then sounded, whipping off more backing.

"Hang on to him, mate," the skipper yelled from the tower, "he's a beauty!"

I fully intended to hang on to the speeding black—my first on a fly.

The marlin was diving for the depths now, and I was impressed with the strength it exhibited relative to its size. The 9-foot, 12-weight fly rod was bent double with the strain. Calvin slipped the engines into reverse and slowly began to back down on the fighting fish.

I had been told by Billy Pate—who caught the first black marlin off Cairns, Australia, on a fly—that small, fly-rod-size fish could be found from about August to November. There is a spawning area off northern Australia, and small black marlin, averaging from twenty-five to fifty pounds, may be found in those months from just south of Townsville up to the Cairns area. Pate holds the world 8-pound-test-tippet record for black marlin: a fish of forty-six pounds four ounces caught on September 4, 1972. According to Captain Tilley, fish in the twenty-five- to fifty-pound class alternate with black marlin from fifty to one hundred pounds each year. The bigger blacks had been caught the previous year, but so far in 1990 only the smaller-sized fish had shown up. Nobody is sure why this happens, he said.

The marlin began to come up slowly. I increased the pressure gradually by turning the drag knob up to the four-pound setting. The line suddenly began to slant toward the surface.

"He's coming up!" Calvin shouted as the black marlin broke the surface about a hundred yards out and climbed into the air, twisting in the bright sunlight. The marlin fell back to the surface, but came out, instantly and began a series of towering jumps. A decade earlier I had caught a one thousand-pound black marlin on eighty-pound line at Lizard Island, just north of Cairns, but it had only jumped once—probably because of its immense size. I was enjoying this fight a lot more!

At the forty-five-minute mark the black was beginning to tire and I had it close to the boat but down about twenty feet below the stern. I was leaning backward, the rod bent into a bow, when the top ferrule gave way and the rod broke with an ear-splitting crack. My heart sank and I thought I had lost the fish, but the 16-pound tippet held. I regained my footing and Alan leaned over with the long tagging stick pointing to where the marlin lay just below us.

"Let me get this tag into his shoulder," the mate grunted, "and he's a legal tagged-and-released fish no matter what happens." He quickly jabbed the long aluminum pole into the water and I could see

Alan Zavodny, mate aboard the Seaducer, *and Jack Samson hold his fifty-pound Pacific black marlin caught off Cape Bowling Green, Australia.*

the marlin surge as the tag went in.

"Got him, mate!" Alan shouted. "He's all yours now."

Unable to hold the small marlin very far from the stern with the broken fly rod, I watched anxiously as the fish dug beneath the boat. It struck the spinning port propellor once, and as it turned and floated to the surface just behind the transom the mate reached out with the gaff, hooked the bill, and led it to the boat. There were whoops, shouts, handshakes, and much back slapping as the mate slid the marlin over the stern and held it aloft, both arms wrapped around it. I have never been as glad to see *any* fish come aboard as I was that little black marlin!

We took its measurements and estimated its weight at about fifty pounds. One can arrive at the approximate weight of a billfish by measuring the girth, multiplying that number by the length from the fork of the tail to the point of the bottom jaw, and dividing that figure by eight hundred. The game little marlin was then released to grow to the size of its one thousand-pound-plus cousins the Aussies call "granders."

The Townsville/Cape Bowling Green area of Australia is a garden spot for the saltwater fly rodder interested in taking a black marlin on a fly. It is the only known area in the world where black marlin can be regularly found in good numbers and just the right size for a fly rod.

In October 1990, Ed Beattie, travel manager for Bass Pro Shops Outdoor World Travel, called me up in Santa Fe. He said he had been reading about my quest for all the marlin species on a fly rod and that he knew a man in Venezuela who had several sportfishing boats and would be happy to have me come down and try for a white marlin.

The peak season for the small whites, he said, was October and November, and the man, Juan Batista Arismendi, had three days vacant on his charters—if I would be interested in going. Interested! Is the pope Catholic? The dates were October 22 through 24.

I needed a good man who could handle the teaser rod and who also spoke Spanish, so I called my longtime fishing chum, the legendary San Juan River fishing guide Chuck Rizuto, who lives in Farmington, New Mexico. Chuck had accompanied me on a number of trips for both flats fishing and blue water and had caught a sailfish on a fly off Costa Rica. He was delighted to go.

The trip was a long and tiring one; the Viasa flight from Miami to Caracas, Venezuela, was delayed and we had to wait four hours in the Miami airport. We arrived late at night in Caracas and were driven the twenty miles or so to the small port city of La Guaira. A huge storm had just passed through and the streets were littered with mud and palm fronds that had washed down the steep, rugged slopes of the mountains towering over the port city. Lightning and thunder were still in the vicinity, making us anxious about the next day's weather. But we were both too travel weary to assemble the fly tackle that night anyway.

There was a gusty wind blowing across the port in the morning. As we put to sea in the 38-foot sportfisherman the *Big Lure,* skippered by Captain Hector Lopez, the seas were running a good six to eight feet high. It was a rough, pitching trip for the hour-and-a-half run to the white marlin grounds. Johnnie, the mate, helped me put the 9-foot Sage and Fenwick rods together and fit them with both a Pate Marlin Reel and an Abel #5 big game reel. I had rigged both reels with thirty-pound Micron backing, one hundred feet of forty-pound, stretchable Schneider mono running line and twenty-five feet of 12-weight, fast-sinking shooting heads. I put the same fly on both: the blue-and-white #3/0 double-hooked flies tied for me by the Fly Factory in Belleglade, Florida. They were the same as the fly with which I had taken the little black marlin off Cape Bowling Green, Australia, in August.

Johnnie ran out two hookless balao baits—one on my long 10-foot fiberglass teaser rod and the other on a 30-pound mono boat rod. He ran a couple of hookless Kona heads off the starboard outrigger, one fluorescent red and the other a bright green.

It seemed as though the baits were just out when the skipper screamed "marlin!" and I stumbled to the corner of the cockpit to grab the big Fenwick rod and black reel. The boat was careening in the swells and it was almost impossible to keep my footing. Chuck was already on the teaser rod and the mate was scrambling for the boat rod.

I dropped the fly into the foamy wake and looked aft. There were two dorsal fins zigzagging back and forth in the white water, alternating between the two teaser baits. Chuck had the middle teaser bait almost up to the boat, and one small white marlin was right behind it.

"Alto!" I shouted to the skipper as I made a quick backcast. I could feel the boat slow as the line came forward, and I saw Chuck's bait sail from the water. The marlin lunged from the water and took the fly as I gave it a fast strip.

As the marlin went off to my left, I quickly set the hook and felt sink in. The fish took off in a series of incredibly quick jumps moving directly away from the boat. I raised the rod and pointed the tip at the fish as it jumped. The drag was set very light as I didn't want much pressure on a fish moving that quickly. There was plenty of time to increase the drag after the fish had gotten all its first jumps out of the way.

When the marlin had jumped at least a dozen times and was about two hundred yards out, it sounded. I set the hooks hard for the second time, but when the small marlin came out of the water again, it threw the fly on the third jump.

"Damn!" said Chuck, off to my left. I began to reel slowly. There wasn't much one could say. Billy Pate, who had caught his world record white here nearly two decades earlier, had warned me these little white marlin were difficult to hook.

If anything, the wind seemed to pick up as the day wore on. I seldom get seasick, but I stayed out of the enclosed cabin—standing high on the port gunwale, holding on to the folded outrigger—for fear of becoming ill. Chuck, who never gets seasick either, was looking pale and also stayed on deck all afternoon. The sun had been shining all day, but the wind tore at the boat rigging and ripped the ocean surface into long white feathers of foam.

No more fish came up and we were both resigned to going back to the marina empty-handed when, about 4:00 P.M., a bill appeared behind Chuck's teaser. We all saw it about the same time, and I was already on the way to the rod when the skipper shouted above the shriek of the wind.

The take of the fly was almost an exact repeat of the first marlin strike and I was fast to the billfish almost before I knew it. Small white marlin are incredibly fast, much more so than sailfish. The fish went off to my right and continued to jump long after I thought it would stop and dive. By the time the series of jumps was over, the fish had nearly four hundred yards of line out.

The skipper had left the twin diesels in neutral and line was peeling off the big black reel rapidly. I was not worried because Steve Abel's big billfish reel carries nearly nine hundred yards of backing and line, but I didn't want to get too big a billow of line out, as that would add pressure to the 16-pound leader tippet.

"Back down, skipper," Chuck shouted as he saw me glancing at the reel.

That small marlin put up as tough a fight as any billfish I have ever hooked. It alternated between greyhounding jumps and deep dives and fought all the way to the boat. It must have taken about twenty minutes to get it close enough for Johnnie to reach out and gingerly grasp the short section of 100-pound shock leader near the corner of the marlin's mouth. A second later he had the bill in his gloved hand and a sudden feeling of relief and elation washed over me as I realized the white was caught.

Mixed with my joy was gratitude to my wife, Victoria, who said she knew I was going to catch that fish and would send me all the light she could. My second thought was that I had finally tied the great Billy Pate with four marlin species and both sailfish on a fly. For years I had fully believed *nobody* would ever match his record!

I no longer felt or cared about the howling wind or the pitching and rolling boat wallowing in great swells off the tiny country of Venezuela. I had done what I came to do—catch my fourth marlin on a fly. Suddenly, for this fly fisherman, all was right with the world.

IGFA International Angling Rules for Fly Fishing

(printed courtesy of IGFA)

Equipment Regulations

A. LINE

Any type of fly line and backing may be used. The breaking strength of the fly line and backing are not restricted.

B. LEADER

Leaders must conform to generally accepted fly fishing customs.

A leader includes a class tippet and, optionally, a shock tippet. A butt or taper section between the fly line and the class tippet shall also be considered part of the leader and there are no limits on its length, material, or strength.

A class tippet must be made of nonmetallic material and either attached directly to the fly or to the shock tippet if one is used. The class tippet must be at least 15 inches (38.10 cm) long (measured inside connecting knots). With respect to knotless, tapered leaders, the terminal 15 inches (38.10 cm) will also determine tippet class. There is no maximum length limitation. The breaking strength determines the class of the tippet.

A shock tippet, not to exceed 12 inches (30.48 cm) in length, may be added to the class tippet and tied to the lure. It can be made of any type of material, and there is no limit on its breaking strength. The shock tippet is measured from the eye of the hook to the single strand of class tippet and includes any knots used to connect the shock tippet to the class tippet.

In the case of a tandem hook fly, the shock tippet shall be measured from the eye of the leading hook.

C. ROD

Regardless of material used or number of sections, rods must conform to generally accepted fly fishing customs and practices. A rod shall not measure less than 6 feet (1.82

meters) in overall length. Any rod that gives the angler an unsporting advantage will be disqualified. Extension butts are limited to 6 inches (15.24 cm).

D. REEL

The reel must be designed expressly for fly fishing. There are no restrictions on gear ratio or type of drag employed except where the angler would gain an unfair advantage. Electric or electronically operated reels are prohibited.

E. HOOKS

A conventional fly may be dressed on a single or double hook or two single hooks in tandem. The second hook in any tandem fly must not extend beyond the wing material. The eyes of the hooks shall be no farther than 6 inches (15.24 cm) apart. Treble hooks are prohibited.

F. LURES

The lure must be a recognized type of artificial fly, which includes streamer, buck-tail, tube fly, wet fly, dry fly, nymph, popper and bug. The use of any other type of lure or natural or preserved bait, either singularly or attached to the fly, is expressly prohibited. The fact that a lure can be cast with a fly rod is not evidence in itself that it fits the definition of a fly. The use of any lure designed to entangle or foul-hook a fish is prohibited.

G. GAFFS & NETS

Gaffs and nets used to boat or land a fish must not exceed 8 feet (2.48 meters) in overall length. (When fishing from a bridge, pier or other high stationary structure, this length limitation does not apply.) The use of a flying gaff is not permitted. Only a single hook is permitted on any gaff. Harpoon or lance attachments are prohibited.

WEIGHTS NEEDED TO DEFEAT OR TIE EXISTING RECORDS

1. To replace a record for a fish weighing less than 25 pounds (11.33 kg), the replacement must weigh at least 2 ounces (56.69 gm) more than the existing record.

2. To replace a record for a fish weighing 25 pounds (11.33 kg) or more, the replacement must weigh at least one half of 1 percent more than the existing record. *Examples:* At 100 pounds (45.35 kg) the additional weight required would be 8 ounces (226.7 gm); at 200 pounds (90.71 kg) the additional weight required would be 1 pound (.45 kg).

3. Any catch which matches the weight of an existing record or exceeds the weight by less than the amount required to defeat the record will be considered a tie. In case of a tie claim involving more than two catches, weight must be compared with the original record (first fish to be caught). Nothing weighing less than the original record will be considered.

4. Estimated weights will not be accepted. (See *Weighing Requirements*.) Fractions of ounces or their metric equivalents will not be considered.

TIME LIMIT ON CLAIMS

With the exception of *all-tackle records* only, claims for record fish caught in U.S. continental waters must be received by IGFA within 60 days of the date of catch. Claims for record fish caught in other waters must be received by IGFA within three months of the date of catch.

Claims for all-tackle records only are considered for catches made in past years if (1) acceptable photographs are submitted, (2) the weight of the fish can be positively verified, and (3) the method of catch can be substantiated. For catches made in the past, as much information as possible must be submitted on an IGFA world record application form with any additional substantiating data.

If an incomplete record claim is submitted, it must be accompanied by an explanation of why certain portions are incomplete. An incomplete claim will be considered for a record if the following conditions are met:

1. The incomplete claim with explanations of why portions are incomplete must be received by IGFA within the time limits specified above.

2. Missing data must be due to circumstances beyond the control of the angler making the record claim.

3. All missing data must be supplied within a period of time considered to be reasonable in view of the particular circumstances.

Final decisions on incomplete claims will be made by IGFA's Executive Committee.

WEIGHING REQUIREMENTS FOR RECORD FISH

1. The fish must be weighed by an official weighmaster (if one is available) or by an IGFA official or by a recognized local person familiar with the scale. Disinterested witnesses to the weight should be used whenever possible.

2. The weight of the sling, platform, or rope (if one is used to secure the fish on the scales) must be determined and deducted from the total weight.

3. At the time of weighing, the actual tackle used by the angler to catch the fish must be exhibited to the weighmaster and weight witness.

4. No estimated weights will be accepted. Fish weighed only at sea or on other bodies of water will not be accepted.

5. Only weights indicated by the graduations on the scale will be accepted. Visual fractionalizing of these graduations is not allowed. Any weights that fall between two graduations on the scale must be rounded to the lower of the two.

6. All record fish should be weighed on scales that have been checked and certified for accuracy by government agencies or other qualified and accredited organizations. All scales must be regularly checked for accuracy and certified in accordance with applicable government regulations at least once every twelve months. If at the time of weighing the fish, the scale has not been properly certified within twelve months, it should be checked and certified for accuracy as quickly as possible, and an official report stating the findings of the inspection prior to any adjustment of the scale must be included with the record application.

7. If there is no official government inspector or accredited commercial scales representative available in the area where the fish is weighed, the scales must be checked by weighing objects of recognized and proven weight. Objects weighed must be at least equal to the weight of the fish. Substantiation of the correct weight of these objects must be submitted to IGFA along with the names and complete addresses of accredited witnesses to the entire procedure.

8. In extremely remote areas where no weighing scales are available, it will be permissible for the angler to use his own scales providing that they are of a quality type and have been properly certified both before and after returning from the fishing trip.

9. IGFA reserves the right to require any scale to be recertified for accuracy if there are any indications that the scale might not have weighed correctly.

Preparation of Record Claims

To apply for a world record, the angler must submit a completed IGFA application form, the mandatory length of line and terminal tackle (described below) used to catch the fish, and acceptable photographs of the fish, the tackle used to catch the fish, the scale used to weigh the fish, and the angler with the fish.

APPLICATION FORM

The official IGFA world record application form or a reproduction must be used for record claims. This form may be reproduced as long as all items are included.

The angler must fill in the application personally. IGFA also recommends that the angler personally mail the application, line sample or fly leader and photographs.

When making any record claim, the angler must indicate the specified strength of the line or tippet used to catch the fish. In the cases of line class and tippet class records, this will place the claim in an IGFA line or tippet class category (see *World Record Categories*). All lines will be examined by IGFA to verify the specified strength of the line. If the line or tippet overtests its particular category, the application will be considered in the next highest category; if it undertests into a lower line or tippet class category, the application will not be considered for the lower line class. The heaviest line class permitted for both freshwater and saltwater records is 60 kg (130 lb) class. The heaviest tippet class permitted for fly fishing records is 10 kg (20 lb). If the line or tippet overtests these maximum strengths, the claim will be disallowed.

Extreme care should be exercised in measuring the fish as the measurements are often important for weight verification and scientific studies. See the measurement diagram on the record application to be sure you have measured correctly.

The angler is responsible for seeing that the necessary signatures and correct addresses of the boat captain, weighmaster and witnesses are on the application. If an IGFA officer or representative, or an officer or member of an IGFA club is available, he or she should be asked to witness the claim. The name of a boatman, guide, or weighmaster repeated as witness is not acceptable.

The angler must appear in person to have his application notarized. In territories where notarization is not possible or customary, the signature of a government commissioner or resident, a member of an embassy, legation or consular staff or an IGFA officer or International Committee member may replace notarization.

Any deliberate falsification of an application will disqualify the applicant for any future IGFA world record, and any existing records will be nullified.

LINE OR TIPPET SAMPLE

All applications for fly fishing records must be accompanied by the lure, the entire tippet, and the entire leader along with one inch of the fly line beyond the attachment to the leader. These components must be intact and connected.

All applications for freshwater and saltwater line class records must be accompanied by the entire leader, the double line, and at least 50 feet (15.24 meters) of the single line closest to the double line, leader or hook. All line samples and the leader (if one is used) must be submitted in one piece. If a lure is used with the leader, the leader should be cut at the eye attachment to the lure.

Each line sample must be in one piece. It must be submitted in a manner that it can be easily unwound without damage to the line. A recommended method is to take a rectangular piece of stiff cardboard and cut notches in two opposite ends. Secure one end of the line to the cardboard and wind the line around the cardboard through the notched areas. Secure the other end, and write your name and the specified strength of the line on the cardboard. Any line sample submitted that is tangled or cannot be easily unwound will not be accepted.

PHOTOGRAPHS

Photographs showing the full length of the fish, the rod and reel used to make the catch, and the scale used to weigh the fish must accompany each record application. A photograph of the angler with the fish is also required.

So that there can be no question of species identification, the clearest possible photos should be submitted. This is especially important in the cases of hybrids and fishes that may be confused with similar species. Shark applications should include a photograph of the shark's teeth, and of the head and back taken from above in addition to the photographs taken from the side. Whether the shark has or does not have a ridge between the dorsal fins should be clearly evident in this photograph.

In all cases, photographs should be taken of the fish in a hanging position and also lying on a flat surface on its side. The fish should be broadside to the camera and no part of the fish should be obscured. The fins must be fully extended and not obscured with the hands, and the jaw or bill clearly shown. Avoid obscuring the keels of sharks and tunas with a tail rope.

When photographing a fish lying on its side, the surface beneath the fish should be smooth and a ruler or marked tape placed beside the fish if possible. Photographs from various angles are most helpful.

An additional photograph of the fish on the scale with actual weight visible helps to expedite the application.

Photos taken by daylight with a reproducible-type negative film are highly recommended if at all possible.